D1766524

Islam and the Politics of Resistance in Algeria, 1783-1992

Ricardo René Laremont

Africa World Press, Inc.

P.O. Box 1892
Trenton, NJ 08607

P.O. Box 48
Asmara, ERITREA

Africa World Press, Inc.

P.O. Box 1892
Trenton, NJ 08607

P.O. Box 48
Asmara, ERITREA

Copyright © 2000 Ricardo René Laremont

First Printing 2000

Cover design: Jonathan Gullery

Library of Congress Cataloging-in-Publication Data

Laremont, Ricardo René.
    Islam and the politics of resistance in Algeria, 1783-1992 / by Ricardo René Laremont.
       p. cm.
    Includes bibliographical references and index.
    ISBN 0-86543-752-1. –0-86543-753-X (pbk.)
    1. Islam and politics--Algeria. 2. Religion and politics--Algeria. 3. Algeria--Politics and government. I. Title.
BP173.7.L37 1999
297.2'72'0965–dc21

                                              99-26862
                                              CIP

11873701

To

Juan Salvador Laremont
Javette Pinkney
Salah Fellah

Table of Contents

✳

Preface

✳

How Islam has inspired movements of political resistance to
social conditions of inequity in Algeria is recounted in this
study. In 1783, Islamic principles were invoked to organize
resistance against injustice in the first modern example of indigenous rebellion in Algeria. Over the next two hundred years Islam
continued to be called upon by those in Algeria who sought relief
from what they considered inequitable and insufferable social, political, and economic conditions. We will see that Islam was used as a
resource for mobilizing resistance to oppression. In addition, we will
also observe that politicized Islam has had manifold expressions
ranging from liberalism to theocracy to socialism.

This book has eight chapters. Chapter 1 is a theoretical chapter
that attempts to explain why the theology of Islam and its definition
of justice have created powerful incentives for organizing political
movements that have been intent upon either the abolition or mit-
igation of inequitable social conditions.

The relationship between Sufism — the mystical branch of
Islam — and the original Algerian resistance against colonialism is
examined in the second chapter. Beginning with the first Algerian
revolt against Ottoman rule in 1783, the chapter concludes with the
Algerian capitulation to the French in 1871. In this chapter we will
review particularly the political themes of Algeria's most successful
resistance leader, the Emir Abd al Qadir, and his Sufi brotherhood,
the Qadiriyya.

The third chapter describes the construction of the French colonial state in Algeria. Emphasis is given to French policies on land tenure and French attempts to coopt clerically led political resistance efforts.

The fourth chapter examines the reemergence of Algerian resistance that began before World War I and continued through the 1950's. Algerian participation in the defense of France in World War I, and President Woodrow Wilson's Fourteen Points, created expectations of self-determination for colonized peoples. After the War, the implied promises of self-determination reignited Algerian aspirations for either political equality or independence. Three important political movements arose in Algeria that represented various strains of politicized Islam. Ferhat Abbas led the liberally oriented *Fédération des élus indigènes.* Sheikh Abd al-Hamid Ben Badis led the more traditional, clerically dominated *Association des Oulemas.* A third group, the *Étoile nord-africaine,* had a nationalist, independence-oriented, and partial socialist orientation. This party was be led by Messali Hadj and initially was associated with the French Communist Party. A fourth movement, the Algerian Communist Party, was present in the resistance movement but never achieved a mass following. Its lack of independence from the Comintern in Moscow and its political and cultural dealings with the French Communist Party inhibited its opportunities to grow as a party in Algeria.

Chapter 5 covers the period from 1954 to 1965. It examines the development of political thought within the leadership of the FLN on two critical issues: the role of the military in government and the role of religion in politics. The incomplete resolution of these issues had serious post-colonial consequences.

After the war against France, factions that had put aside their ideological differences during the war split again into diverse groups. The clerics returned to neo- conservative politics, some liberals and less authoritarian socialists formed parties such as the *Front des Forces Socialistes* (FFS) and the *Parti de la révolution socialiste* (PRS), and the more authoritarian socialists remained within the FLN. While all these groups agreed that Islam and Arabic should play important roles in Algeria's politics, none of them ever clearly articulated what those roles would be. The sixth chapter examines how the FLN and the army under the leadership of President Houari Boumedienne used Islam to try to extend their base of popular support while creating an authoritarian society with extensive controls over all aspects of society, especially religion. The chapter begins with Boumedienne's June 1965 *coup d'état* and ends with his death in December 1978.

Chapter 7 examines the period from 1979 to 1992. During that time the FLN's and the army's attempts to centralize control of religion and religious groups weakened, and independent grass-roots political and religious movements emerged. The successful Islamic revolution in Iran, the rise of such groups such as Hizbollah in Lebanon, and the emergence of powerful Muslim Brotherhood groups in Egypt, Jordan, and the Sudan all contributed to energizing religio-political movements in Algeria. In February 1989, Abbasi Madani and Ali Belhadj established the *Front Islamique du Salut* (FIS) that became the first explicitly religious political party to be recognized by the state. On December 26, 1991, the FIS was elected to govern Algeria in the first multi-party nationwide elections to be held in that country during the independence period. On January 11, 1992, two weeks after this electoral victory, the army led by General Khaled Nezzar annulled the election results and pressured President Chadli Ben Jedid to resign. Chapter 7 explores why the FIS emerged between 1990 through 1992 as the preferred electoral choice of the Algerian people. The chapter also examines the consequences of annulment of the elections.

Chapter 8 summarizes our essential arguments: first, that Islam played a remarkably continuous role in the organization of political resistance in Algeria; second, that Islam's definition of justice as equity has played a critical role in stimulating the organization of these movements in Algeria and elsewhere; and, third, that Islam, in its search for justice, has had diverse ideological expressions.

This third point is probably one of the most important that can be made within this book. Many Western educated citizens terribly misunderstand Islam, believing that Islam when it is expressed politically is either monolithic in its expression or that it poses an essential political and ideological menace to the West. While many residents of the West may not fully believe in the tenets of Islam, it is patently false to believe that all Muslims create or imagine their politics similarly. Islamic politics are wonderfully diverse in their expression. Second, Islam does not pose a menace to the West. Certain Muslim leaders may oppose Western political or economic interests either militarily or politically. While these Muslim leaders challenge the West's alleged prerogatives, other Muslim leaders and states regularly cooperate and maintain pacific relations with western countries. So where is the Muslim menace?

This book has been written with the hope that it enhances the reader's understanding of the role of Islam in Algeria's politics. It has also been written so that the question of Islam in politics more generally can be understood. It is my hope that I have accomplished both objectives.

Acknowledgments

✳

No book is the work of a single person. This book would have been impossible without the help of family, friends, professors, and even strangers who lent moral and material support to make it possible. Let me thank the following individuals in particular.

First, to Javette Pinkney, I would like to express my sincerest thanks for her many years of support. She helped me realize this work. Second, I would like to thank my parents. My father, Juan Salvador Laremont, died before this book was completed. His constant insistence that I needed to finish it encouraged me to work longer hours and work more diligently. As always, my mother, Ana Maria Laremont, has provided the guidance and support that have made her an ideal mother.

Friends and professors also helped along the way. The entire political science faculty at Yale University was extraordinary. Especially to be thanked are Professor William Foltz who provided persistent encouragement, Professor David Apter whose enthusiasm and global vision were boundless, and Professor Juan Linz whose brilliance as a teacher and advisor is only matched by his humility. I also thank Professor David Cameron at Yale.

The faculty and staff at my new academic home — the Institute of Global Cultural Studies at Binghamton University, State University of New York — must also be thanked. Professor Ali A.

Mazrui, the Director of the Institute, has been a friend and mentor now for almost ten years. His wife, Pauline Mazrui, has always been supportive. The staff at the Institute has been most helpful. I would like to thank especially Ruzima Sebuharara, Robert Ostergard, Fouad Kalouche, Aldrin Bonilla, Parviz Morewedge, Danielle Blas, Nancy Levis, and Barbara Tierno. They have all helped make my professional life infinitely more pleasant.

Others who have helped along the way and who need to be mentioned include Grace Houghton who helped enormously with brilliant editing, Redha Fellah, Adrian Kirk, and the numerous helpful librarians at Yale University, Harvard University, Columbia University, the Colonial Archives in Aix-en-Provence, the National Archives in Algiers, the National Library in Paris, and the Arab Institute in Paris.

Last and certainly not least I must thank my wife, Dr. Lisa Yun, who is a constant source of joy, inspiration, intellectual camaraderie, and fidelity. She has taught me to laugh again.

Chapter I

✳

The Politics of Islam

Since the successful Islamic revolution in Iran in 1979, and more recently since the demise of the Soviet Empire in the 1990's, Western political commentators have refocused upon political Islam as a "problem" to be solved.[1] The number of analyses that has claimed to explain this phenomenon has been legion.[2] Most of these studies, however, have characterized Islam as a religion and a political movement that should be feared and confronted by the West. Many of these analyses have ignored the larger reality that most Muslim countries and most Muslims are peaceful rather than warmongering. This introduction will explain why the social and political goals of Islam and the institutions created by that religion may pose initial intellectual challenges to their being understood by Western-educated thinkers and policy makers.

The first essential element to recognize about the social and political community of Islam is that — in contrast to the liberal societies of the West — it is a community in which its political discourse and political institutions that emerge from that discourse are founded upon a vision emphasizing justice as substantive rather than procedural, that justice has origins in a moral order that is derived from religion, and that its delivery is possible through the application of scriptural laws. In Euro-American societies, by con-

1

trast, justice is a concept that is more formal both in its adjudication and administration. Its system for the delivery of justice is more structured and bureaucratized than that which exists in Islamic law, and its moral vision, while having origins in scripture, has since the eighteenth century, A.D., been partially divorced from it.

Second, in this book we will observe that there are often critical political linkages among the creation of systems of law, the mass acceptance of systems of law, and the eventual stabilization and legitimation of states. From the nineteenth century in Algeria (and from even earlier times in other Muslim countries) dissidents and critics from within the community of Islam have consistently questioned the legitimacy of laws, politics, and states that have borrowed political ideas or jurisprudential principles from the legal and political traditions of Europe or the Americas.[3] The demise of European colonialism accelerated this process of scrutiny. Some political dissidents have claimed that Muslim politics cannot possibly be authentic or functional when it borrows political ideas or jurisprudential principles from outside the realm of Muslim thought.

These dissidents have claimed that the systems of law and politics that operate in Europe and the Americas simply do not deliver real substantive justice. They believe that justice, when it is real, is fair, substantive, and equitable rather than procedurally formal. They argue that foreign legal and political systems simply do not fit within the moral order of Islam. They claim that these systems apply the law mechanistically and that they do not achieve substantive justice. They allege that these systems tolerate high levels of inequality, with prevalent racial, ethnic, and economic discrimination. Because of their failure to deliver their view of justice, they urge the rejection of European and Anglo- American systems of law and politics and their substitution with Islamic law and politics.

The Islamic law tradition — in contrast to the European and Anglo-American legal traditions — is more informal in its institutional operation. Substantive justice and equity are its principal goals.[4] In informal systems of law "the administration of justice . . . is oriented not towards fixed rules of a formally rational law but toward the ethical, religious, political, or otherwise expediential postulates of a substantively rational law."[5] Dragan Milovanovic said that in informal legal systems

> Decision making . . . is based upon the specific factors of a particular case. It is substantive to the degree that some external political, ethical, moral, emotional, etc. criteria is applied. Little generalization exists. No general norm is applied. It is irrational to the degree that even similarly situated [cases] are treated differently. In other words, case-by-case decision making takes place rather than the attempt to apply universal standards. An outsider cannot predict the outcome of the decision.[6]

Max Weber claimed that the Islamic legal system operated informally because its judges settled disputes on a case-by-case basis.[7]

This method of decision-making focussed on case-by-case deliberation and did not require that judges refer to fixed principles of law such as statutes or legal precedent *(stare decisis)* for rendering decisions. Being freed from the mechanistic application of formal principles of law, Islamic law judges were more easily empowered to create and deliver equitable solutions. Equity rather than formalism was enshrined as the principal jurisprudential objective. European or Anglo-American judges, by contrast, must decide their cases by reference to more rigid principles of positive law. This more formal approach — with fixed references to positive law — inhibits the reaching of equitable solutions. Judges in Europe and the Americas also do not refer to scripture for rendering their decisions. In Islamic law, by contrast, judges systematically refer to either scripture or the religious law (the *sharia*).

Theorists of jurisprudence have asserted that in European and Anglo-American law there is a high concern for formality in decision making.

> The form of legal reasoning is logical to the degree that decisions or rules are consciously arrived through a highly developed systematized set of rules; formal, to the degree that decision-making criteria is intrinsic to the legal order; and rational, to the degree that decision-making is based and justified on rules that treat all those similarly situated within a "gapless system of rules, under which . . . all conceivable fact situations must be capable of being logically subsumed.[8]

The procedural formalism of European and Anglo-American law has stabilized liberalism and helped legitimate bourgeois capitalist regimes. Marx and Weber agreed, albeit for different reasons, that there was a close nexus between the successful institutionalization of European and Anglo-American law and the stabilization of liberal bourgeois capitalist states. Karl Marx said in his *A Contribution to the Critique of Political Economy:*

> The general conclusion at which I arrive and which, once reached, continued to serve as a leading thread in my studies can be briefly summed up as follows: In the social production which men carry on they enter into definite relations that are indispensable and independent of their will; these relations of production correspond to a definite stage of their material powers of production. The sum total of these relations of production constitutes the economic structure of society — the real foundation, on which rise *legal and political superstructures* and to which correspond definite forms of social consciousness. The mode of production of material life determines the social, political and spiritual processes of life. It is not the consciousness of men that determines their existence but, on the contrary, their social existence determines their consciousness. At a certain stage of development, the material forces of production forces come in conflict with the existing relations of production or — what is but a legal expression for the same thing — with the property relations within which they have been at work before. From forms of development of the forces of production these relations turn into their fetters. Then begins an epoch of social revolution. *With the change in the economic foundation the entire immense superstructure is more or less rapidly transformed.* In considering such transformations a distinction should always be made between the material transformation of the economic conditions of production which can be determined with the precision of natural science, and the *legal, political, religious, aesthetic or philosophic — in short, ideological forms in which men become conscious of this conflict and fight it out.*[9]

Max Weber agreed with aspects of Marx's analysis in Economy and Society. In that work he said that formally administered, bureaucratized, and autonomous systems of law were needed to support liberalism and capitalism. Weber claimed that the systems of law that developed in Europe and the Americas provided this kind of institutional support. Capitalism needed efficient judicial systems that would enforce commercial contracts in a predictable way.

> The rationalization and systematization of the law in general and . . . the increasing calculability of the functioning of the legal process in particular, constituted one of the most important conditions for the existence of capitalistic enterprise, which cannot do so without legal security.[10]

By enhancing the predictability of legal outcomes, European and Anglo-American law stabilized commodity markets and capitalist enterprises. Weber claimed that liberal bourgeois interests demanded "an unambiguous and clear legal system, that would be free of irrational administrative arbitrariness as well as irrational disturbance by concrete privileges, that would also offer firm guarantees of the legally binding character of contracts, and that, in the consequence of all these features, would function in a calculable way."[11]

Marx and Weber agreed upon the nexus between the legal formalism of European and Anglo-American law and the creation of liberal capitalist states. They also agreed that these regimes of formal justice may also fail to deliver substantive justice. Max Weber said,

> Formal justice guarantees the maximum freedom for the interested parties to represent their formal legal interests. But because of the unequal distribution of economic power, which the system of formal justice legalizes, this very freedom must time and again produce consequences which are contrary to the substantive provisions of religious ethics or of political expediency.[12]

The advantage of European and Anglo-American law's legal formalism was its capacity to deliver more predictable legal outcomes. Its disadvantage, according to Marx and Weber, was its weakness in the delivery of substantive social justice. Formal justice has not been substantially preoccupied with the ethical, moral, or religious issues.[13]

The Qur'an, however, specifically directed judges to concern themselves with the delivery of substantive justice and the resolution of equitable issues in the cases presented before them.[14] This search for substantive justice and equity is sought within a judicial procedure that is more informal than those that apply in European and Anglo-American law. This different method of judicial deliberation has empowered Islamic law judges to create and provide equitable solutions more easily than his European or Anglo-American colleague. The Islamic law judge's procedure of deciding cases more informally, however, while enhancing the probability for the creation of equitable solutions, has made jurisprudential consistency much more difficult. Predictability of legal outcomes has been less certain. The European and Anglo-American legal traditions of formal deliberation, while enhancing the predictability of the outcomes, inhibit the application of equitable solutions.[15] These different processes of judicial decision-making reveal that the systems of law in Europe and the Americas may display higher levels of tolerance for what critics of these systems may claim are inequitable judicial results.

If we accept the argumentation and approach of Muslim critics of Western law and politics, we begin to understand how dissidents within the community of Islam have argued that Western systems of law and politics are simply unjust. We can also understand how these critics have used the discourses of law, legitimacy, and politics to create logical relationships among the establishment of systems of law, the mass acceptability of systems of law, and the eventual legitimation of states. These dissidents have claimed that the European and Anglo-American law traditions, with their more formal and mechanistic application of the law, and European and Anglo-American politics, with their tolerance of higher levels of socioeconomic inequity, will not work within the moral order of *Dar al-Islam* (the world of Islam). They claim that only the traditions and institutions of Islam, which are aimed specifically at the provision of substantive justice and equity as political and religious objectives, will work.

What the Muslim critics of European and Anglo-American law are doing politically is engaging in what semioticians call the *politics of replacement discourse.*

Using analytical approaches that have been developed by Gramsci, Althusser, Poulantzas, and Habermas, we can say that these critics are trying to replace the political discourse of the dominant class, which is grounded in the language and the discourse of the old European colonial order, with another discourse, grounded indigenously in Islam, that they claim represents the desires and aspirations of the oppressed classes. Antonio Gramsci emphasized that ruling classes create a *hegemonic superstructure* of social control that employs *education, culture, religion,* and *ideology* along with coercion of *law* and the courts to invoke *social compliance* with its rules.[16] Using class analysis, Gramsci argued that within this superstructure of control, dominant classes used courts and formal positive law to repress the aspirations of substantive justice demanded by the masses.[17] Later, theoreticians Louis Althusser and Nicos Poulantzas agreed with and then amplified Gramsci's analytical approach.[18] Jürgen Habermas, reinforcing this line of reasoning, claimed that there indeed was a difference between procedural justice and substantive justice when he said, "The moral principle must be distinguished from the principle of legality, which specifies, a process of legitimate lawmaking. It states . . . that only those laws can claim validity which can achieve the agreement of all citizens in a discursive process of legislation that is itself legally constituted."[19]

Using this method of analysis, we can see that dissidents within the so-called community of "fundamentalist" Islam are rejecting the *linguistic and ideological superstructure* that has been imposed upon them by ruling classes. The rejection of these linguistic, legal, and ideological superstructures involves, from their view, the final stage in the revolution for true cultural, linguistic, legal, psychological, and political emancipation. This process of liberation requires the rejection of all political ideas and jurisprudential principles having origins in either Europe or the Americas. By engaging in this kind of revolution, the critics of established regimes are not just changing the terms of the political discourse; they are also transforming the underlying psychological and linguistic meaning of law and justice and, what is more important, the bases for legitimation of the state itself. This is a truly revolutionary approach. Their shifting of the paradigms for political discourse from the *legal formalism* and *procedural justice* of European or Anglo-American law and justice (which is historically and ideologically tied to colonialism) to the

legal informalism and *substantive justice* demands of Islam has politically empowered leaders who claim to represent oppressed classes.
This shift in the discourse has also simultaneously weakened the
defenders of status quo regimes who willy-nilly may have adopted
political and jurisprudential ideas that they inherited from previous
colonial regimes. In psychological and linguistic terms, this is the
political process of delegitimation. Linguistics specialist Benjamin
Whorf said,

> . . . the users of markedly different grammars are pointed by
> their grammars toward different types of observations and dif-
> ferent evaluations of externally similar acts of observation and
> hence are not equivalent observers but must arrive at some-
> what different views of the world.[20]

This approach to justice and delegitimation espoused by Muslim political dissidents is linguistically and politically similar to
approaches espoused by Catholic liberation theologians.[21] Muslim
critics of formal European and Anglo-American law and justice and
Catholic liberation theologians have revealed to us with substantial
clarity that there can be a great difference between the formal justice of European and Anglo-American law and substantive justice
demands having origins in religion. This search for substantive justice drives most "fundamentalist" Muslim political movements.

Last, we can observe that ever since the fifteenth century, A.D.,
lawyers and judges emerged in Europe as a class that began rendering decisions independently of religious law or the preferences of
clerics.[22] In the history of Islamic jurisprudence, however, lawyers
and judges have not emerged as a class that has been able to operate autonomously of either religion or the religious establishment.
The following chart summarizes differences between Islamic law
and Euro-American law.

CHART I

Differences between Islamic Law and Euro-American Law

ISLAMIC LAW	EURO-AMERICAN LAW
Search for substantive justice	Operation of formal justice
Focus on equitable solutions	Focus on the application of fairly rigid principles of law (statute & *stare decisis*)
Less predictability of outcomes	More predictability of outcomes
Less bureauciatized	More bureaucratized
Law derived from scripture	Law originally derived from scripture, then partially divorced from it
Meaning of law obtained with references to religious law tradition	Meaning of law articulated by elected representatives without references to a religious law tradition
Lack of autonomy between legal and clerical professions	Autonomy between legal and clerical professions

According to the fundamentalists, substantive justice and its realization are the real issues. Within the community of Islam these issues of substantive justice have been raised repeatedly. Across the centuries dissidents and critics have asked whether justice can ever be achieved when European and Anglo-American concepts of law and politics are incorporated into Muslim politics. Efforts to delegitimate political regimes have revolved around the questions of whether regimes have failed to deliver substantive justice and whether this failure is caused by ideas having origins in Europe and the Americas. Regimes that have failed to deliver substantial socioeconomic justice and that have also incorporated Western jurisprudential principles or political ideas into their methods of governance have been challenged for their "inauthenticity" and "illegitimacy." When political challenges are articulated in these terms we begin to understand how Islam and Islamic principles are invoked to bring down political regimes.

The Relevant Political Actors

Although substantive justice is the goal of Islamic politics, we must recognize that, in this search for substantive justice, two sets of actors, clerics and secular elites, have been engaged in real struggles to determine who will define justice and who will rule the states that will administer justice. While some scholars have claimed there is no distinction between religious and secular affairs in Islam,[23] a closer examination of history reveals that religious leaders and secular agents have been engaged in a continuous power struggle on the questions of politics and justice.

For most of the period from the Ommayad (661–750 A.D.) and Abassid (749–1258 A.D.) dynasties through the Ottoman dynasty (1444–1922, A.D.), both caliphs and sultans obtained stability for their regimes and legitimated their political authority by collaborating with and receiving the approval of religious authorities.[24] Both pre-colonial indigenous leaders and nineteenth and twentieth century European colonizers practiced an identical policy of trying to obtain the permanent political support from the men of religion regarding political and justice issues. As Habib Boularés said, "In Africa, in the north and south of the Sahara, it depended on the brotherhoods. In India, Great Britain courted the great scholars and did not hesitate to knight some of them."[25]

Even in the post-colonial period, secular leaders have negotiated with the *ulema*.[26] Presidents Sadat and Mubarak of Egypt both intermittently negotiated with religious authorities at the University of al-Azhar, Islam's leading institution of higher learning based in Cairo, to obtain official clerical support for their policies. In Tunisia and Algeria, Presidents Bourguiba and Ben Ali and Presidents Ben Bella and Boumedienne undertook different strategies. In those countries, the state attempted to coopt religious support by assuring the appointment of their preferred candidate as chief religious officer within the cabinet. By having their own person placed in charge of religious affairs, the political leadership attempted both to control and receive support from a clerical community that it could not ignore. In Morocco, King Hassan II, despite his considerable political power, has continued to consult with the *ulema* to build a consensus for his policies. In Saudi Arabia, the kings of the Saudi Kingdom have regularly worked with religious advisors who counsel them on the law. And in Iran, the clerics have had direct influence over the formulation of governmental policy.

While the Qur'an does not provide for a scripturally mandated clergy, the *ulema* nonetheless emerged as a professional class of religious leaders by the eighth century, A.D. "Their prestige and authority were based upon a reputation for knowledge and learning: Qur'an, prophetic traditions, law. As jurists, theologians, and educators, they became the interpreters and the guardians of Islamic law and tradition."[27] The political leaders (the sultans) and the *ulema* established a political relationship of uneasy symbiosis, with religious leaders advising in the regulation of private and moral behavior, while the sultans governed the state. This pattern of symbiosis and power-sharing has been observable across the entire geographical expanse of the medieval Muslim world from Timbuktu to Fez to Nishapur.[28] A *cooperative* relationship eventually emerged between sultans and the religious leaders. The *ulema* granted the use of their imprimatur to secular leaders, (thereby facilitating the creation of legitimacy), while the political leaders provided the *ulema* with protection and patronage. Rather than fusing religion and society *(din* and *dawla)* as required by the Qur'an, what emerged was a tenuous symbiosis between secular leaders and the *ulema*. Occasionally their relationship was harmonious; sometimes it was not. This pattern of symbiosis, which began in the ninth century, A.D., has continued through the present.

To understand this contentious relationship, we should realize that from the eleventh through the fourteenth centuries, A.D., a shift in political power occurred, with sultans becoming more powerful while the *ulema* as a class became politically marginalized. After all, the sultan had armies and the capacity to enforce the collection of taxes; the *ulema* only had moral and religious authority. The *ulema*, recognizing the weakening of their authority and influence, reacted by trying to delay this trend. They did this by trying to devise creative compromises of political power between themselves and the sultans. From neither a practical nor a political standpoint, however, could the *ulema* claim exclusive jurisdiction over politics. The power and prestige of the sultans had simply expanded while theirs had contracted.

During those centuries, prominent theologians including Muhammad al-Mawardi, Abu Hamid al-Ghazali, and Ahmad Ibn Taimiyya developed philosophical and theological rationales for sharing political authority between the clerical community and the caliph.[29] The caliph and the religious establishment arrived at a power-sharing arrangement that deviated from the Qur'anic ideal of unified political authority. The *ulema* defended this shared power arrangement in elegantly argued treatises such as al-Mawardi's *Al-Ahkam al-sultaniyya* and al-Ghazali's *Ihya ulum al-din*. In these treatises the *ulema* revealed subtextually the weakness of their own political position vis-à-vis the caliph. Pragmatically they compromised the Qur'an's desired fusion of *din* and *dawla* (religion and society) by conceding to an incomplete separation of power between themselves and secular leaders. This separation of powers never reached the degree of separation that it did in Christian Europe. Nevertheless, it is important to recognize that the union of the secular and the religious that was theoretically mandated by the Qur'an was historically compromised during this period. A symbiotic political relationship emerged between sultans and the *ulema*. Each side respectively began playing major and minor parts in a chess game of politics, with the *ulema* capable of "checking" but unable to "checkmate" the sultan's political moves. Sultans emerged with greater independence for the expression of their prerogatives, but they continued to find it difficult to proceed politically without the support, advice, and approval of the *ulema*.

Despite the instability and the variations in the relationships between the *ulema* and secular leaders over the centuries, and despite the changes forced by colonialism, the *ulema* endured and survived as guardians and interpreters of a tradition of religious law that the masses continued to respect and revere. Because of the vibrancy and the relevance of religious law, the *ulema* have emerged in the twentieth century as symbolic and institutional constants who have represented continuity, stability, and tradition during periods of turbulent social change. Because of their institutional capability for political survival, their position as arbiters of the definition of substantive justice, and their function as co-guarantors of political stability and legitimacy to secular political leadership, they have been difficult to displace politically.

Besides fixing themselves as co-guarantors and co-counselors to political regimes, the *ulema* have attempted to carve out for themselves two other important areas of authority that potentially can undermine what ordinarily would be considered critical prerogatives of the state. First, in the important area of law and legal administration, the agents of the sultan have been engaged consistently in a continuous struggle with religious authorities to establish autonomous and parallel systems of law. These systems have been initiated or created by the secular leaders to serve as alternatives to legal services provided by the *ulema* on matters of personal status such as marriage, divorce, and inheritance.[30] The *ulema* have tried to counteract this effort by trying to reestablish their jurisdiction over these matters of personal status. The first secular ruler who established a separate court system that was not under the control of the *ulema* was Suleiman the Magnificent (1520-1566) in Turkey.[31] He codified his laws in a separate code called the *Qanun* or *Book of Laws.* Suleiman created a system of law and legal administration that was controlled by secular agents. His creation of a legal system outside of the control of the *ulema* was a significant political development. States that aim to be independent of clerical authority must eventually establish systems of legal administration that are under governmental rather than clerical control. Since Suleiman's initial legal innovations, the *ulema* have persisted in their attempts to recapture jurisdiction of the law. In the twentieth century this issue has again become important. To the extent that the *ulema* can assert jurisdiction over discrete elements of the law, the realization of that achievement diminishes the capacity of what otherwise would be legal systems controlled by secular agents. If religious courts become viable, and if these clerically controlled courts satisfactorily resolve legal disputes, they provide a basis for undermining the state's authority.

Second, the *ulema* have had funds available to them that have been used to help address the social service concerns of their constituents. They derive these funds from internal taxation of the Muslim community (the *zakat)* or from external sources (Muslim charitable institutions). They amass these monies from internal and external sources into a fund called the *waqf.* The *ulema* have used the *waqf* to provide food, clothing, and housing for the widowed, the unemployed, and other needy persons. On occasion the *ulema* have used *waqf* funds to provide free books, tutoring, scholarships, and housing to needy students. Both by their creation of a parallel court system and by their establishment of an alternate social service system, the *ulema* have created institutionalized political and social infrastructures that occasionally rival those provided by the state. If the *ulema* can provide these services more efficiently and more effectively than the state, the provision of these services may eventually undermine the state's effectiveness, authority, and legitimacy.

Because of their capacity to survive as an institution, because of their efforts to create systems of law that rule on questions of substantive justice, and because of their provision of needed social services, the *ulema* have emerged in the twentieth century as potent political actors. They have enjoyed considerable symbolic legitimacy and they have demonstrated considerable institutional capabilities. They have become icons of moral authority because of their interpretation of religious law tradition and they have become institutionally powerful because of their success in creating alternate legal and social service systems. In the twentieth century, they have expanded their own authority and legitimacy while seriously challenging the authority of secular leaders. For institutional, ideological, religious, symbolic, and social reasons they have become formidable political actors. The challenge for contemporary political actors who are not members of the class of clerics is to cooperate with rather than ignore the *ulema*.

The Diversity of Political Islam

Stability and legitimacy in the politics of Muslim countries require creative power-sharing compromises between secular political elites and the *ulema*. From this pragmatic need for political compromise and from the doctrines of the Qur'an emerge three ideological possibilities: liberalism, socialism, and theocracy.

Before entering into a discussion and analysis of the relative significance of liberalism, socialism, and theocracy in Muslim countries, non-Arabic readers need to become familiar with certain Arabic terms. Liberals, socialists, and theocrats alike use these terms to justify their own positions within an Islamic framework or to deny the same to their political adversaries.

The first term is *shura*. *Shura* is the word in Arabic for "consultation." It is described in the Qur'an as a worthy activity, and it is the prescribed procedure for decision-making.[32] *Shura* requires that Muslims arrive at decisions by mutual consultation. Liberals have invoked the concept of *shura* in the twentieth century as the scriptural basis for parliamentary democracy.

Our second term, *ijma*, means consensus. According to the Qur'an, Muslims can adopt and carry out a decision only after they have reached a consensus. The Qur'an does not suggest a specific procedure for reaching a consensus nor does it provide a specific set of institutions for doing the same. It does, however, require a consensus within the community of believers before the implementation of a decision. Because of the lack of specific guidelines regarding the procedures for *ijma*, the process itself may often seem obscure. For Western observers, *ijma* may seem most akin to the Quaker "sense of the Meeting." In Quakerism, the Friends converse and discuss issues until a "sense of the Meeting" is reached. The Friends take no votes and they do not follow specific procedures for reaching a consensus. Because both groups use consensus for decision-making, there may be a transcultural parallel between Quakerism's "sense of the Meeting" and Islam's *ijma*.

Last, our third term, *ijtihad*, means independent reasoning. Neo-traditionalist commentators within the Muslim community have periodically asserted that the "door of *ijtihad*," or independent reasoning for the interpretation of scripture, has been closed since the tenth century, A.D. They have claimed that the "door" has been closed because all necessary scriptural exegeses of the Qur'an were completed by that time. They have claimed that contemporaneous examinations or commentary of scripture would be redundant. These critics have also used the idea of "closing the door of *ijtihad*" in attempts to prevent the adoption or implementation of legislation that they believe innovates from the body of Islamic law known as the *sharia*.

Liberalism was introduced into the political vernacular of the Muslim world after its encounter with European colonialism. The colonizers introduced liberal parliamentarism into the regions where they settled. In the French colonial world, indigenous members of the colonial community who were sufficiently evolved or *évolué* could be considered as candidates for citizenship in the French imposed liberal parliamentary regime. In the more racist British colonial system, indigenous members of the colonial community were often ineligible for citizenship.[33] In the colonized Muslim world, two indigenous intellectual movements emerged as either reactions or alternatives to European liberalism: one movement attempted to reform Islam by urging that it adopt liberalism and Western technological innovation; the other rejected Europe and European ideas, urging Muslims to return to a purer practice of their faith so that Muslims could reacquire cultural and political independence. The first movement was best personified by Muhammad Abduh (1849–1905) and Muhammad Iqbal (1875–1938). The second movement's leading theorists were Muhammad Ibn Abd al-Wahhab (1703–1792), the founder of the Wahhabi movement in Arabia, and Shah Wali Allah (1703–1762), a reformer in India.[34]

The movement in favor of reconciling Islam to liberalism was first expressed by Jamal al-Din al-Afghani (1838–1897) and Muhammad Abduh.[35] Of these two writers, Muhammad Abduh was the more thorough political theorist. He addressed the question of compatibility among Islam, liberalism, and openness to scientific innovation. He believed that inflexible adherence to tradition *(taqlid)* was the enemy of Islam and that Islam should be open to innovation, independent analysis *(ijtihad),* and especially scientific discoveries.

It was Abduh specifically who suggested the use of the Qur'anic principles of *shura* (consultation) and *ijma* (consensus) as scriptural bases for the creation of parliamentary democracies. Other authors, writing later, elaborated upon Abduh's ideas. Muhammad Iqbal, for example, in his article entitled "The Principle of Movement in Islam" agreed with Abduh that the principle of *ijma* offered a scriptural basis for the creation of parliamentary democracies. Additionally, Iqbal insisted that eligibility for candidacy to parliament should not be the exclusive province of the *ulema*. Rather, he urged the extension of eligibility for candidacy to a larger section of the male population.[37]

In contrast to the liberals Abduh and Iqbal, in eighteenth century Arabia Muhammad Ibn Abd al-Wahhab set out to reform his society by urging his fellow man to return to a pristine practice of Islam based upon pure monotheism and the rejection of innovations provided either by the mystical branch of Islam known as Sufism or by the West. Wahhab argued for the unadulterated practice of monotheism, the complete adoption of the *sharia* as law, a radical adherence to Muhammad's prophetic tradition, and the rejection of accretions or innovations emerging from Sufi thought. The objects of Wahhab's religious and ideological animus were primarily the Sufi tradition and what he felt was an apathetic and obscurantist class of *ulema*. His reform measures were not directly targeted at the West. His religious commitments, however, impelled him towards exclusive reliance upon the Qur'an and Muhammad's prophetic tradition. The exclusivity of his references required the rejection of "deviant" ideas such as Sufism and, by extension of his logic, Western political ideas.

Shah Wali Allah, a contemporary of Muhammad Abd al-Wahhab, echoed many of Wahhab's views in India. He, too, railed against the apathy and backward traditionalism of the *ulema*. He, too, called for a return to the social egalitarianism mandated by the Qur'an and a rejection of the feudalism and hierarchy tolerated and sanctioned by the *ulema*.

Critics such as Abdel Wahhab and Wali Allah who disparaged the political status quo, the entrenched *ulema*, "deviant" Sufism, hierarchy and social inequality; the West and Western political, economic, cultural, and ideological influence shared a common theme: a return to purity in the practice of Islam. Despite their doctrinal differences, these eighteenth-century reformers from Abdel Wahhab in Arabia to Wali Allah in India to Al-Hajj Umar in Senegal to Muhammad al-Sanussi in Libya to Uthman Dan Fodio in Nigeria to Shihab al-Din Marjani in Kazakhstan all made it clear that a return to the pure principles of Islam was needed, without innovations or accretions from Sufism, from the West, or from other branches of thought.

These two approaches to Islam, one intent upon innovation and the other intent upon reversion to the purest tenets of monotheism, reflected a division of thought in the Muslim world that had its intellectual origins in Islam's other confrontation with an alien culture: the Greeks. In the eleventh and twelfth centuries, Abu Nasir al-Farabi and Abu Hamid Muhammad al-Ghazali engaged in another, similar debate about whether Muslims could modify the precepts of statecraft in Islam by importing Hellenic philosophical concepts into the practice of government. Al-Farabi was a neo-Platonist who in his *Ara ahl al-madina al-fadila* tried to use both neo-Platonic and Aristotelian ideas to create a revised Muslim political philosophy.[38] In the tenth century, al-Ghazali and Ibn Taimiyya attacked al-Farabi's Hellenically inspired ideas.[39] They argued for a rejection of al-Farabi's intellectually syncretic project of Islam and neo-Platonism. They insisted upon an interpretation of politics grounded entirely upon the Qur'an rather than neo-Platonism. This contest between reformers and conservatives of political Islam, observable from the ninth through the nineteenth centuries A.D., has repeated itself in the twentieth century and most likely will continue into the twenty-first century.

Moving from the tenth century back to the twentieth century, we have found essentially three schools of political thought in Islam.[40] One group has wanted to reform Islam to make it compatible with liberalism, a second has wanted to wed Islam to socialism, and the third has urged the full implementation of the *sharia* and the creation of either a theocracy or a clerically influenced government.

Liberals such as Abduh and Iqbal, socialist intellectuals such as Salah al-Din al-Bitar and Michel Aflaq, and leaders including Gamal Abdel Nasser, Sékou Touré, and Ahmed Ben Bella have been among political personages who have intermittently incorporated the symbols and rhetoric of Islam into their own ideological systems. By fusing liberalism and socialism with Islam, they have been successful from time to time in broadening their political appeal to the masses.

Besides those liberals and socialists who have used Islam ideologically, there has been another group of neo-traditionalists led by such intellectual luminaries such as Abu al-Ala al-Mawdudi, Sayyid Qutb, Ayatollah Ruhollah Khomeini, Rashid Ghannoushi, Hassan al-Tourabi, and Abbasi Madani. These men have claimed that the socialists and liberals have perverted Islam and have used Islam instrumentally to keep themselves in power illegitimately. They assert that a return to a true and pure form of Muslim state is required for the realization of justice.[41] These writers have demanded the creation of a Muslim state based upon the full implementation of the *sharia*. Second, they have insisted upon either the election or appointment of a leader (a *khalifa)* who will govern the state. Third, they have claimed that a legislature or advisory council (a *majlis)* must advise this leader.

These twentieth-century neo-traditionalist writers have also differed among themselves. Specifically they disagree over the composition of the *majlis* and whether the *khalifa* should have an absolute right to veto the *majlis'* advice. Some authors (for example, Ayatollah Murtada Mutahari) have claimed that only members of the *ulema* are eligible for candidacy to the *majlis*. Other authors (Abu al-Ala al-Mawardi and Fazlur Rahman) have claimed that candidacy to the *majlis* should not be the exclusive province of the *ulema* but rather should be open to a broader cross-section of the adult male Muslim population.[42] On the important question of the absolute veto power of the khalifa, Ayatollah Khomeini and Abu al-Ala al-Mawardi supported the idea, while Fazlur Rahman and Ali Shariati rejected it. These are examples of important, substantive ideological differences within the neo-traditionalist community. This diversity of views has been lost in the more general discussions about "fundamentalist" Islam.

Throughout the latter half of the twentieth century many socialist, ostensibly secular movements in the Muslim world have assumed the mantle, the rhetoric, and the symbols of Islam within their politics. For example, the Ba'ath parties in both Syria and Iraq officially incorporated Islam into their ideologies. (During the Gulf War of 1990- 1991, the Iraqi regime even added the words "Allahu Akbar" or God is the Greatest to its flag). Algeria adopted Islam as the official state religion in 1964. The socialists could not avoid the incorporation of Islam into their politics. John L. Esposito has said,

> Muslim governments employed Islamic symbols, values and institutions to legitimate and justify reforms. However, this was not a return to classical ideology for an Islamic polity. Islam was not the central principle, but rather it emerged as "a" component of the state's national ideology. There was a growing tendency to assert national independence by shunning the posture of wholesale reliance on the West and to appeal more to cultural pride and identity. Acknowledgment of indebtedness to the West for governmental structures and institutions as well as science and technology was distinguished from acceptance of Western values. Government leaders were coming to grips with the political and social reality of their countries in which the vast majority of their citizens (in urban as well as rural areas) were spiritually and psychologically indebted to and influenced by the beliefs, practices, and values of their common Islamic heritage. The governments sought to legitimate their policies through a controlled use of religion.[43]

These socialists have used Islam instrumentally in two senses: First, they have called upon Islamic traditions as a means of trying to restore historical and cultural continuity to peoples whose identities may have been fractured by some of the racist policies of colonialism.[44] Second, Islam's principles, with its emphasis upon universal brotherhood and social egalitarianism, provided an auxiliary ideological framework that meshed well with the goals of socialism.[45] In societies historically riven by familial and clan affiliations, the socialists were attracted by Islam's appeals to unity, egalitarianism, and universal brotherhood. These principles could serve the purposes of national unification quite well. The socialists believed that Islam would help them consolidate the polity, thereby making the struggle for a more just and egalitarian society easier. The traditions of Islam were wedded to an ideology of revolutionary socialist change and nationalism. For leaders such as Gamal Abdel Nasser in Egypt, Ahmad Ben Bella in Algeria, Sékou Touré in Guinea, and Sukarno in Indonesia this wedding seemed to make sense.[46]

Initially, socialists in Syria, Algeria, Iraq, and other countries with their programs of "Arab Socialism" and "Islamic Socialism" were able to improve the lives of their citizens. The new socialist regimes built roads and dams, they extended education and health care, and they brought electricity to the countryside. Eventually, however, socialist state planning ran into inefficiencies for both internal and external reasons. Economic and social progress slowed or was even reversed. Disparities in wealth became more apparent. Shortages became common. In this environment, a grass roots, *ulema*-led reaction against the socialists was born. Sayyid Qutb, the leading ideologist of the Muslim Brotherhood, issued his clarion call for fundamental political and social change. In his *Maalim fil Tariq* (Signposts on the Road) he urged Muslims to return to their authentic, indigenous religious and political traditions. He argued for the complete rejection of both the Communist east and the Capitalist west.[47]

Radical reform of politics and of society became the objective of neo-traditionalist politicians who argued that progress and prosperity would be restored to the Muslim community when it returned to piety and fear and obedience of God. The socialists, according to the neo-traditionalists, had steered from the path of righteousness. Both the socialists whom the Godless Karl Marx and Vladimir Lenin had inspired and the liberals who had collaborated with the heathen West were equally condemnable. These liberals and socialists were to be condemned because, in varying ways, they had steered away from the Qur'an's requirements of government based upon the principles of substantive justice. They urged that Muslims reject these movements and return to their own more authentic religious and political practices.

Neo-traditionalist Islamic reformers such as Ayatollah Ruhollah Khomeini in Iran, Rashid Ghannoushi in Tunisia, Abbasi Madani in Algeria, and Hassan al-Tourabi in the Sudan directly challenged the political authority and legitimacy of either liberal reformers or the inheritors of the socialist revolutionary legacy. They claimed or intimated that they, as leaders and scholars more fully versed in the Qur'an and Islamic law, would be better qualified and able to lead their societies towards the creation of a truly just Muslim state.

Debate within the neo-traditionalist community, however, has been complex. Some writers, including the Ayatollah Khomeini, plainly have favored a theocracy or substantial political oversight by clerics.[48] Other authors, including Ali Shariati, Abu al-Ala al-Mawdudi, Hassan al-Tourabi, Rashid Ghannoushi, and Ayatollah Shariatmadari, have wanted Qur'anically inspired governments and the implementation of the *sharia* as law. They have not, however, preferred clerically supervised governments. Similarly, concerning the question of the composition of the *majlis* or parliament, some authors (e.g., Mutahari) claim that it should be open to candidacy by clerics only while others (Iqbal, al-Tourabi, Shariati) have claimed that candidacy should be open to a much broader section of the population.

The Qur'an itself does not create a class of clerics; nor does it arrogate political authority to such a class. The Qur'an says that only the virtuous and pious, not just the learned, are eligible to lead politically or interpret the law.[49] The strict application of this scriptural mandate would make it difficult for clerics to claim that they have any special prerogatives either to lead politically or to interpret the law. The mandates and logic of the Qur'an make it tenable for both secularly trained technocrats as well as religiously trained *imams* to claim that anyone, if pious, is qualified to lead politically or interpret the law.

This is the conundrum: who is truly eligible to rule upon political and legal conformity with the Qur'an and the *sharia?* Because the Qur'an does not authorize the establishment of a class of clerics, any pious Muslim believer can claim the right to interpret the law and apply it to politics. In this context of real egalitarianism, both defenders of the status quo and revolutionaries and reformers claim authority to interpret the law and apply Islam to politics. Revolutionaries and reformers invoke the Qur'an to assail status quo regimes. Defenders of established regimes do the same. All cite the Qur'an. Contending and contradictory political forces make use of the tenets, the symbols, and the rhetoric of Islam to claim their sole right to express Islam in politics. Behind this rhetoric, however, lies a raw struggle for political power.

Widespread in the Muslim world is a desire for the creation of a politics that conforms to Islam and local traditions. Both the West (liberal capitalism) and the East (socialism) have either been rejected or are on the verge of repudiation. A new ideological foundation that is based upon a reassessment and reformulation of the Muslim tradition seems necessary. It is entirely unclear, however, what form this new ideology will take. What is clear, is that these new Muslim political ideologies will emerge in different political and social contexts.

The combatants of political Islam battle in six different sociopolitical arenas. Variations among the partisans, their resources, and the nature of their struggles suggest the following typology: (1) monarchical-rentier regimes; (2) monarchical-charismatic regimes; (3) military-authoritarian regimes; (4) bureaucratic-authoritarian regimes; (5) populist-authoritarian regimes; and, (6) clerically-informed regimes.[50] Examples of monarchical-rentier regimes include Saudi Arabia, the Sultanate of Brunei, UAE, Kuwait, Oman, Bahrain, and Qatar. Monarchical-charismatic regimes Jordan and Morocco. Military-authoritarian regimes include Syria, Iraq, and Algeria. Tunisia and Egypt represent bureaucratic-authoritarian regimes. Populist-authoritarian regimes include Libya. Iran and the Sudan comprise the final category: the clerically informed regimes. The nature of the struggle between status quo and challengers varies according to the regime.

Monarchical-rentier regimes such as Saudi Arabia and Kuwait have used extensive patronage systems for the distribution of petroleum rents coupled with their declared public fidelity to the Qur'an and Islamic law to counteract resistance to their regimes. Monarchy is not an Islamic institution. Yet, ". . . the monarchy has been rationalized by the claim that all, even the king, are subservient to Islamic law. The Qur'an and the *sharia* provide the basis and fundamental structure of the state — its constitution, law, and judiciary."[51] By swearing their allegiance to the Qur'an and Islamic law, these monarchs have thus far fended off attacks from more "fundamentalist" challengers. Because they have declared themselves on record as upholders of the principles of Islam, contesting the monarchs' sincerity has been difficult for political challengers. What is more important however, is that these regimes have absorbed criticism because they have the financial capacity to provide generous social and economic benefits to their citizens. These regimes have a surplus of economic resources to finance extensive social and economic programs. This financial capacity helps mitigate challenges to their authority (and legitimacy).

Monarchical-charismatic regimes including Morocco and Jordan have lacked the petrodollar resources of the monarchical-rentier regimes. Consequently, the Kings of Morocco and Jordan have found it necessary to bolster their regimes by alluding to their claims of ancestry from the Prophet Muhammad.[52] Kings Hassan and Hussein have also learned to play the role of leader as astute diplomat and warrior to mobilize mass support. King Hussein has often responded deftly to challenges to his regime by maneuvering in the arenas of diplomacy and warfare. King Hassan used Morocco's claim to the former Spanish Sahara to mobilize the populace in support of his regime. Both kings are aware of the need to fulfill their roles of royal leadership.

Military-authoritarian regimes include Iraq, Syria, and Algeria. In these regimes the military has proven that it was and still is willing to bind together, by force if necessary, states in which social forces tend to explode or implode. The social and political costs of unity by these methods are high. These military elites have viewed liberalization and democratization as costly political options that may lead to social chaos.

Bureaucratic-authoritarian regimes include Egypt and Tunisia.[53] These regimes are less repressive than the military-authoritarian regimes yet there is real fear of reprisal for either anti-governmental criticism or activity. In these countries there are greater opportunities for freedom of expression and freedom of assembly than in military-authoritarian regimes, yet the freedoms afforded by these regimes do not approximate real democracy.

In both military-authoritarian and bureaucratic-authoritarian regimes, political leaders have often pursued agendas of economic and industrial growth within the context of a one-party or one-party dominant state. While these leaders have focussed primarily upon secular economic and social development, these "socialist" or nationalist states have often tried to incorporate the symbols of Islam into the substance and style of their governance. Their resources for legitimacy have been either the legacies of their historical role as the party of revolution against colonial or indigenous bourgeois oppression, or as the party of economic and social progress. The challenges to their legitimacy have occurred when their historical legacy of revolutionary or reform leadership wanes (as it must over time) or when these regimes have been unable to deliver on their promises of continued economic progress. When both occur concurrently, as they did in Algeria, the consequences can be seriously destabilizing.

A populist-authoritarian regime describes Muammar Qadafi's Libya. His regime is an atypical hybrid. He invokes Islam prominently to attempt to legitimate his political agenda, yet, because of his own charismatic resources and his ability to negotiate a consensus among political elites, he has not found it necessary to resort to pervasive repression. Charisma, an ability to lead and negotiate with dissident factions, Islam, and petrodollar resources all mix to stabilize the regime.

The only two clerically led or clerically informed governments, Iran and the Sudan, comprise our final category. Differences between the two regimes are discernable. Although both are regimes in which clerics have political influence, in Iran the clerics or ayatollahs serve as jurisconsults to the political regime who can exercise a veto power over government policy. In the Sudan, the role of clerics in government is less institutionalized, more indirect and informal. Eventually, the role of clerics in that regime may wane. Reformers in the Sudan and Iran seem to have enjoyed substantial popular support. These regimes have been willing to constrain economic development when that development has seemed to conflict with their interests in cultural or religious revival. These regimes, of course, have had a shorter life-span. It remains to be seen exactly how challenges to their legitimacy will be framed.

Within these varying political and social contexts in the Muslim world, demands for substantive justice are prevalent. These demands provide the bases for most political challenges to status quo regimes. In the politics of challenge and counterchallenge, contending ideologies have vied for the attention and allegiance of the masses. Theocrats, socialists, and liberals all have claimed that they provided coherent ideological solutions for the economic, political, and moral dilemmas that confront the masses. In this book we will see how substantive justice demands have motivated the politics of Islamic resistance in Algeria. We will also see how liberals, socialists, and theocrats all have claimed that they truly expressed the correct version of political Islam.

Chapter II

⁂

Sufism and Resistance to Colonialism (1783–1871)

Introduction

I slam has played a consistent and central role in the stimulation of political movements in Algeria for over two centuries. It predates the arrival of the French on Algerian territory in 1830. Using Islam and its demands for justice as its moral compass, the indigenous people of Algeria rallied against Ottoman injustice and oppression as early as 1783. Throughout the nineteenth and twentieth centuries Algerians have referred to the political and social mandates of Islam to question whether the social orders that had been imposed upon them were justifiable. Islam has catalyzed demands for fairness and justice; Islamic institutions have contributed substantially to the organization of the political and military forces that confronted oppression.

In eighteenth and nineteenth century Algeria, indigenous political ideology found inspiration in the principles and practices of the Sufi brotherhoods. They also provided logistical resources that made military resistance possible.

The Sufis comprise Islam's mystical branch.[1] During the nineteenth century, the practice of Sufism was widespread in North Africa. In contrast to the Middle East where traditional Sunni legal-ism has created a well-established class of clerics that has ruled upon acceptable and unacceptable modes of religious expression, in North Africa and West Africa decentralized, polycentric Sufism has been well established as an acceptable mode of religious expression.[2] In Sufism, formally trained *imams* and *qadis* — who can often play conservative roles in society and politics — play less important roles. Direct, intimate, and often ecstatic worship of God is experienced directly without the assistance of an imam. This chapter will describe the resistance activities of five major Sufi brotherhoods in Algeria. It will also examine the exploits of the most successful of the Sufi politicians and warriors: the Emir Abdel Qadir.

The Sufi Orders

Both the Ottomans and the French imposed systems of colonialism in Algeria. Although their systems were different, both groups of colonizers subjugated the indigenous people of Algeria to second-class status. This subjugation, with its accompanying economic squalor and psychological dehumanization, provided substantial motives for political resistance.

The Algerian people resisted both the Ottomans and the French and they were able to sustain this resistance because they had in their possession institutions known as *zawiyas* that were run by the Sufi brotherhoods.[3] These *zawiyas* can be understood as a combination monastery-school-hostel. There, the Sufis educated students in Arabic and Islam, they cared for the sick and for the poor, and they eventually trained soldiers for combat.[4] Indigenous North Africans ran these *zawiyas* and managed them independently of either the Ottomans or the French.[5]

The five largest Sufi brotherhoods in nineteenth century Algeria were the Rahmaniyya, the Qadiriyya, the Tayibiyya, the Tijaniyya, and the Darqawiyya.[6] Of these five brotherhoods, the Rahmaniyya was the largest. It was originally founded in Algeria in 1793 by Muhammad bin Abd al-Rahman in Aït Smail.[7] The Rahmaniyya were quite influential in the Kabylie, a region ensconced in a mountainous area in eastern Algeria that creates a natural geographical enclave. Within this enclave, primarily Berber-speaking

Algerians live. Besides the Kabylie, the Rahmaniyya also obtained support in the important eastern city of Constantine.[8]

Abd al-Qadir al-Jilani founded the second brotherhood, the Qadiriyya, in Baghdad in the twelfth century, A.D.[9] It is one of the oldest Sufi brotherhoods and has worldwide membership. In nineteenth century Algeria, its strength was primarily in the western part of the county in the province of Oran. We will discuss this brotherhood in greater detail later in this chapter.

Moulay Abdallah bin Ibrahim al-Sharif established the Tayibiyya brotherhood in Ouezzan, Morocco (near Tangier) in 1678.[10] It was closely allied to Moroccan royalty during the eighteenth and nineteenth centuries. A prominent King of Morocco, Moulay Idriss, (Idriss I) was a member of this brotherhood.[11] Because of this royal connection, this brotherhood became the most influential in Morocco. Its followers in Algeria could be found primarily in western Algeria, especially in the city of Tlemcen.[12]

Ahmad bin al-Mukhtar al-Tijani created the Tijaniyya brotherhood in Aïn Mahdi, Algeria in 1781.[13] The Tijaniyya was an expansive and dynamic brotherhood having followers in Morocco, Algeria, Tunisia, Mauritania, Mali, Senegal, and the Sudan. After the death of its founder, the Tijaniyya had two principal centers. One was in Aïn Mahdi and the other was in Tamassin, Morocco.[14] From their center in Aïn Mahdi, the sons of the founder of the brotherhood, Muhammad al-Kabir and Muhammad al-Saghir, waged war against the Ottomans, the French, and other brotherhoods that tried to dominate or affiliate themselves with them.[15]

The Darqawiyya was a small, radical brotherhood based in Morocco and Algeria that preached and pursued what the other brotherhoods perceived as political and social policies of extreme social egalitarianism. The Darqawiyya was the offshoot of another, older brotherhood called the Chadeliyya that Abu Hassan al-Chadeli founded in R'Mara, Morocco in 1258. The Darqawiyya itself was founded by Moulay al-Arbi al-Darqawi in Bou Berih, Morocco in 1823.[16] Its principal *zawiya* was in Bou Berih.[17] Because of its emphasis upon radical social egalitarianism, this brotherhood attracted many members who came from the poorest classes in Morocco and Algeria.

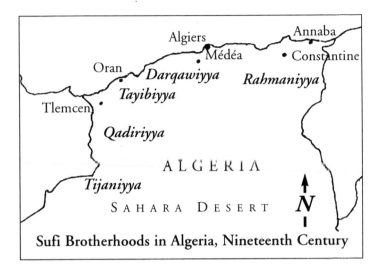

Sufi Brotherhoods in Algeria, Nineteenth Century

The first Algerian revolt against colonial rule was directed against the Ottoman Empire in 1783. Before recounting that revolt, however, we should describe how the Ottomans first arrived to assert political control over Algeria.

Ottoman Rule

The Ottomans arrived in Algeria in 1519 when Kheir al-Din, the ruler of Algiers, petitioned them to help him in the defense of the city against Spanish invaders. Kheir al-Din (also known as Barbarossa) himself was not a native Algerian but rather was a Turk born on the Greek island of Lesbos, who became the leader of Algiers by the consent of its Andalusian community. The Andalusians asked Kheir al-Din and his brother, Uruj, to defend the city of Algiers from the first set of Spanish invaders who had arrived in 1509. The Spaniards had invaded Algiers because of harassment of their merchant ships by pirates based in the area. The struggles and controversies between the Spanish and the Andalusians of Algiers were both significant and threatening because King Ferdinand and Queen Isabella had only recently expelled the Andalusians from Spain in 1492. In exchange for their defense of the city, the politically influential Andalusian community in Algiers accepted Kheir al-Din and Uruj as their leaders. When Uruj was killed in battle in 1518, Kheir al-Din became sole ruler.

The Ottomans later negotiated a treaty with Kheir al-Din in 1525 that gave them political sovereignty of the area. They then went on to create a society in Algeria that was based upon ethnic discrimination. The Ottomans or Turks placed themselves (that is, pure-blood Turks) in the highest positions of political, economic, and social power. They then created an intermediary category of privilege of mixed race persons known as *kulughlis*. (Those were persons born of a Turk father and Algerian mother). Pure-blood native Algerians, however, were placed at the bottom rung of this socioeconomic ladder. The Ottomans practiced ethnic discrimination against their Muslim co-religionists. They elevated themselves and remained aloof. They created an ethnically based hierarchal society that was not compatible with the ethnic, racial, and social egalitarian ethos of Islam.[18] They also imposed burdensome taxes. Because of these social and fiscal practices, they were widely disliked.

The Darqawiyya brotherhood's lineal predecessor, the Chadeliyya, was the first to revolt against the Ottoman Empire. From 1783 to 1805 the Chadeliyya/Darqawiyya brotherhood rebelled in Algeria's western province of Oran.[19]

The Chadeliyya/Darqawiyya brotherhood and the Rahmaniyya brotherhood instigated a second rebellion against the Ottomans in the Kabylie that lasted from 1804 to 1809. Because of their continuous participation in uprisings against Ottoman rule, the Darqawiyya provoked massive retaliation. After being flattened militarily, the Darqawiyya retreated to a region of Algeria known as the Médéa (just south of Algiers).

The third brotherhood to rebel against the Ottomans was the Tijaniyya. From their center in Aïn Mahdi in southern Algeria, the Tijaniyya resisted the payment of taxes to the Ottomans from 1822 to 1827. In 1827, the Tijaniyya attacked the Ottomans in Mascara, a city in western Algeria. The Ottomans defeated the Tijaniyya there. Their leader, Muhammad al-Kabir, was killed in battle and then decapitated. The Ottomans then displayed his head in public as a warning to those who would rebel against Ottoman rule.[20]

The French Invasion and Algerian Resistance

French forces arrived on Algerian soil on 14 June 1830. On that day they invaded at the beach of Sidi Ferruch, near the city of Algiers. They assaulted the city five days later, using plans that Napoleon had devised in 1808. The battle for the city of Algiers was quick yet it was quite bloody. One-fifth of the entire French expeditionary force — six thousand Frenchmen — died or were wounded in battle. On the fifth of July, the Turkish *dey* of Algiers, Hussein, surrendered to General de Bourmount, the commander of the French forces.

For many years, apologetical colonial historians claimed that the French invasion took place because Hussein had struck Pierre Deval, the French consul, with a hand-held fan. The jingoistic press in the southern French city of Marseilles characterized this blow to the body of a representative of France — with a fan — as a blow to the honor of France. They cited this minor bodily assault as justification for an invasion of 35,000 soldiers. This temporary invasion to restore the honor of France turned into 132 years of colonial occupation.

The assault with the fan did indeed take place on 30 April 1827 during an argument between Hussein and Deval about a debt owed by the government of France to two of the *dey's* subjects. These two subjects, who were Jewish merchants, had previously delivered grain to France 27 years earlier. As of 1827, France still had not paid in full for the delivery of the grain, though their debt had been renegotiated so that France would pay less than the amount originally owed. In the midst of an argument concerning the resolution of this debt, Hussein struck Deval with a fan. This apparently trivial scuffle initiated war and colonial domination.

Underlying this story of physical assault were more complex economic and political reasons for invasion. France did not launch a war and then maintain 132 years of colonial occupation simply because of an assault involving a fan. For many years, merchants in the port city of Marseilles in southern France had been agitating for colonial expansion into northern Africa for commercial reasons. [21] Napoleon himself had considered invading Algiers as early as 1808.

Apart from these two factors, there were substantial agricultural interests for the invasion of Algeria. The littoral across the northern edge of Algeria between the Atlas mountains and the Mediterranean Sea can be, because of the prevalence of somewhat more regular rain, a more productive area for agriculture than many areas of southern France. Further, merchants in Marseilles goaded France to invade Algeria because they feared that England would move into the area by either commercial treaty or force.

France's successful invasion provoked a real political and psychological crisis among Algerians in the city.[22] Historically, Algerians had been accustomed to periodic European invasions of their territory. They had also been confident of their ability, usually with the assistance of co-religionists, to expel the invader. In the midst of this crisis, two brotherhoods emerged in the western part of Algeria as leaders in the resistance to French colonial rule. These brotherhoods were the Qadiriyya and the Tayibiyya.

Although the Rahmaniyya brotherhood was much larger than either the Qadiriyya or the Tayibiyya, it did not participate initially in the resistance against the French. The reason for their absence from the resistance movement was largely geographical. The Rahmaniyya resided primarily in the mountainous enclave of the Kabylie. This region, because it is mountainous and geographically remote, has been relatively inaccessible to invasions by outsiders. Because of their geographical placement, the Rahmaniyya could function semi-autonomously within this enclave.[23] They were able substantially to ignore either the Ottomans or the French, both of whom had established their governmental center in Algiers.

Farther west in Oran, the Qadiriyya and the Tayibiyya brotherhoods were well established and struggled between themselves for political influence among the people there. To understand fully the relationship between the Qadiriyya and the Tayibiyya in western Algeria, however, one must examine that relationship in the context of a geopolitical struggle between the King of Morocco and the Ottomans in the nineteenth century.

At the beginning of the nineteenth century, the King of Morocco based in Fez viewed the Ottomans as rivals and usurpers in the western part of Algeria. Throughout the period of Ottoman rule, the king consistently challenged Ottoman efforts to control the area. From the king's perspective, western Algeria or Oran was part of Morocco. To enhance his own position there and to challenge the Ottomans, the King supported the growth of the Darqawiyya, the Tijaniyya, the Qadiriyya, and the Tayibiyya brotherhoods at different periods. Being himself a member of the Tayibiyya brotherhood, however, he often favored that brotherhood.

Despite (or, perhaps, because of) the king's dispersed support of each of these four brotherhoods, the Darqawiyya and Tijaniyya brotherhoods suffered military losses in the eighteenth and nineteenth centuries in Oran that were inflicted upon them by either the Ottomans or by rival brotherhoods. The Darqawiyya retreated towards central Algeria and the Tijaniyya returned to their principal *zawiya* of Aïn Mahdi in the south.[24]

With the Darqawiyya and the Tijaniyya removed from the scene in western Algeria, the rivalry between the two remaining brotherhoods, the Tayibiyya and the Qadiriyya, became intense.[25] The Moroccan monarch, being a member of the Tayibiyya, was aware of this rivalry. He began a policy of supporting both groups as part of an effort to advance his own interests in the area. By supporting both groups he envisioned dividing and controlling both. We will provide the details of this strategy later.

Mustafa bin Muhammad (date of birth unknown, died 1797/8) founded the Algerian branch of the Qadiriyya brotherhood in the eighteenth century. Bin Muhammad joined the Qadiriyya after having made a religious pilgrimage to both Mecca and Baghdad. Baghdad was the headquarters of the Qadiriyya. Upon returning to Algeria, Mustafa bin Muhammad founded a Qadiriyya *zawiya* in Guetna (near Mascara) in western Algeria. This *zawiya* eventually housed an 800-volume library. The Guetna *zawiya* was dedicated to the teaching of Arabic, Islamic law, and Islamic theology. The Sufis at the *zawiya* also cared for the sick, the indigent, and the itinerant.

Upon the death of Mustafa bin Muhammad, his son, Muhi al-Din, assumed the leadership of the Qadiriyya brotherhood. Muhi al-Din was a religious and political leader who eventually asserted substantial territorial control in western Algeria. Because of his presence in the area and because of the prowess of his military forces, both the Ottomans and the Moroccan royalty tried to limit the growth of his influence.[26]

The latent rivalry between Muhi al-Din and the Ottomans was first exposed in 1823 when Muhi al-Din asked Hassan, the Turkish *dey* of Oran, for permission to participate in a religious pilgrimage to Mecca.[27] Hassan, fearing that Muhi al-Din's request for pilgrimage for his large entourage was a subterfuge for a military operation against his rule, denied Muhi al-Din's request. Instead he arrested Muhi al-din and his son, Abdel Qadir, and he placed them in house detention for almost two years. Finally, in November 1825, he released them and granted them permission to travel to Mecca.

Upon obtaining their freedom, Muhi al-Din and his entourage traveled to Tunis and Cairo where they stayed and studied at al-Zaytouna and al-Azhar, both of which are Muslim centers of higher learning. In Cairo, they met with Muhammad Ali, the independence-oriented leader of Egypt.[28] They then traveled to Mecca where they fulfilled their pilgrimage obligations. While in the Middle East, they also visited Damascus and Baghdad where they studied with the Naqshbandiyya and Qadiriyya Sufi brotherhoods. In 1828, they returned to Algeria.

The trip to the East was highly significant in the development of the intellectual, organizational, and spiritual careers of Muhi al-Din and Abdel Qadir. From their studies at the mosques-universities of al-Zaytouna (Tunis) and al-Azhar (Cairo), they enriched their knowledge of Islamic law and jurisprudence. From Muhammad Ali in Egypt they observed how a highly organized, militarily oriented leader could rapidly and fundamentally transform a society. They were also able to observe how Ali was beginning to assert his independence from the Ottoman Empire. Their visits to the Naqshbandiyya and Qadiriyya brotherhoods (in Damascus and Baghdad, respectively) deepened their Sufi connections. Their trip enabled them to enhance religious and political credentials that would prove useful in the organization of resistance to French colonial rule.

When they returned to Algeria in 1828, Muhi al-Din and Abdel Qadir maintained their network of *zawiyas* in the province of

Oran. Within these *zawiyas* they continued educating the believers and feeding and protecting the poor. Later, after the French invasion, they converted these *zawiyas* into centers for political and military resistance against the French.

As was mentioned earlier in this chapter, the sudden French military success at the battle of Algiers in 1830 seems to have thrown the Muslim community of Algeria into disarray. The military loss provoked a real crisis of confidence. In the panic of defeat and retreat, the defeated Muslim community sought solutions for their security, military, and psychological concerns. In this context, the Qadiriyya brotherhood, of all the brotherhoods in Algeria, provided the best organized network of *zawiyas* that contributed to the organization of political and military resistance.

The Qadiriyya were politically and militarily successful for several reasons. First, the Qadiriyya, because of their well-maintained networks of *zawiyas,* could provide housing and care for refugees. They could address the refugees' primal concern: physical security. Second, the Qadiriyya had centers both for propagandizing against the French and for organizing forces for armed resistance. Third, the Qadiriyya put forward an ideological program that resonated with the masses. Their ideological program had four elements: first, an appeal for *jihad* or struggle against the foreign aggressor;[29] second, a promise of the creation of a more socially just and egalitarian society than had been provided by the Ottomans; third, the establishment of Islamic law *(sharia)* as the law of the land; and, fourth, the appointment or election of a political leader who would be both morally impeccable and knowledgeable of Islamic law. These four elements of the ideological program were the bases for organizing the masses in the nineteenth century. Some of these themes relating to *jihad,* social justice, and the creation of an Islamic legal system reemerged in the late twentieth century.

In April 1832, Muhi al-Din declared that the Qadiriyya brotherhood would begin a *jihad* or armed struggle against the French in western Algeria. Soon afterwards he began leading the Qadiriyya and their allies in assaults against the French.[30] It soon became apparent, however, that Muhi al-Din, because of his advanced age and his waning physical vigor, could not continue to command armed forces. He then turned over the leadership of the Qadiriyya brotherhood and the *jihad* to his son, Abdel Qadir. On 21 November 1832 the Qadiriyya brotherhood and the leaders of neighboring tribes invested Abdel Qadir as imam with the *ulema* supporting his appointment.[31]

Abdel Qadir was able to lead the Qadiriyya and to sustain support for his religious and political leadership because: (1) he had earned the respect of his co-religionists due to what most observers claimed were his impeccable moral credentials;[32] (2) he was learned in Islamic law and, consequently, could obtain the support of the ulema who, in turn, urged their followers to support Abdel Qadir;[33] (3) he maintained his religious order's network of *zawiyas* enabling him to train an educated cadre of judges, leaders, and administrators who supported his rule; (4) he was willing and able to use the concept of *jihad* to mobilize the masses against foreign invaders;[34] (5) he established a system of law based upon the sharia that his followers widely respected;[35] and, (6) he created a more egalitarian society than had existed under the Ottomans.[36] Abdel Qadir ideologically and pragmatically weaved together the promises of *jihad*, social justice, and leveling egalitarianism with effective programs of military resistance, legal administration of *sharia*, and the provision of social welfare benefits through the *zawiyas*. As he said upon his investiture on 27 November 1832,

> I accept this position as emir, although with reluctance, hoping it will be a vehicle for Muslims, for preventing strife and dissension among them, for assuring the safety of the roads, for terminating activities that are contrary to the sharia, for protecting the country from the enemy, and for establishing law and justice for the powerful and the feeble alike. . . . Know that my utmost goal is the unification of the Islamic community and the execution of the Islamic practices. In all this my trust is in God.[37]

Abdel Qadir's promises of a more just society founded upon the principles of Islam would eventually be realized. His promises became real policy. His political legitimacy became established because he had proposed an ideology and programs that were firmly rooted in Islam.

Abdel Qadir's resistance effort began in 1832 and ended in 1847. Within that period he signed a peace treaty with General Bugeaud that lasted from 30 May 1837 to 18 November 1839. When he reinitiated armed conflict, Abdel Qadir and his forces fought for another eight years before finally surrendering to the French on 23 December 1847.

Calculating that the French would eventually be successful in defeating Abdel Qadir on the battlefield, King Abd al-Rahman eventually abandoned Abdel Qadir's war efforts and shifted his support entirely to the Tayibiyya brotherhood. Because the King feared the eventual defeat of Abdel Qadir, he acted to cut his losses. On 10 September 1844 he signed a peace treaty with General Bugeaud wherein he promised not to support Abdel Qadir. In Article 4 of the treaty he also promised to pursue and capture Abdel Qadir in the Kingdom of Morocco. If captured by the Moroccans, they would prevent Abdel Qadir from taking up arms against the French; if captured by the French, they promised that they would treat him with respect and dignity. The King's shifted his entire support to his own brotherhood, the Tayibiyya, which substantially weakened Abdel Qadir's resistance efforts.

Abd al-Rahman decided to negotiate with the French because he wanted to try to assure that his political rule would continue in western Algeria in case of a French victory. By preparing for the defeat of Abdel Qadir, he hoped to obtain his principal goal: the limitation of French colonial expansion to central and eastern Algeria while reserving western Algeria for himself. Abd al-Rahman and the French conducted and concluded their negotiations in secret. Given Abdel Qadir's influence and prestige within Algeria, they could not have revealed such a treaty publicly without seriously damaging the King's reputation.

When we contrast the Qadiriyya and the Tayibiyya brotherhoods, notable differences are observable in their doctrinal orientations. These doctrinal differences affected the organization of their political resources. The Qadiriyya's doctrines placed great emphasis upon charitable work, driving them to build large networks of *zawiyas* to fulfill that mission.[38] These networks of *zawiyas* were then converted into staging ground for the organization of military forces.

The Tayibiyya placed greater emphasis upon veneration of and devotion to descendants of the Prophet Muhammad, among whose number included the King of Morocco.[39] This difference in orientation caused the Tayibiyya to rely upon the political resources of charismatic or messianic leadership. Because of this fundamental difference in doctrinal orientation, the Tayibiyya were not as driven as the Qadiriyya were towards the building and maintenance of networks of *zawiyas*. These differences in orientations meant that the Qadiriyya would be able, through their networks of *zawiyas,* to wage war systematically. In contrast, the Tayibiyya could not.

This emphasis upon messianism vitalized a separate revolt against French colonialism in the Dahra mountains of Algeria in 1845. Throughout the history of Islam, the notion of a *Mahdi,* or a restorer of political and religious righteousness, has been prevalent.[40] From within the Darqawiyya brotherhood a leader named Bou Maza arose who claimed that he was the *Mahdi.* Bou Maza's real name was Si Muhammad bin Abdallah.[41] For more than two years Bou Maza led a revolt that spread from the Dahra to the Ouarseni and Titteri mountains, to the Kabylie and then to the Saharan rim. This rebellion was independent of efforts led by Abdel Qadir. In fact, Abdel Qadir refused to support Bou Maza after concluding that Bou Maza could not possibly be the *Mahdi.* One French intelligence officer, Charles Richard, writing at the time of the rebellion, asserted that Bou Maza may have been operating under orders from El Hajj al-Arbi, the leader of the Tayibiyya brotherhood. Richard asserted that the Tayibiyya brotherhood's support of Bou Maza's rebellion was part of a political effort to create independent centers of power away from Abdel Qadir's resistance movement.[42]

After the resistance efforts of Abdel Qadir and Bou Maza, one last Sufi rebellion led by Muhammad bin Ahmed al-Hadj al-Mokrani would took place in the Kabylie mountains in 1871. He was sustained in his efforts by the Rahmaniyya Sufi brotherhood. This revolt began on 15 March 1871 and ended on 5 May. Finally, it was met and vanquished by overwhelming French firepower.

Conclusion

From these events in the nineteenth century, we can make several observations concerning the role of Islam in Algerian politics. First, Islam, with its doctrinal emphasis upon egalitarianism, provided an ideological basis for the rejection of hierarchy as created by the Ottomans and the French.

Second, the Sufi brotherhoods, through their management of networks of *zawiyas,* created logistical resources for the organization of military resistance. Although the *zawiyas* were originally centers for education and charity, they were eventually converted into venues for the organization of military resistance. Of the five major brotherhoods in Algeria, the Qadiriyya had the best organized network of *zawiyas* and, therefore, it became the group that was most effective in organizing resistance.

Third, in the nineteenth century we see themes emerging that reappeared in the twentieth century. These themes included *jihad,* or struggle against a foreign aggressor; social justice, in the form of the desire for the creation of a more egalitarian society; and morally based religious-political leadership, in the form of the election or appointment of a political leader who would be both morally incorruptible and knowledgeable in Islamic law.

After the last Sufi revolt of 1871, the French subjected the Algerian people to brutal and systematic colonialization. French colonialism continued until the end of the Algerian revolution in 1962. The following chapters will describe how the French installed their system of colonialism in Algeria and how the Algerians eventually rejected it.

Chapter III

✳

Political Islam in Hibernation: The Effects of French Colonialism (1870–1919)

Nous avons vaincu les Arabes avant de les connaître.[1]

— Alexis de Tocqueville

Introduction

In the last quarter of the nineteenth century Algerian political resistance movements entered a period of quiet hibernation. After the last major Sufi-led rebellion of 1871, the forces of Algerian political resistance entered a gestational period and found renewed expression after World War I. Minor rebellions occurred in April 1876 (in Biskra), in May and June 1879 (in Aurès), and from 1881 to 1882 (in the Northern Sahara and the Oran). Rather than considering these smaller revolts as real threats to the colonial regime, the French suppressed them as police actions.

Beginning in 1870, France's Third Republic embarked upon legal, taxation, and forced labor programs that displaced indigenous Algerians from their lands while simultaneously empowering and enriching a newly arrived community of colonizers, or *colons,* from Europe. From 1870 to 1919 this community of *colons* grew and became the most influential political community in Algeria, often

41

challenging and blocking metropolitan efforts at colonial reform. During this period, indigenous Algerians became substantially poorer. We will describe this process of impoverishment.

During the last quarter of the nineteenth century, while Algerian resistance quieted superficially, participation in Sufi brotherhoods continued to grow. Colonial authorities in Algeria noticed this membership growth and developed effective policies to undermine the incipient political threat posed by the increasing Sufi membership. We shall examine these policies.

French policies to force Sufi brotherhoods into political compliance were politically successful. From 1870 to World War I, political resistance in Algeria remained disorganized, with the French authorities imposing their will where they wished. On the eve of World War I, however, rumblings of resistance began with French attempts to conscript Algerians into the French army. The imposition of involuntary military service upon an indigenous community discriminated against them both racially and religiously and provoked demands for fairer treatment. From an international perspective, the Algerian movement for political rights for World War I army veterans mirrored the same struggle waged by African-Americans in the United States during the same period. The Algerian political rights movement also received an additional and unexpected boost from President Woodrow Wilson when he endorsed the principle of the right of self-determination for nations in his "Fourteen Points." This declaration, although not intended as a principle for the colonial world, encouraged the formation of groups of politicized Algerians who challenged the colonial order.

After the turn-of-the-century period of political quiet, Algerian political resistance began to revive just before World War I. A political reform movement started by a minuscule Algerian *petite bourgeoisie* expressed itself through formal political channels rather than through armed resistance. Because this movement was the expression of a very small class and because it was largely disconnected from the masses, it could be ignored by the colonial regime. The failure of colonial authorities to respond to the demands of the reform movement pushed Algerians to convert their demands from peaceful methods to armed resistance. The *Guerre d'Algérie* would begin in 1954.

The Process of Colonialism, 1870–1919

The French Chamber of Deputies issued a decree on 4 October 1870 that legally integrated Algeria into France. With that decree the Algerian colony became, according to French law, part of France. The decree provided political representation for French *colons* in Algeria by granting them the authority to elect six deputies to France's Chamber of Deputies. Another decree legislated on 24 October 1870 established the office of the Governor General and the *départements* of Algiers, Oran, and Constantine.

Three years later, on 26 July 1873, the French Chamber of Deputies in Paris enacted the Warnier law. This law changed the legal regime governing land transactions in Algeria. Before the enactment of that law, Algeria was, from a French legal perspective, a disorganized colony. It was unclear whether indigenous Muslim law, Ottoman law, or French law applied to the governance and adjudication of real estate transactions. The Warnier law, with the law of 22 April 1887, became the principal legal instruments for the systematic displacement of the Algerian people from their land.

These two laws broke up jointly held, family-owned properties into smaller, less productive, individually owned lots. These laws permitted purchase of up to 400,000 hectares of land by individual *colons* and they authorized seizure without compensation by colonial authorities of so-called "unproductive" fallow lands. Further, under these laws, Algerians became responsible for the administrative costs of their displacement from their own lands. From 1875 onwards, because of the operation of these two laws, French authorities exacted 750,000 francs per year from the indigenous Algerian community to pay for the costs of their own expulsion.[2]

Land records show that after the enactment of these laws, from a period from 1878 to 1914, Europeans purchased 1.22 million hectares of land at an average cost of 119 francs per hectare.[3] During the same period, Algerians purchased 337,000 hectares of land at an average price of 223 francs per hectare. The following table details land distribution to the *colon* community from 1841 to 1920.

Expropriation of Land and *Colon* Population, 1841–1920

Years	Hectares of land distributed to colons	Colon Population
1841–1850	115,000	131,283
1851–1860	250,000	192,746
1861–1870	116,000	245,177
1871–1880	401,000	412,177
1881–1890	176,000	530,924
1891–1900	120,000	633,850
1901–1920	200,000	791,370
Total	1,378,099	

Source: *Annuaire statistique de 1933*

Hectares of Land Distributed to *Colons*

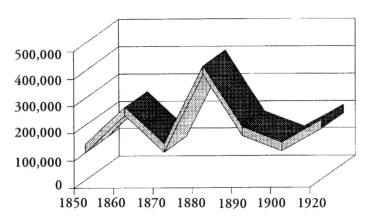

Transaction Costs, 1877–1919

	Land Sold to Colons		Land Sold to Algerians	
	Hectares	Cost (ff)	Hectares	Cost (ff)
Before 1877	54,000	n.a.	31,878	n.a.
1878–1898	563,762	56,495,302	131 374	20,087,471
1899–1908	277,428	31,329,295	125,794	25,887,329
1909–1914	382,749	59,271,977	79,953	28,884,400
1915–1919	80,963	34,943,880	79,608	55,245,310
Totals	1,358,902	182,040,454	448,607	130,104,510

Source: *Abdellatif Benachenhou, Formation du sous-développement en Algérie* (Alger: OPU, 1976), p. 172.

From 1873 to 1919, 1.35 million hectares were sold or transferred to the *colons*.[4] In this process Algerians were left with the less fertile lands. The more arable lands were sold or transferred to the colons. During this period land cultivated by Algerians fell from 2.57 million hectares in 1876 to 1.96 million hectares in 1916 1920.[5]

Not only did these legal devices displace indigenous Algerians from their lands, but the French system of taxation also forced Algerians to pay much higher taxes than the *colons*. From the beginning of their period of colonialization, French authorities had collected income taxes from Algerians originally imposed by the Ottomans and the Emir Abdel Qadir. These taxes were called the *impôts arabes*. In addition to these taxes, however, the French required the payment of French income taxes by indigenous Algerians. By contrast, the *colons* who arrived in Algeria were responsible only for the payment of French income taxes. A much higher tax burden had been placed on the indigenous community. Algerians also had to pay French taxes on real estate; the *colons* did not. In fact, the *colons* did not start paying real estate taxes until 1891. Even when the French imposed real estate taxes upon the *colon* community, they were only liable for taxes on developed real estate; any undeveloped lands that they owned remained entirely non-taxable until 1918.[6] These tax advantages to the *colon* community enabled it to accumulate wealth while this discriminatory and burdensome tax system systematically reduced the indigenous community into poverty. John Ruedy noted:

> From 1901 to 1919, the [indigenous Algerian] tax contribution increased by 26 per cent, while population only grew by 16 per cent, this at a time when economic productivity of the native sector was slipping. By 1909, Muslims were paying nearly half of all the taxes in the colony, contributing about one-third of the central budget, two-thirds of the département budgets, and half of the communal budgets.[7]

An Algerian jurist concluded in 1912 that while Algerians owned 38 per cent of the land and capital goods in the colony, they paid 71.19 per cent of its direct taxes.[8]

Besides their displacement from their lands and their imposition of a higher tax burden, involuntary recruitment into forced labor obligations (the *corvée*) frequently diverted indigenous Algerians from productive private economic activity. The *corvée* was mandated by the *code de l'indigènat* (the Indigenous Code) that was put in place in Algeria in 1881. This law empowered French colonial administrators to conscript indigenous Algerians to work in civic projects against their will. These projects included building roads and other public facilities, fighting fires, controlling pests such as grasshoppers and locusts, and providing human labor for transport when animals were either insufficient or unavailable. The French practiced the *corvée* across the entire geographical expanse of their colonial empire from Guyana to Viet Nam.

This combination of systematic dispossession of their land by legal machinations, higher taxation, and involuntary recruitment into forced labor reduced the Algerian people, who had been primarily agriculturalists and pastoralists, from being owners of their own communally owned farms into sharecropping. By 1914, the percentage of Algerians who were forced into becoming sharecroppers rose to 32 per cent of the total agricultural labor market.[9]

Workers who were not absorbed into the agricultural labor market were pushed by economic necessity into wage labor in the larger Algerian cities. Their pay in these cities was usually one-quarter to one-half of the amount paid to *colons* for the same work.[10] Women also entered the urbanized working class after 1902. By 1911, 21,397 women were working as wage laborers in Algerian cities. Most of them were engaged in the garment industry and in domestic work.[11]

Algerians who did not find work in the cities departed for Europe. The first Algerian workers seem to have appeared in France and Belgium in 1871.[12] Algerian workers were drawn to Europe because wage rates were much higher there than in Algeria. By the start of World War I, more than 30,000 indigenous Algerians had already moved to France to seek employment.[13] During World War I, another 119,000 Algerians as well as 155,000 Algerian *colons* were requisitioned to work in France.[14] The pull of immigration from Algeria to France continued throughout the twentieth century.

The colonization process created a community of richer *colons* and a community of poorer indigenous Algerians. The economic distance between the two communities created substantial hostility. The foundations of hostility between these two communities were not, however, entirely economic. Antagonistic relations were aggravated by persistent French attempts to assert political control over indigenous religious and cultural institutions. Political and administrative measures undertaken by the French during this period initiated a cultural confrontation between *colon* and Algerian that became permanent.

From 1871 to 1919, French colonial administrators extended their political authority over religious institutions. They did this by creating and appointing an official Muslim clergy — keep in mind that an organized clergy had never existed before in Algeria — and then the authorities determined that only they had the authority to pay this group of clergymen.[15] French authorities seized religious properties and foundations (the *hubus* and the *awqaf*), thereby depriving mosques, *zawiyas,* and schools of the revenue that they needed to survive. French officials monitored the activities of their own officially appointed clergy and they enforced surveillance over the leaders of the quasi-independent Sufi brotherhoods. They did this to ensure that Algerians would not organize resistance to colonialism within religious institutions. Religious leaders were subjected to intermittent internment, often on capricious grounds. Strict immigration controls were placed upon religious pilgrimages to Mecca because of fears that the *hijra* afforded opportunities for political organization among Muslims. For four years, from 1897 to 1900, colonial officers banned pilgrimages to Mecca entirely.[16] Muslims had to wait until 1914 to have their right of religious pilgrimage fully restored.[17] These measures controlling religion widened the distance between Algerian and *colon,* making reconciliation between the two communities difficult.

In 1905 French officials became concerned briefly about whether they would have the legal authority to continue their political control over Muslim institutions in Algeria. On 9 December 1905, the French government in Paris enacted a law requiring the complete separation of church and state affairs in metropolitan

France. This law, intended for France, could have had unpredictable consequences for the political control of the Muslim religion in Algeria. The colonial authorities in Algeria became concerned that, if this law were to be applied to Algeria, it would deny them the authority to regulate Muslim religious institutions. The *colon* community became quite alarmed about these political developments. Governor General Jonnart immediately wrote this letter to the Minister of the Interior in Paris:

> The greater interest of our domination requires that we preserve direct control over the functioning of the Muslim religion . . . this control manifests itself in our right to nominate the clergy. . . . I must insist that — for a period of ten years — I remain capable of filling vacancies [in the clergy] as they arise.[18]

This letter from the Governor General never received a response from the Interior Ministry. Religious policy in Algeria, despite changes in the relationship between church and state in metropolitan France, remained unchanged. French authorities continued their control and regulation of the Muslim religion.

As the French imposed their political control over religious institutions, indigenous Algerians reacted by affiliating with the quasi-independent Sufi brotherhoods. The historian Charles-Robert Ageron analyzed the question of regulation of religion during this period this way:

> Faced with this situation, with its clergy recruited and compensated by the Infidel, with its [religious properties] either confiscated or closed, with religious holidays, pilgrimages and schools at the mercy of the colonial administration . . . European observers thought that conscientious Muslims would resign themselves to deploring the miserable state of their condition. The believer, however, in a spirit of resistance, could also join a Sufi brotherhood. It became increasingly evident that Muslims had begun returning to initiation in the Sufi brotherhoods because of dissatisfaction about the social and religious order. European commentators began to suspect that these "secret societies" had aims that were political.[19]

Political persecution of the official practice of religion pushed

Muslim Algerians to abandon the traditional mosques that French administrators now regulated. As part of an effort of cultural, religious, and political resistance, they began practicing their religion in locations that were partially outside the control of the French. Real freedom to worship and to organize could be found in the *zawiyas* of the Sufi brotherhoods.

During the last quarter of the nineteenth century, indigenous Algerians, when faced with political and religious persecution, refused to retreat into submission. They continued to resist, even if passively, on religious and cultural, rather than on military, grounds. Between 1870 and the First World War, Islam remained a cultural and organizational resource for resistance. Islam, as experienced within the Sufi *zawiyas,* provided solace and opportunities for political organization in the midst of an enemy that was politically, militarily, and economically dominant.

Towards the end of the nineteenth century, membership in the Sufi orders or *tariqas* increased markedly[20]. This increase in Sufi membership seems attributable to the fact that the traditional venues for worship, the mosques, were under the administrative control of the French. Membership in the Sufi *tariqas* enabled Algerians to practice their religion without as much interference from the government. Participation in the *tariqas* enabled believers to exercise both their independence and their defiance of France. From 1870 to 1919, the Sufi orders provided a venue where men could congregate both to pray and to provide mutual assistance. Throughout this period, the brotherhoods mentioned in the previous chapter, including the Rahmaniyya, the Tijaniyya, the Darqawiyya, and now also the Senoussiya, survived.[21] In contrast, the Qadiriyya, which had been affiliated with the vanquished Emir Abdel Qadir, and the Tayibiyya, which had resisted the French under the leadership of Bou Baghla, were punished by colonial authorities as enemies of the state.[22]

Over time the French became aware of the growing popularity of the Sufi *tariqas.* They also became concerned about the possible political role that these brotherhoods might play in insurrection. To discourage this possibility, the French developed a policy for bringing these *tariqas* and their *zawiyas* under their control. Rather than confront these brotherhoods with military force, however, the French decided that they would try to undermine the Sufi movement.

Louis Rinn, the Chief of Services for Indigenous Affairs, developed a policy to reward brotherhoods that cooperated with the regime by granting them favors. These favors included, for example, the lowering of their taxes, the granting of a reprieve from the closing of a *zawiya,* or the loosening of restrictions on internal travel. Brotherhoods that remained uncooperative with the colonial regime did not receive the same benefits.[23]

Besides trying to control the official Muslim clergy and the Sufi brotherhoods, the French also began dismantling the Muslim system of education. The French closed many schools, especially schools attached to *zawiyas.* Colonial agents blocked the appointment of teachers of the Qur'an. Alexis de Tocqueville had observed earlier:

> We have seized their revenues (those religious foundations whose purpose is charity and public instruction). We have let their schools fall apart, we have dispersed their seminaries. All around us the lights are going out . . . . That is to say that we have rendered the Muslim society much more . . . ignorant than that which we first encountered.[24]

The purpose of these activities was to dismantle the Muslim system of education and to encourage Muslim students to attend French-run schools. The French succeeded in weakening the Muslim system of education but they were unsuccessful in recruiting Muslim students for the French run schools.[25] From the 1880's through the end of World War I, although they offered scholarships to Muslim students to attend French schools, attendance was much lower than the colonial planners desired. Attendance by Muslim students quintupled from 10,577 in 1890–1891 to 49,071 in 1917–1918.[26] The percentage of Muslim students enrolled, however, remained disappointing. In 1892, 1.7 per cent of Muslim children were enrolled in French schools. By 1918, that percentage had reached only 5.7 per cent of the Muslim school-age population.[27] French educational policies failed to recruit significant numbers of

Muslim students. When French policies are viewed as part of a com-
prehensive program to control the growth of the political power of
the Muslim community, however, we must conclude that these policies were largely effective. The French successfully dismantled the
Muslim system of education. Before the French invasion of 1830,
because of the existence of Qur'anic schools, literacy rates among
Muslims were higher than literacy rates among Frenchmen.[28] After
1830, because of the French disassembly of the Muslim educational
system, illiteracy among Muslims increased. These increases in illiteracy made the task of political and economic organization much
more difficult for indigenous Algerians. Illiteracy inhibited Algerians from breaking the hegemony of French colonial control.

The French enjoyed considerable success in controlling Muslim
institutions in the nineteenth and early twentieth centuries. Two
events occurred on the eve of World War I, however, that jarred
French colonial control and opened up the political process. The
more important of these two events was the compulsory conscription of Muslim Algerians into the French army in 1912; the other
was the mass exodus of Algerians from the western city of Tlemcen
in 1911.

On 17 July 1908, George Clemenceau, the President and the
Minister of the Interior of France, signed a decree ordering a census
of indigenous Algerians for conscription into the French army.
According to France's plans, actual conscription would begin in
1909. Leaders within the Muslim community in Algeria responded
to Clemenceau's census and conscription decrees by formally
informing the French administration that conscription would be
acceptable only if France offered citizenship and full political rights
to those who served in the French army. Clemenceau responded by
saying that these demands seemed reasonable.[29]

The *colon* press in Algeria responded to Clemenceau's proposed
policy of granting political rights to Muslim conscripts with
incredulity. The *Dépêche algérienne* of 1 October 1908 said, "This
red Vendéen, Mr. Clemenceau, who has never crossed the Mediterranean . . . wants to impose the grand ideas of the Third Republic
upon us."[30] A local mayor in Algeria, a Mr. Picinbino, said in the

newspaper, *Petit Parisien,* "According to the laws of conscription, every member of the French army must be either French or naturalized. I do not know any Arabs who are either French or naturalized. What's next!"[31]

Adverse *colon* reaction and political timidity in Paris delayed conscription of soldiers until 1912. On 24 January 1912, Governor General Jonnart issued another decree for the conscription of indigenous Muslim troops. Two thousand four hundred men were to be called up. The term of conscription would be three years per Muslim soldier. (Frenchmen and Algerian Jews only had to serve for two years). The French did not offer naturalization or full political rights to Muslim Algerians who would be conscripted.

After the issuance of the decree, Muslim-led anti-conscription demonstrations flared up around the country, especially in the city of Constantine. The colonial authorities repressed these demonstrations. The leaders of the demonstrations were then placed under police surveillance. The religious leadership in Algeria whom the French called the *Vieux Turbans* denounced Muslim participation in the French army altogether; the assimilationist bourgeoisie leadership known as the *Jeunes Algériens* demanded that the French government either grant full political rights to the conscripts or give them permission to leave Algeria for another Muslim country *(hijra).*

The colonial government responded to these anti-conscription protests by offering partial political rights to the conscripts. If they could prove that they had been discharged from the army honorably, indigenous Muslims who had served in the French army would be eligible to vote for advisors to the Governor General who were called *Conseillers généraux.* They would not allow participation by soldiers in elections for provincial or national representatives. Muslim army veterans would also be exempt from the application of the indigenous code (the *code de l'indigénat).* The *Jeunes Algériens* accepted the government's offer of partial citizenship; the *Vieux Turbans* rejected it.

The other important event that opened up the political process in Algeria was the large exodus of Muslims from the city of Tlemcen in 1911. Muslims who live in what they consider to be an impious regime have always had the religious option of exodus or hijra. The Qur'an provides this option.[32] The Prophet Muhammad moved from Mecca to Medina when the Meccans refused to answer his call to monotheism. For Muslim believers who can no longer tolerate life in the land of the unbeliever, *hijra* is a canonically acceptable option.

The census of 1908, which was a prelude to the planned conscription of indigenous Algerians into the French army in 1909, was the first event that triggered the beginning of an exodus from Tlemcen. After issuing the order for a census in 1908, Governor General Jonnart received 321 requests for emigration from the city of Tlemcen.[33] Local *colon* and Muslim opposition to conscription, however, caused a postponement of conscription plans until 1912. Just before the beginning of conscription in 1912, Governor General Jonnart issued another decree on 28 February 1911 ordering a census for conscription. This 1911 decree was the event that catalyzed the residents of Tlemcen into exodus.[34]

On 17 September 1911, the local newspaper, *L'Écho d'Oran,* published an article saying that a census would take place in the department of Oran. The same newspaper also reproduced an article from the newspaper *La France militaire* that said that, after the census, conscription would be demanded but that political rights would not be granted to Muslim conscripts. On 20 September 1911, the *L'Écho d'Oran* reported that 130 Tlemçanis had already clandestinely left the city. Within a short period, 164 families (526 persons) had sold their possessions, quit the city of Tlemcen, and moved to Morocco clandestinely, with their ultimate objective being emigration to Syria or Turkey. These exodi were not limited to Tlemcen. The Tlemcen exodus was simply the largest. Between 1910 and 1912 seven hundred and ninety-four families (some four thousand persons) had successfully emigrated from Algeria.[35]

The Tlemçani exodus and the other exodi created a pattern of Muslim emigration that alarmed the *colon* community and the French administration. A discussion arose for the first time in the *colon* press about the need for real reforms in the colonial system.

The Governor General ordered a commission of inquiry. In 1914 it issued a report called *L'Exode de Tlemcen en 1911*.[36] While this report acknowledged that resentment of military conscription without the provision of political rights was one reason for the exodus, it went on to recommend that the entire colonial system in Algeria needed reform to prevent future exodi. The report specifically mentioned the seizure of religious properties, the appointment of religious officials, the substitution of French law for Muslim law, the *code de l'indigénat*, emigration controls, the system of double taxation, the education system for Muslims, and even the denial of the right to vote as items that needed reform. This prescient report was in the *avant-garde* of colonial thought at the time. Needless to say, it was not adopted.

At the time of the Tlemçani exodus and the demonstrations against conscription, Muslims were only partially eligible to vote in Algeria. The right to vote was automatically available only to the *colons* and Algerian Jews.[37] Those Muslims who were allowed to vote were limited to a very small class of *évolués* or "evolved" Muslims who, to obtain French citizenship, had to renounce, in contrast to the Jews, their religious law (the *sharia)*. In reaction to both the Tlemcen exodus and the anti-conscription demonstrations, Governor General Lutaud announced a plan for political reform on 26 March 1913. He first suggested an increase in the quota of *Conseillers généraux* who were Muslim.[38] He proposed raising their number from three to twelve persons. He also recommended the amendment of the *code de l'indigénat* so that Muslims who were either veterans of the army, or decorated soldiers, or university graduates, or members of another category of educated people called *lettrés*, would be eligible to vote for these *conseillers généraux*. Despite these changes, other Muslims, who comprised the vast majority of the indigenous people, would still not be able to satisfy these amended electoral requirements. They would be denied their full political rights. Under Lutaud's reforms, these newly eligible Muslim voters could vote only for these twelve Conseillers généraux. Most Muslims would not be able to vote for other positions within the government, including mayors, legislators, and other officials.

The arrival of World War I with its attendant conscription of

Muslim Algerians into the French army, however, put aside Lutaud's recommendations and further pushed the agenda for political reform. By 1917, in the third year of the war, 115,000 to 120,000 Muslim Algerians had been sent to fight in France.[39] A report issued after the war showed that 19,075 Muslims from Algeria had died in action and that 6,096 were missing in action.[40] Muslim Algerian military service and Muslim deaths in the battlefield in the defense of France seemed to create a sense of moral obligation on the part of the metropolitan French government to begin addressing the political complaints of Muslims in Algeria. After the war, in 1918 and 1919, a series of reforms called the Jonnart reforms were introduced that expanded political rights of Muslims.

The Jonnart reforms did not grant full political rights to all Muslims. They simply amended the right to vote as defined by the 1865 *code de l'indigénat*. These reforms were quite restrictive. To vote, a Muslim had to (1) be more than 25 years of age; (2) be monogamous or a bachelor; (3) never have committed a crime; and, (4) have a fixed domicile for at least two years. If a candidate to vote met these requirements, he then could vote if he belonged to one of the following categories of Muslims: (1) military veterans; (2) owners of property or farms or sedentary merchants; (3) government employees; (4) members of the Chambers of Commerce or Agriculture; (5) holders of certificates of primary school education or of a university degree; (6) decorated soldiers; or, (7) winners of prizes in agricultural competitions. Further, the French administration did not grant the right to vote automatically to these categories of persons. Rather, eligible Muslim voters from these categories had to apply for French citizenship and the right to vote. In addition, and this is very important for our discussion in this chapter, the Jonnart reforms continued to require that eligible Muslim voters renounce the *sharia* or Muslim personal law to obtain French citizenship. This requirement was unconscionable to many Muslim applicants for the vote. This legal requirement effectively prevented many of them from applying for French citizenship.[41] Second, the Jonnart Reforms' requirement of two years of fixed residence barred most Muslims — who often had to move from place to place in search of work — from applying for citizenship.

Despite these barriers, 421,000 Muslims were eventually registered as voters because of the Jonnart Reforms. By contrast, before the war, in 1914, only 57,044 Muslims had been registered to vote.[42] We should remember, however, that despite these reforms, Muslim voters were eligible to vote only for candidates who would participate in the *Conseils généraux* (General Councils) and the *Délégations financières* (Financial delegations). Muslims could have their concerns represented to the Governor General within these legal bodies. These institutions were not independent, deliberative legislatures that enacted laws; they functioned essentially as advisors to the Governor General.[43]

Despite what we could characterize as very limited political reforms, the immediate post-World War I environment in Algeria revealed that demographic and political forces created during the war had fundamentally fractured the practices of European colonialism. Muslim participation in the defense of France provided proof both to the colonized and the colonizers that hierarchy founded upon distinctions of race or religion would be of waning relevance either on the battlefield or in the post-battlefield domestic environment.

When *colons* and indigenous Muslims returned to Algeria after World War I, they found that the rules of the political and social game had been altered by what had occurred during the war itself. The *colons* and the Muslims began to adjust to these new political and social realities. The *colons* reacted to the beginning of the reform of the colonial system with considerable trepidation; the Muslims looked forward hopefully to a postwar period of substantive political change. The *colon* community's politics would remain conservative and would remain essentially united in one reactionary and resistant political bloc. Muslims would organize themselves into three political groups that would unite episodically. These groups were the *Étoile nord-africaine*, the Association of the Ulema, and the *Jeunes Algériens*. We will discuss these three groups in the next chapter.

Chapter IV

✳

Politicized Islam:
Proletarian Nationalists, Clerics, and
Bourgeois Liberals
(1902–1954)

Introduction

In the first half of the twentieth century three political movements emerged in Algeria that led Muslims to challenge French colonialism. These movements were (a) a proletarian led, nationalist, and independence oriented movement founded with the assistance of the Communist Internationale; (b) a clerically led movement that was initially interested in religious, cultural, and linguistic revival and then later became involved in politics; and (c) a liberal colonial reform movement led by a petite bourgeoisie class that originally was not interested in independence but rather was concerned with equal rights for Muslim Algerians. These three diverse groups, with different political programs, all invoked Islam to validate their politics with the masses.

It is important to bear in mind that for most of the twentieth century the largest social group in Algeria available for political organization was the peasantry. This peasant class was also Algeria's most traditional, most conservative, and most religious group. Consequently, all political movements within Algeria found it necessary to refer to Islam, either symbolically or substantively, to capture this critical mass of potential political actors. This chapter explains how the proletarian and peasant nationalists, the clerics, and the liberals all invoked Islam to obtain mass support. It also delineates the specific political positions taken by these groups in their resistance to colonialism.

This chapter is divided into four sections. The first section describes the political development of the *Étoile nord-africaine* or North African Star party. Algerian proletarian nationalists in France founded this party. It was the intellectual and political predecessor of the National Liberation Front (FLN) that eventually led Algeria towards independence. The second section will describe the role that Muslim reformist clerics played in the intellectual, religious, political, educational, and cultural revival of the Algerian nation. The third section describes the political activities of Algeria's numerically small and liberally oriented bourgeoisie. The last section, the conclusion, will offer a theoretical analysis of changes in the structure of Algerian society and polity during the first half of this century. The successes and failures of these three political movements during the first half of this century had long-term consequences for Algeria. An analysis of these movements helps us understand why liberalism had such a numerically small base of support. It also explains why Islam has played such an important role in Algerian nationalist politics from the 1930's onwards.

This chapter attempts to establish five propositions. First, it claims that the most important political development of the first half of the twentieth century in Algeria was the cultural, historical, and educational work undertaken by the Association of the Ulema. This organization helped reestablish Islam and Arabic as the cultural bases of Algerian nationalism. Before the cultural intervention by the Association of the Ulema, Algeria was developing culturally and linguistically, under French aegis, into a French-speaking nation. The Association's extensive cultural and educational work partially reversed this process. They reestablished Algerian nationalism upon the foundations of Arabic and Islam. Second, from the 1920's through the 1950's, the Association of the Ulema, which was centrally organized, replaced the organizationally decentralized Sufi Brotherhoods as the principal religious organization participating in politics. When the centrally organized Association of the Ulema replaced the decentrally organized Sufis, a better organized clerical group emerged that challenged the state. This outcome fundamentally reoriented the relationship between the Muslim religion and the state. After the political empowerment of the Association of the Ulema, the potential always existed in Algeria for the creation of other centrally organized, clerically led groups that might challenge the state. If the political capacity of religious groups had remained decentralized — as it had been during the period of Sufi political leadership — it would have been much more difficult for clerically led groups to organize on religious and political questions. Third, by imbedding Islam and Arabic themes as elements of Algerian nationalism in their political programs, the proletarian nationalists were enable to expand the membership of the North African Star rapidly. Their embrace of Arabic and Islam assured that these two cultural icons would remain an essential part of the definition of Algerian nationalism both by themselves and by its successor: the *Front de libération nationale* or FLN. This form of religion-based and language-based nationalism provided political dynamism in the short and medium term but destabilized the post-colonial socialist and secular state in the long term. Fourth, the Communist Party's failure to recognize that Arabic and Islam were essential elements of Algerian identity guaranteed that this party would not enjoy either electoral or ideological success among indigenous Algerians. As a result, their sister party, the North African Star, became a nationalist party with a proletarian and agrarian constituency rather than an ideologically consistent socialist or communist party. Fifth, the Young Algerians, whose class base was bourgeois and whose political orientation was liberal and democratic, never emerged into a successful mass movement despite their periodic success at the polls. We can explain their failure for two critical reasons: first, their core constituency was limited to a numerically small class of the Muslim bourgeoisie; and, second, for a long period, their cultural affiliation was French rather than Arab. The masses of Algerians, being poor, politically oppressed, and resentful of the French, tended to resist both French culture and those who identified with it. The Young Algerians' francophilia inhibited their success.

The *Étoile Nord-Africaine:* Independence Oriented Proletarian Nationalists

After World War I a party named the *Étoile nord-africaine* (North African Star) emerged that catalyzed Algerians into militant, independence oriented political action. This party, both intellectually and politically, was the progenitor of the National Liberation Front (FLN). The FLN eventually led Algeria to independence in the *Guerre d'Algérie* which lasted from 1954 to 1962.

The North African Star party had political and intellectual predecessors in Algeria. The Socialist party began organizing and agitating for political change in Algeria as early as 1902. Before World War I, several socialist newspapers had been founded in Algeria including *l'Avenir Social* (1902), *L'Évolution Sociale* (1903), *Le Réveil de l'Esclave* (1904), *La Réforme* (1904), and *Le Socialiste Algérien* (1905). *Le Socialiste Algérien* was the official publication of the Algerian Socialist Party. It was renamed *Le Travailleur* (1906-1909) and, later, *La Lutte Sociale* (in 1909). The Socialist Party held its first congress in Algeria in 1908.[1]

The Algerian Socialist Party was profoundly influenced by Marx and Engels and contemporaneous European socialist thought. In its attempts to reform capitalism in Algeria, the Socialist party discussed the possibility of creating a political alliance between the Algerian peasantry and the European proletariat. It sought to create linkages between these very different groups because it saw this alliance as a key element in the struggle for worldwide social change.[2] The Socialists welcomed collaboration with Muslim political activists because of the asserted compatibility between Islam's emphasis upon social egalitarianism and its denunciations of hierarchy, and the Socialist party's own social and political objectives.[3] As the socialist newspaper, *Demain,* said:

. . . Islam does not pose a barrier to Communism, but to the contrary it is its most certain support. The history of Muslim civilization proves this point.

The rapid conquest of the world by Muslims may seem extraordinary to those who do not know Islamic theory. The first Arabs did not fight wars of brutal annexation. They fought for one idea, monotheism, and for one means of organization, collectivism. They wanted to liberate the masses of various superstitions and reduce social oligarchy. Those were the objectives of the first partisans of Muhammad. . . .

. . . No more hatred of the races! No more difference between conqueror and conquered, between rich and poor . . . .

What were the ideas of the Muslims? On matters of religion: one sole God. On social matters: communism.[4]

Many Socialists may have been agnostics or atheists, but they were unwilling to let belief in God be an obstacle to political organization or the creation of political alliances.

Outside Algeria and just after the Russian Revolution, European Socialists and Communists in Berlin and Moscow began organizing on the Muslim question. In 1918, a League for the Liberation of Islam was founded in Moscow. In 1919, Lenin founded a Special Commissariat for Muslim Affairs. In August of 1919, this Commissariat organized a conference in Kazakhstan where they obtained a *fatwa* inviting Muslims to consider the Union of Socialist Soviet Republics as the friend and protector of Islam.[5] The creation of the Commissariat and organization of these meetings reflected the fact that political activists within the socialist community were beginning to examine the relationship between socialism and Islam.

The creation of the Third Socialist Internationale in July and August of 1920, however, created political divisions between Socialists and Communists on the question of political organization in the colonies. At the conference in Moscow that created the Third Internationale, Lenin issued several theses unequivocally declaring that Communists and the Soviet Union would support "revolutionary movements of national liberation" in the colonies of the capitalist metropole. This revolutionary stance created splits between the socialists and the communists in Algeria, with the communists following the Third Internationale's call for revolutionary national liberation within the colonies, while the socialists first formally adopted and then quickly abandoned this position. The Socialists in Algeria had not envisioned an Algeria that would have been separate and independent of France. Also, the Socialists had not endorsed revolution as a means of political change. The Socialists preferred reform of the colonial system rather than revolution. They also endorsed the complete political integration of Algeria into France.[6] For these reasons, they abandoned the Third Internationale's call for revolution and independence.[7]

After the organization of the Third Internationale, Communists in Europe began supporting independence-leaning "Young Islam" movements. These movements were called Young Egyptians, Young Tunisians, Young Algerians, Young Turks, et cetera. While the Communists endorsed these movements because they found a fundamental compatibility between Islam and communism on the question of social egalitarianism, their endorsement of these movements was not complete. The Communists and the Young Islamists split on the essential question of nationalism. The communist revolutionary world view specifically endorsed internationalism and class struggles. These ideological commitments required them to criticize nationalism as a basis for political organization. The Young Islamists, on the other hand, were specifically nationalists. While the Communists and the Young Islamists shared interests in destroying imperialism, colonialism, and perhaps capitalism, they were unable to agree on the question of nationalism.

While the Communists in most of Europe were lending support to the independence oriented "Young Islam" movements, the Communist Party of France was dragging its feet. The French Communist Party determined, at variance with stated directives of the Third Internationale, to invest the bulk of its revolutionary activities in France rather than in its colonies. The French Communist party concluded that the revolution would start in France and then extend itself to the colonies rather than vice versa. At the Fifth Congress of the French Communist Party in June 1924, many Communist Party members from the colonies including Nguyen Al-Quoc (later known as Ho Chi Minh) roundly criticized the French Communist party for its faulty strategy.[8]

When the French Communist party did turn its attention to Algeria, it focussed on recruiting Algerian workers into labor unions and distributing leaflets and documents to Algerian workers on the nature and importance of the international class struggle. Their task was formidable, however, because given the lengthy period and the discriminatory structure of French colonialism, solidarity among Algerians was based upon religion (Islam) and language (Arabic) rather than class. The Communists' efforts to reorganize Algerians upon the basis of class proved perplexing.

By 1927, the Communist party had adjusted to the protests of its colonial cadres and unequivocally declared itself in favor of independence for the colonies. In Algeria, this position was revealed in the pages of *La Lutte Sociale.*[9] Throughout 1927 and 1928 the Communist party agitated for abolition of the *code de l'indigènat,* freedom of the press, freedom of assembly, the right to organize unions, the eight-hour work day, and universal suffrage.[10] The Communist Party also made it a point to reject alliances with all reformers of the colonial system, whether Muslim or European. At the same time the Communist party decided to support Algerian nationalism and the nascent North African Star party.

Algerian immigrants in France founded the North African Star party in 1926.[11] By 1926 France had a sizeable Algerian population. By the end of World War I, 119,000 Algerians had already moved to France to work.[12] During the economic boom of 1920 to 1924, another 136,000 to 174,000 Algerians left to work in France.[13] The arrival of colonial workers from Algeria, Viet Nam, Madagascar, Senegal, and elsewhere in the French colonial world encouraged both the anarchists and the communists to create leagues of solidarity and mutual assistance between colonial and French workers.

Although the North African Star was officially formed in the spring of 1926, discussions for the creation of a North African, Muslim, and nationalist political party that would cooperate with — yet be independent — of the Communist party seem to have begun in 1924.[14] The founders of the party were Hadj Ali Abdelkader, Messali Hadj, Chabila Djillali, Si Djilani Mohamed Saïd, and Banoune Akli. The Emir Khaled Abdelkader also supported the founding of the party.

On ideological issues, the North African Star party wanted to distinguish itself from the Communist party. The North African Star was explicitly nationalist — its membership was open only to Tunisians, Algerians, and Moroccans — while the Communist party, being internationalist, encouraged membership from all nationalities. The North African Star also had a religious orientation (its membership was overwhelming Muslim) while the Communist party, on the other hand, was officially atheist.

The ideological rupture between the North African Star and the Communist party was only partial. Whereas the North African Star and the Communist parties disagreed on questions of nationalism and religion, they did agree to fight colonialism, imperialism, and the exploitation of workers. The two parties had points of agreement and points of disagreement.

The leader of the North African Star party who also emerged as a seminal national leader in Algerian history was Messali Hadj. He assumed the presidency of the party in 1926 shortly after its founding. Hadj was born in 1898 in Tlemcen, Algeria, where he attended Qur'anic school and where he joined the Darqawiyya Sufi order.[15] Military obligations took him to France where he married and established himself as an industrial worker in Paris. The egalitarian social ethos of the Darqawiyya Sufis and by the Arab nationalism of Shakib Arslan and the Emir Khaled Abdelkader profoundly influenced his intellectual formation. For him, political liberty, Algerian nationalism, independence for North Africa from colonial rule, and Islam were themes that drove his ideological programs. His background as an industrial worker and his themes of independence, nationalism, and Islam were a combination that appealed to the North African industrial working class of France. His call for a North African independence party, allied with the Communists but also independent of them, was also well received within the North African community.

As time passed, however, membership in the North African Star party — despite its objective of trying to become a pan-North African party — became overwhelmingly Algerian. This movement accelerated when the Tunisians formed their own party (the *Destour*) and when the Moroccans did the same (the *Action Marocaine*). The North African Star was also overwhelmingly proletarian. It was comparatively unsuccessful in recruiting bourgeois intellectuals. Intellectuals tended to affiliate themselves with a group called the Young Algerians, whom we will discuss later in this chapter.

The North African Star's political program was in some ways similar to the program demanded by the Young Algerians. Here is a summary of the North African Star demands:[16]

(1) Abolition of the *code de l'indigènat*;

(2) Amnesty for prisoners;

(3) Freedom of the press and association;

(4) Political and labor rights equal to those offered to French Algerians;

(5) Abolition of the separate *Délégations financières* and the creation of an Algerian parliament based upon universal suffrage;

(6) Elimination of residential and political segregation and the abolition of militarily administered regions within Algeria;

(7) The end of discrimination against Muslims to political office and the civil service;

(8) Universal Education. Creation of Arabic language schools and the simultaneous publication of public documents in French and Arabic;

(9) Equality of terms of military service for Muslims and Europeans;

(10) The application of French social and labor laws to Muslims; and

(11) The expansion of agricultural credits to Algerian peasants, the rational organization of irrigation, and the enhancement of the means of transportation and communication in rural areas.

In contrast to the Young Algerians, however, the North African Star went on to add these demands:

(1) The independence of Algeria;

(2) The complete removal of French troops;

(3) The creation of an Algerian national army; and,

(4) The return of all property, including banks, mines, and lands, et cetera, to the Algerian state.[17]

The North African Star cited President Woodrow Wilson's Fourteen Points and the sacrifice of Algerian soldiers in the defense of France during World War I as principles justifying their political program.[18]

The celebration of the centenary of French colonialism in 1930 in Algeria was the next event to encourage the North African Star in its political activities.[19] The centenary provoked condemnations of the event by the North African Star and the Communist party. The Young Algerians tried to use the event to plead for equality with the French under French law.

The contrast in the reactions between the North African Star and the Young Algerians during the centenary revealed the distance that existed between them on the questions of identity and nationalism. For example, at an official centennial celebration the Young Algerian counselor Ben Abdellah said, "The indigenous people are French in their hearts." Doctor Bendjelloul added, "We are French before anything else. All the world should know that this celebration in the motherland has made me feel the power and the depth of the ties that unite France with the French Muslims of Algeria."[20] In contrast, the North African Star sent a letter to the League of Nations protesting the centenary of colonialism.[21] Articles were written for the French communist newspaper *L'Humanité* denouncing the centenary and urging Muslim soldiers to fraternize with their fellow Muslim Algerians.[22] The North African Star founded its own newspaper in Paris, *El Ouma,* in which it called for armed liberation for independence.[23] It urged Algerian workers returning to Algeria from France to set up clandestine groups called *Les Amis d'El Ouma.* It was from these groups that the first clandestine, nationalist, and militant party working for independence in Algeria was formed.

The world-wide economic depression of 1932–1935 further exacerbated the conditions of colonialism in Algeria. During the period between 1926 and 1936, the Muslim population of Algeria grew from 5.1 million to 6.2 million while the European population increased from 833,000 to 946,000. Average growth of the Muslim population from 1926 to 1931 was 87,000 persons per year. From 1931 to 1936, this average increased to 122,000 persons per year.[24] While this population was growing, European demand for Algerian exports including wheat and tobacco (but excluding wine) dropped significantly.[25] The conjunction of population growth and depressed agricultural exports created the threat of famine in the Algerian countryside and increasing unemployment in the cities.

When the depressed economic conditions intensified the discrimination already imbedded in the French colonial system, Algerians became more motivated to participate in demonstrations and riots. The first large riot after World War I period took place Friday, 24 February 1933 in Algiers. This demonstration took place after Friday midday prayers when two clergymen were arrested upon orders of the Governor General. The arrests of the two clergymen prevented them from preaching to the assembled congregation.[26] A year later, on 6 February 1934, Muslims rioted in Algiers again. A few months later, on 5 May 1934, Muslim and European workers, supported by both the North African Star and the Communist party, united to stage several strikes in Algiers.[27]

These strikes and riots, however, paled in comparison to the Constantine riot of 1934. This revolt must be considered as one of the turning points in Algerian history. The riot of Constantine was provoked when an intoxicated Jewish soldier named Kalifa Eliaou assaulted several Muslims on 3 August. These Muslims were completing their ablutions before prayers at the Sidi Lakhdar mosque when they were assaulted. The Muslims retaliated by stoning Eliaou's house in the Jewish quarter of the city. Shots were exchanged during the stoning and approximately 30 persons were injured. On the next day, 4 August, Muslim and Jewish leaders met to exchange regrets for the incident. All was believed to be calm. On

5 August, however, a scuffle broke out between Muslims and Jews, shots were again fired, and several Muslims and French soldiers were wounded. The Jews then attacked and pillaged Muslim shops in the Arab quarter. The Muslims counterattacked by doing the same in the Jewish quarter. The fighting escalated and the army was forced to close off the city for two days. On 24 August, twenty-one days after the original incident, fighting spread to other cities in the province of Constantine. The second round of rioting resulted in the deaths of 23 Jews, four Muslims, and 81 wounded of all religious denominations.[28]

The riots in Constantine reflected long-standing tensions between the Muslim and Jewish communities about the relative economic and political power of the Jews compared with the Muslims within the French colonial regime. As in other colonial situations, the French granted Jews certain economic and legal privileges not granted to Muslims so that they could divide the two communities against each other.[29] This tactic of creating a middle tier, an economically powerful yet politically debilitated non-indigenous merchant class, was used, in other examples, by the French in Viet Nam (with the Chinese community) and by the English in Malaysia (again with the Chinese community) and Kenya (with the Indian community).

Besides this structural explanation, the riots were also an expression of Muslim disgust with the colonial system. The riots of Constantine must be viewed as part of a series of demonstrations and riots in 1933 and 1934 that gave initial expression to the commitment of various Algerians to change the colonial system by violent means.

Although the Constantine riots were not instigated by either the North African Star or the Communist party, both parties analyzed the event as an indication of the latent revolutionary potential in Algeria.[30] The two other extant political groups within Algeria, the Association of the Ulema and the Federation of the Elect (the successor to the Young Algerian movement) both denounced the riots and preached peace.[31]

During the 1930's and the 1940's the North African Star and the Communist party competed for affiliation and support of Muslim Algerians. The Communist party wanted to build a militant alliance between European and Muslim workers that would bring down the state. The Communists' objective of building a biracial alliance was frustrated, however, for several reasons. First, European workers feared that the creation of such an alliance would only result in the political and social empowerment of Muslim workers, thereby costing European workers their advantaged position within the society. Second, Communist organization of Muslim workers was made more difficult because many of these workers could not read either French or Arabic and few Communist party organizers were fluent in the Algerian dialect of Arabic.

Additionally, the Communist Party was at a disadvantage because, in terms of ideology, the North African Star offered a program that was more appealing to the masses of Muslim workers. Communist ideology emphasized the primacy of the abolition of private property, the abolition of social and economic classes, and atheism as intrinsic parts of their ideological program. These propositions were fundamentally incompatible with the religious beliefs of Muslim workers. First, Islam recognizes the right of private property. Second, whereas Islam does impose an explicit religious obligation upon the rich to care for the poor, it does recognize the existence of different economic classes. Third, and this is most important and obvious, Muslims are required to believe in God. For workers who were Muslim, the Communist ideology did not make sense in light of their religious upbringing. For these reasons, the Communist party could not possibly enjoy success among Muslim workers in Algeria.

Further, the Communist party recruitment efforts were hobbled when, in the midst of the anti-Fascist struggles in Europe, Prime Minister Laval and Stalin signed their 1936 Laval-Stalin accord, which required the abandonment of calls for Algerian independence. The reversal in Communist policy on the question of liberation for the colonies caused widespread disaffection with the Communist party among independence-minded Algerians. The signing of this treaty quickly reversed the small gains the Communist party had made.

Shortly after the signing of the Laval-Stalin Accord, Léon Blum and his Popular Front movement won control of the French Chamber of Deputies through elections. The Popular Front, led by Socialists, seemed oriented towards the left on political issues. The victory of the Popular Front inspired Muslim Algerians of various ideological persuasions to believe that change in the colonial system might be imminent. In July 1936, Léon Blum floated the idea that he might encourage a reform proposal originally suggested by Maurice Viollette that would have extended the right to vote to 25,000 *évolués* or "civilized" Muslim Algerians. This proposal became known as the Blum-Viollette reform proposal.

The Association of the Ulema and the Young Algerians enthusiastically supported the Blum-Viollette proposal. The North African Star decided initially not to challenge directly either the proposal or the left-leaning government of Léon Blum because it felt that challenging Blum and the Popular Front would have been imprudent at a time when leftists were challenging fascism in Spain, Germany, and Italy.[32]

The North African Star demurred on the Blum-Viollette proposal, although it would have preferred independence for Algeria. As Messali Hadj said in Paris in 1936,

> The politics of assimilation [as envisioned in the Blum-Viollette plan] cannot be realized. It is condemned because of reason, because of justice, and because of history. The only solution is the total emancipation of North Africa. We say frankly that we want and hope for emancipation because it is in our interests and it is in France's interests that it be accomplished.[33]

At first, the North African Star responded to the Popular Front's presentation of the Blum-Viollette reform plan and the Front's reticence concerning their independence demands by remaining patient. When it seemed that the Front might begin actively mobilizing for the enactment of the Blum-Viollette reform proposal rather than for independence, however, the North African Star began organizing demonstrations for independence in both France and Algeria.

The first large Algerian demonstration in favor of independence took place on 2 August 1936 when Messali Hadj spoke before 8,000 people in Algiers. Hadj had just returned to Algeria. The Association of the Ulema and the Young Algerians had organized the Algiers gathering as a rally to support the Blum-Viollette reforms. Instead Hadj turned the rally into a rally for independence. The crowd received his political positions warmly. He said, "We will never accept that our country would be connected to another against its will. We will not under any pretext mortgage the future, which is the national liberation of the Algerian people."[34] His speech for independence, which did not have the support or the consent of the organizers of the rally, surprised them. One of the members of the Association of the Ulema, Tayyib al-Uqbi, later chastised him at the podium for his actions.

Hadj then set about organizing further the North African Star in Algeria. In less than a year he had organized 30 sections of the party and was planning 31 more.[35] The North African Star held political meetings where its leaders and members invoked the Qur'an to justify its independence principles. Hadj and the North Africa Star consistently wedded the rituals and the language of Islam with its political goals for independence.

Hadj's success in political organization, his categorical rejection of the Blum- Viollette plan, and his enthusiastic reception by Algerian youth provoked a negative response from his political competitors. His ideological commitment to independence was avant garde in comparison to his political peers. His political leadership and his ideas were attacked particularly by the Young Algerians and the Association of the Ulema who, in 1937, had united into the *Congrès Musulman Algérien* or Muslim Algerian Congress. One goal of this Congress was to support the Blum-Viollette plan. Apart from Hadj, the rest of the Algerian political elite were not ready to fight for independence. Because of his views, which in 1936 and 1937 were considered extreme, he provoked castigating responses from the Young Algerians.[37] The colonial administration, which was even more alarmed by his activities and his popularity, dissolved the North African Star on 27 January 1937. Hadj then went to Paris where he filed legal papers on 11 March 1937 creating a new party called the *Parti populaire algérien* (PPA) or the Algerian Peoples' Party. He then returned to Algeria where, on 27 October 1937, he was arrested upon orders of the Governor General for "reconstituting a dissolved league."

After its founding, the PPA continued to refer to Islam as the basis for justifying its refusal to assimilate into France. As part of a political ritual replete with religious symbolism, participants at their rallies would dedicate themselves to the independence cause while raising their index fingers skyward. This physical gesture, using the skyward-oriented index finger, is the same physical sign used when one affirms being a Muslim. The Muslim raises his right index finger skyward while reciting the *shahada,* or the profession of the faith. By using the rituals of Islam and the language of the Qur'an in its political work, the PPA was consciously wedding Islam into its political program and practices. In its party newspaper, *El Ouma,* the PPA declared,

> . . . [c]olonialism works to destroy Islam and not to collaborate with it. But Islam is not assimilable. It imposes its humane and just doctrines with institutions that over the centuries have benefitted Muslims if they follow Islam to the letter. It is the anchor to which we must attach our hope.[38]

While Hadj was in jail, the PPA continued to organize. Its support in Algiers and elsewhere swelled. Faced with the growing popularity of the PPA and its vocal opposition of the Blum-Viollette plan, the Blum government continued its arrests, harassment, and imprisonment of party organizers. From October 1938 to March 1939, the Popular Front government systematically arrested and imprisoned thirty-six of the PPA's leaders. On 29 September 1939, the colonial administration legally dissolved the PPA. On 29 September it prohibited the publication of the party's newspapers, *El Ouma* and *Le Parlement Algérien.*

On 10 May 1940, Hitler's forces invaded France. After having their troops quickly overrun by German troops, the government of Daladier surrendered to the Germans on 17 June. According to the terms of the French-German armistice, the Germans directly occupied the north of France while Marshall Phillipe Pétain established what was known as the Vichy government in the south of France. Pétain, according to the armistice, had legal jurisdiction over the south of France and the colonies, including Algeria. From the beginning of Vichy rule in 1940 until the American liberation of Algeria in November 1942, Messali Hadj articulated from his jail cell a policy of non-cooperation with the Fascists.[39] Several PPA activists, however, including Mohammed Taleb, Hadj Cherchalli, Si Djilani, and Amar Khider, broke ranks with Messali Hadj and cooperated with the Vichy regime and the Germans.[40]

After their territorial liberation of Algeria, the Americans freed Messali Hadj from prison on 24 April 1943. In the period from 1943 to 1945, the PPA developed a dual plan for political action. On the one hand, the PPA decided to lend support to Ferhat Abbas who had created a new organization called the *Amis du Manifeste et la liberté* or Friends of the Manifesto and Liberty (AML). The AML was a coalition of parties that united Abbas' liberal, assimilationist supporters with the Association of the Ulema and the PPA. The AML's objective was the creation of an autonomous Algeria federated with France. Although Messali Hadj expressed doubts about Ferhat Abbas' probability for success in this matter, he nevertheless recommended that the PPA support Abbas' federation plan.

As part of their second track of political action, the PPA began organizing a subgroup within their party called "The Organization." The "Organization's" purpose was the preparation of armed revolution. The "Organization" operated clandestinely. It was organized pyramidally and in cells, with members of each cell not knowing many other members of the larger clandestine organization. This was done purposefully so that if a party member were arrested, interrogated, and compromised, the collateral implication of other party members would be limited. Additionally, the party created "Special Committees" within the party whose missions in propaganda, recruitment, and security were secret even to other party initiates. The creation of these secret organizations within a clandestine party was part of an organizational strategy that would provide the necessary elements for the creation of an armed revolutionary movement in the 1950's.

When the French authorities remained unresponsive to Ferhat Abbas' proposal for an autonomous Algeria federated with France, the climate for resistance within Algeria and within the PPA changed. The liberation of Algeria by the anti-colonialist-oriented Americans, the anticipated liberation of France by the allies, and the discussions of independence in other African and Asian colonies encouraged the spirit of resistance in Algeria.

On 1 May and 8 May 1945, in response to continued French resistance towards change on the issue of colonialism, the PPA organized demonstrations throughout the country. The PPA called these demonstrations to display Algerian support in favor of independence and to protest against the deportation of Messali Hadj, whom the French authorities had transported from Algeria to Brazzaville in the Congo on 23 April 1945.[41] Violence accompanied these demonstrations. The bloodiest was in Sétif where twenty-nine persons were killed.[42]

Emboldened by their success in organizing the demonstrations of 1 May and 8 May, the central committee of the PPA decided to call for a mass insurrection by the Algerian people on the night of 23 May 1945. The PPA hastily devised military operations for 23 May and, as a result, its plan for a mass insurrection was unsuccessful. A general uprising did not occur. The PPA was successful only at cutting off phone service to various parts of the country.

The colonial administration responded to the events of 23 May with its only policy: brutal repression. Overwhelming force was used. The French administration claimed that, as a result of its military operations, 1,500 Muslims were killed. Its own military, however, declared that it had eliminated 6,000 to 8,000 Muslims. The Americans in Algeria estimated that 35,000 were massacred. Algerians have claimed that 45,000 died. Human carnage of such a dimension had never been seen before in Algeria. In the Mediterranean region, mass violence on such a scale had only been observed during the civil war in Spain.

Shortly before the repression of the rebellion of 23 May, the Governor General suspended Ferhat Abbas' AML on 14 May 1945.

He then ordered the suppression of the newspaper *Egalité* on 18 May.[44] From the administration's point of view, the more moderate AML and the more militant PPA were indistinguishable. They were both enemies of France that needed to be extinguished. The entire colon community, from conservative landowners to members of the French and Algerian Communist parties, condemned both the PPA and the AML for the "troubles."[45]

After the liberation of Paris on 25 August 1944, it became one of the tasks of the new French government to redefine its relationship with its colonial empire. In some colonies and protectorates, notably Morocco and Tunisia, the new French government decided that eventually it would loosen its imperial control. In others, notably Algeria and Viet Nam, the French decided they would try to maintain colonial domination.

After World War II, France tried several ad hoc policies to hold on to Algeria. At first France experimented with giving Algerians the right to elect two official delegations, one Muslim (called the *collège des non-citoyens*) and one European (called the *collège des citoyens*), to the French Chamber of Deputies in Paris. These separate delegations had the same number of representatives (13) and were coequal. In the first election of 21 October 1945, the PPA and AML urged their members not to vote. They pleaded for mass abstention because the French had jailed both Messali Hadj and Ferhat Abbas, the leaders of the PPA and AML. Despite their pleas for abstention, 54.5% of the Muslim electorate participated in the vote. With the PPA and the AML absent from the electoral process, a group of Muslim *évolués* led by Doctor Bendjelloul of Constantine won seven seats, the Socialists won four, and the Communists obtained three.[46]

In March 1946 the French released Messali Hadj and Ferhat Abbas from jail. In the second election for the French Chamber of Deputies scheduled for 2 June 1946, Abbas' AML, which he had now renamed the *Union Démocrate du Manifeste Algérien* or Democratic Union for the Algerian Manifesto (UDMA), fielded a list of candidates that, because of the continued abstention of the PPA from the elections, was elected overwhelmingly. With 49% of eligible Muslims voting, the UDMA won 11 of the 13 seats available and the Socialists won the two remaining seats.

Election Results for *Collège des non-citoyens*
2 June 1946

	P.C.A.	%e	Coop.	%	UDMA	%
Alger	23,456		68,439		101,007	
Oran	13,295		4,537		98,068	
Constantine	20,815		13,867		254,986	
Totals	57,566	8.9%	86,843	13.4%	454,061	70.3%

Source: *Le Monde,* 14 November 1946
N.B.: P.C.A. was the *Parti communiste algérien.* Coop. was an abbreviation for *Coopérants,* a category for candidates in favor of a "cooperative" relationship with France. UDMA was the *Union Démocrate du Manifeste Algérien* led by Ferhat Abbas.

Upon the arrival of the UDMA representatives in Paris in 1946, Ferhat Abbas, as an elected representative, proposed the enactment of a new law reconstituting Algeria as an autonomous republic federated with France. The French Chamber of Deputies rejected this proposal. Abbas also proposed laws that would have returned Messali Hadj from his forced exile in Brazzaville and that would have reinstated the legality of the PPA. The Chamber of Deputies enacted these proposals.

After Messali Hadj's return from internment in Brazzaville in August 1946, the PPA renamed itself the *Mouvement pour la triomphe de la liberté démocratique* or the Movement for the Triumph of Democratic Liberty (MTLD). It also, in a change of policy, decided to participate in the electoral process by fielding candidates in the third election for the Muslim Algerian delegation to be sent to the French Chamber of Deputies. This election took place on 10 November 1946. This time, with Ferhat Abbas' UDMA abstaining from participation in the election, Hadj's PPA-MTLD won 30.8% of the vote and 5 of the 15 seats in the Muslim delegation. Less than 38% of the Muslim electorate participated in the vote.

Election Results for *Collège des non-citoyens*
11 November 1946

	P.C.A.	%	Coop.	%	PPA	%
Alger	14,150		108,874		99,385	
Oran	32,852		47,938			
Constantine	32,802		68,581		43,768	
Totals	79,804	17.1%	225,393	48.5%	143,153	30.8%

Source: *Le Monde,* 14 novembre 1946 (N.B.:The P.P.A. was the *Parti Populaire Algérien* led by Messali Hadj.)

The newly elected Muslim Algerian delegation went to Paris in August of 1947 to deliberate a new Organic Law for Algeria. During the parliamentary deliberations, Messali Hadj's PPA-MTLD argued for an independent Algeria; Ferhat Abbas' UDMA, while not elected to the chamber, informally lobbied for Communist and Socialist support for an autonomous yet federated Algeria, and the *colon* delegates resisted any change in the colonial system.

On 20 September 1947, the French Chamber of Deputies enacted a new Organic Law for Algeria. This law affirmed the colonial relationship between France and Algeria. It declared that France's principal political officer in Algeria would be the Governor General. It created an Algerian Assembly of 120 members that they divided into two coequal Muslim and *colon* colleges. These separate yet "equal" electoral colleges gave the smaller European community of 510,000 voters the same number of legislators as the larger Muslim community of 1,500,000 voters. Under this new Organic Law, Algeria remained a legal *département* of France. The law also determined that Paris rather than Algiers would retain control over defense, the running of elections, local government, judicial administration, land policy, and customs.[48] Laws enacted by the newly constituted Algerian parliament would not be effective unless accompanied by an implementation decree signed by the Governor General.[49] Budgets passed by the legislature needed the approval of the Governor General, the Minister of the Interior, and the Minister of Finance.[50]

While in 1947 the French government was moving forward timidly with this belated and insufficient reform of the colonial system, earlier in February of the same year the PPA-MTLD held an organizational meeting in which it decided that the party would continue to have two aspects. One facet of the party would be legal and would participate in elections (the MTLD). The other would be clandestine and oriented towards military and guerrilla activities (the *Organisation Spéciale* or OS). This clandestine organization was founded by Mohammed Belouïzdad, Hocine Aït Ahmed, Belhadj Djilali, Ahmed Ben Bella, Mohamed Boudiaf, Djilali Reguimi, Ahmed Mahsas, and Mohammed Maroc.[51] These men later participated in the creation of the *Front de libération nationale* or National Liberation Front (FLN).

In the same 1947–1950 period, the PPA-MTLD sharpened its articulation of its political objectives. Whereas before World War II the PPA and the Communists shared similar if not consonant views about the exploitive nature of capitalism and the importance of the class struggle, during and after the war the PPA-MTLD shifted ideological emphasis even more from class struggle towards nationalism and independence. After the war, both within the organization and outside of it, the PPA-MTLD emphasized that class struggle would take a secondary and perhaps irrelevant role in its ideology and programs. The PPA-MTLD made it clear that its efforts would be directed towards independence and sovereignty rather than class struggle.[52] For these reasons, we can classify the PPA-MTLD as a proletarian-led nationalist party committed to independence rather than a socialist party committed to internationalism and class struggle. This nationalist position clearly put them at odds with the French administration and also the French Socialist and Communist parties.[53]

The municipal elections of 20 October 1947 were the first elections held after the enactment of the Organic Law of 1947. In the first round of these municipal elections, the legalized wing of the PPA, the MTLD, won an outstanding victory. Campaigning on a platform of independence, the MTLD won all the seats in the large cities (Algiers, Oran, Constantine, Bône, Tlemcen, Blida, Tizi Ouzou) and in 110 municipalities.[54] Frightened by this overwhelming success of the independence-oriented MTLD, colonial authorities sabotaged the outcome of the second round of the voting scheduled for April 1948. Between January and April, Governor General Naegelen ordered the arrest of 32 of the MTLD's 59 candidates. On the day of the election, ballot boxes were stuffed. Others simply disappeared.[55] Because of these tactics, the MTLD, which had won overwhelmingly in the first round of voting, was granted only nine seats in the separate Muslim electoral college after the second round. Of the nine legislators elected, five were in jail. Using these tactics, the colonial authorities distorted the electorally expressed will of the people.

Similar tactics of harassment were permitted by Governor General Naegelen in the elections of 1949, 1950 and 1951. As in the election of October 1947, Muslim candidates were harassed or imprisoned, Muslims were turned away from the polls, and ballot boxes were either stuffed or destroyed. The colonial government, in a desperate effort to maintain control of the political process, continued to manipulate the elections fraudulently. Although the Organic Law of 1947 theoretically granted Muslims an expanded right to vote, French officials in Algeria were denying Muslims that same right.

The denial of the full and honest exercise of the vote in June 1951 pushed the Muslim community to organize a new response. On 5 August 1951, the MTLD, the UDMA, the Association of the Ulema, and the PCA (Algerian Communist Party) joined to create the *Front Algérien* (Algerian Front). The objectives of the *Front* were the abrogation of the results of the legislative elections of 17 June 1951 and the assurance of fundamental liberties for Muslims in Algeria.[56]

After the government's electoral trickery of June 1951, The MTLD, the UDMA, and the *ulema* urged their members in the *Front Algérien* to abstain from the elections of October 1951. The Algerian Communist Party (PCA), not wishing to antagonize its European constituency, urged participation in the election. Because of the Front's efforts, participation rates by Muslims in the election dropped to between 14% and 25% across the country.[57]

The denial of the right to vote by the colonial administration pushed Muslim Algerians into alternate modes of political expression. One road, more moderate and less violent, urged abstention from the electoral process as a means of expressing mass discontent. This approach was taken by most of the members of the *Front Algérien*. Another approach, encouraged by the independence oriented MTLD, involved the selective use of violence. The MTLD, having played by the rules of the electoral game since 1946, decided they had learned the lesson that the colonialists wanted them to learn: participation in elections was irrelevant. Encouraged by the success of guerrilla warfare tactics at the 1954 battle of Dien Bien Phu, the MTLD decided that it would try to emulate its Vietnamese colleagues. It would abandon the strategy of contesting elections and resort to clandestine guerrilla warfare.

The Association of the Ulema: Clerics Trying to Reform Society

After World War I another group, this one led by Muslim clerics, rose first to reform and then to reject the colonial system. This group was founded on 5 May 1931 in Algiers and its name was the Association of the Ulema. Its principal leader was Sheikh Abdel Hamid Ben Badis of Constantine. Other leaders within the organization included Bashir al-Ibrahimi, Tayyib al-Uqbi, Mubarak al-Mili, Lamine Lamoudi, and Tawfiq al-Madani. In its founding charter, this group established itself as a religious and as a social party. It explicitly stated that its objectives were apolitical.[58]

The Association of the Ulema, however, engaged in critical educational and cultural activities in Algeria that would have penetrating political implications. Without the Association's work in education and culture, the Algerian movement for independence in the 1950's would have had to have been postponed. Without their efforts to establish a cultural basis for Algerian nationalism, the Algerian revolution would never have been successful.

The members of the Association of the Ulema were social reformers profoundly influenced by other Muslim reformers who were based primarily in Egypt. Most prominent among these reformers were Jamal al-Din al-Afgani, Muhammad Abduh, and Rashid Rida.[59] Throughout the Muslim world this reform movement was known as the *Islah* movement.

The Association of the Ulema's work in reeducation and historical research was among its most prominent contributions to the Algerian nationalist project. It was from the Association's work in political culture that Algerian nationalism obtained a cultural foundation. Before the Association's trail blazing educational and cultural work, the French government systematically tried to deny the existence of an Algerian nation separate from France. The Association restored that critical idea.

By the 1930's, French colonial administrators and French intellectuals attempted, after almost 100 years of French colonialism and especially within the context of the 1930 centenary celebration of French colonialism in Algeria, to deny the existence of an Algerian nation. The Association of the Ulema, along with separate but less significant efforts waged by the previously mentioned North African Star, restored the notion that there was an Algeria separate and independent of France. These two groups recreated the cultural bases of Algerian nationalism. To use Benedict Anderson's mode of analysis in *Imagined Communities,* they helped "reimagine" the Algerian community.[60]

Debates about culture can have enormous political significance. In one of the more famous debates that occurred in the 1930's, Sheikh Ben Badis, the leader of the Association of the Ulema, dissented from the views held by Ferhat Abbas, the leader of the Young Algerian movement. The issue for their debate concerned the question of whether Algeria, as a nation, existed separately from France. Abbas, a liberal reformer whom we will discuss later in this chapter, had this to say:

> If I had discovered the "Algerian nation," I would be a nationalist. . . . This motherland does not exist; I have not discovered it. The men who died for a patriotic ideal are honored and respected on a daily basis. My life is not more valuable than theirs. Nevertheless, I will not die for an "Algerian fatherland" because that fatherland does not exist. I have not discovered it. I have looked in history. I have asked the living and the

dead. I have visited the cemeteries: no one spoke to me . . . .
One cannot build upon air. We have rejected once and for all
such lofty and fanciful notions to definitely tie our future with
France's work in this country.[61]

Ben Badis had this response:

History has taught us that the Muslim people of Algeria have
been created like all others. It has its own history marked by
great accomplishments. It has its own religion and language,
its own culture, its own traditions, its own customs of which
there are good and bad . . . .

The Muslim Algerian nation is not France. It cannot be
France. It does not want to be France. And, even if it wanted
to, it couldn't. To the contrary, it is completely remote from
France because of language, customs, ethnic origins, and religion. And it doesn't want to assimilate with France at all.[62]

These separate notions about nationhood were staked out in
the 1930's. Muslim liberals, with their dreams of assimilation into a
France that did not and would not welcome them, could not con-
ceive of an Algeria separate from France. The reformist clerics and
the proletarian nationalists, because of their different experiences
and because of their contacts with the masses of Algerians, understood that Algeria was not France and could not be "even if it
wanted to." The Association staked out its positions for a separate
Algeria in its newspapers and journals, *Al Muntaqid* (The Critic), *Al
Shihab* (The Meteor), *Al Bassair* (Vision of the Future) and *Al
Nahda* (The Renaissance).

Besides the cultural criticism encouraged in its newspapers and
journals, the second element of the Association's cultural work
involved the establishment of schools run by the Association. In
these schools both children and adults learned Classical Arabic and
Muslim theology. The restoration of a language that was separate
from the language of the imperialist metropole was a critical element of the nationalist project.[63] The clerics understood that. The
teaching of Arabic and theology gave the students in the Association
schools the cultural tools they needed to redefine themselves in
terms that were not influenced by or imported from France.

By promoting the establishment of schools and enlarging the debate about political culture in its newspapers and journals, the Association encouraged historians, poets, and other intellectuals in their efforts to restore Algerian history and culture on indigenous terms. Among the more prominent writers actively supported by the Association were Lamine Lamoudi, Mubarak al-Mili, and Tawfiq al-Madani. Here is an excerpt from Lamine Lamoudi that interrelates religion and nationalism:

> Algerian, your country is dead. What means do you have to revive it! It is with religion that you can reawaken the country. You have abandoned the two links that tie you to your brothers: religion and patriotism. All the evils that have overtaken us: contempt, poverty, and the denial of all the good of the world is due to the abandonment of religion and our country.[64]

Besides Lamoudi, the Association actively encouraged Mubarak al-Mili and Tawfiq al-Madani. Mubarak al-Mili was the author of *Tarikh al-Jazair fil qadim wa'l hadith* (History of Algeria in the Past and the Present) and Tawfiq al-Madani wrote *Kitab al- jazair* (History of Algeria). These two historical works by al-Mili and al-Madani were important in establishing the foundation for the intellectual construction of Algerian nationalism. Both works included references to the nineteenth-century exploits of the Emir Abdel Qadir as part of their effort to create a "foundation myth" for the Algerian state. These authors contributed histories that redefined Algeria in indigenous rather than in French terms. They helped Algerians reappropriate their own history and cultural legacy. With their reacquisition of their own definition of the past, the Algerian people could then move forward more coherently toward national independence. The Association of the Ulema helped liberate Algerians intellectually before they proceeded with territorial liberation.

Despite its professed apoliticism, the Association did, however, intervene in traditional politics — as opposed to cultural politics — when its critical interests were at stake. Three issues provoked the Association into political action. First, the Association engaged in difficult negotiations with colonial authorities when these authorities tried to regulate both the number of Association schools and the teaching of Arabic within those schools. The *colon* press viewed Association schools as incubators for nationalist politics.[65] This was indeed true because within these schools Algerians learned the grammar of their language and they memorized poems that often had a nationalist orientation.[66] Despite governmental obstructionism, by 1935 the Association established 70 elementary schools and three *medresas* (a more advanced school) in Algeria. By 1947, the Association increased its number of elementary schools to 90. By 1955, it had established 181 schools, 50 *medresas,* and 441 educational centers with branches in Algeria, Paris, and Cairo.

The second issue that provoked the Association into political action was the application of French nationality laws toward Muslims. The Association objected to French naturalization laws because they required Muslims to renounce the *sharia* or Muslim personal law in favor of French law to obtain citizenship. Muslims felt that this law was particularly onerous because Algerian Jews, by virtue of a preexisting decree called the Crémieux decree of 1870, had been automatically granted French citizenship without having to renounce their personal religious law, the *halakah.*

Third, and this is an important issue, the Association engaged in a political and ecclesiastical battle against the marabouts of the Sufi brotherhoods for influence among the Algerian people.[67] High on the Association's religious and social agenda was its belief that the practice of Islam in Algeria needed purification. The Association decided that, to attain this objective, the marabouts and the maraboutic practices of the Sufi brotherhoods needed elimination.

The ideas of the *Islah* or reform movement based in Cairo profoundly influenced the activities of the Association of the Ulema. These *Islah* reformers, while being quite progressive on scientific and technological, could be quite capable of adhering to a rigidly conservative social and religious agenda. This dynamic of being progressive on some issues while conservative on others explains how the *Islah* reformers could simultaneously embrace scientific, technological, and institutional innovation while espousing social and religious conservatism. Whereas the reformers' predilection for technological and institutional innovation moved them to embrace change in the scientific and political arenas, their social and religious conservatism impelled them to challenge and persecute persons and groups that they deemed were practicing deviant forms of Islam.

As early as 1903, Muhammad Abduh, one of the *Islah* reformers, while visiting Algeria, denounced the widespread practice of maraboutism and the prevalence of marabouts in Algeria. The writings of the *Islah* reformers encouraged the Association of the Ulema to try to revivify the practice of what they thought would be a purer and more correct practice of Islam in Algeria. They tried to purge Algeria of Sufism and maraboutism, which they felt had led believers in Algeria to go unconscionably astray.

The leaders of the Association of the Ulema primarily were educated clerics from the universities of Zaitouna (in Tunis, Tunisia) and Qarawiyyin (in Fes, Morocco). For these educated clerics, the practices of Sufism with its esoteric spiritualism induced by chanting or dance and its allegedly saintly marabouts who dispensed blessings or divinely inspired favors to the faithful were expressions of deviant forms of Islam. Despite Algeria's long tradition of Sufism and despite the widespread popularity of Sufis and marabouts among the masses, the *ulema* viewed Sufism and maraboutism as impure and rife with superstition.

The veneration of the marabout by the faithful as a person either occasionally or perennially endowed with *baraka,* or powers to grant blessings and divinely granted favors was tantamount to heresy for these educated men of the *ulema.*[68] They were contemptuous of the marabouts who, they thought, were deceiving the faithful by engaging in the practice of superstitious magic. They were also concerned about the potential for pecuniary abuse involving a reputed "spiritually endowed" marabout and "spiritually needy" believer.

In the 1930's a seminal political, religious, and ecclesiastical battle emerged in Algeria between the *ulema* and the Sufi brotherhoods. During this period political and ecclesiastical power shifted from the religiously heterodox and organizationally decentralized Sufi brotherhoods to the religiously orthodox and organizationally centralized *ulema.* This shift in political and ecclesiastical power was a turning point in Algerian history. From the 1930's to the 1950's the Association of the Ulema displaced the Sufis for political leadership of the religious community. There were three reasons for their success. First, the *ulema* had at their disposal their own newspapers that they used to disseminate and propagandize their social and political views. Second, they became more prominent than the Sufis because of their episodic collaboration with two other major political actors: the *Étoile nord-africaine* (The North African Star) and the *Jeunes algériens* (The Young Algerians). Third, their creation of a large network of schools enabled them to develop a cadre of followers. For these reasons, political power shifted. This shift in ecclesiastical power fundamentally reoriented politics between the Muslim community and the state for the 1930's and throughout the rest of the century. After this shift of power, clerical groups in Algeria were centrally organized, enabling them to challenge the state more easily.

The move against the Sufis revealed an elitist orientation within the Association of the Ulema. Sufism and maraboutism were popular expressions of Islam in Algeria. The move against the Sufis by the *ulema,* while motivated by a sincere interest in purifying religion, also revealed class biases against the Sufis, who were less formally trained than the *ulema.*

Despite its indispensably important work in political culture, the Association of the Ulema was initially less politically militant than the North African Star party. For example, it did not, in contrast with the North African Star, immediately advocate independence. At the same time, however, it was less francophilic and less pliant politically than the Young Algerians. Ben Badis and his colleagues hesitated initially on the independence issue, urging their followers to remain faithful to France and to work for reform of the colonial system.

The Association of the Ulema's first official entry into organized political action occurred in June 1936 when the Association joined with the *Federation des Élus* (the successor group to the Young Algerians) and other parties to create a coalition of parties called the

Congrès des Musulmans Algériens (The Muslim Algerian Congress). Within this new congress, the Association decided to work officially for the attainment of political objectives. The new Congress began mobilizing from 1937 onwards for the adoption of the Blum-Viollette bill. This bill, as mentioned previously, would have extended the right to vote to about 25,000 "evolved" Muslim Algerians.

The Association of the Ulema worked with the Young Algerians within the context of the Muslim Algerian Congress for the passage of the Blum-Viollette bill because, despite differences that they had with the Young Algerians concerning the existence of an Algerian nation separate from France, they believed that the new Popular Front government of Léon Blum might be sincere about reforming the colonial system.[69]

After participating with the Young Algerians in the Muslim Algerian Congress for more than two years, the Association of the Ulema gradually began breaking away from the organization. After almost two years of lobbying in favor of the Blum-Viollette plan, little had changed in Algeria. The *ulema* eventually determined that the Blum government did not intend to follow through upon its original intention to reform the colonial system. On 25 December 1938, Ben Badis withdrew his support of the Blum-Viollette bill.[70] After this two-year period, the Association began moving from the assimilationist ideas of the Congress and towards the independence-oriented and nationalist ideas of the North African Star-PPA.

Sheikh Ben Badis had become both fatigued and impatient with the French government and its delays on colonial reform. The next month, on 14 January 1939, he intensified his quarrel with the French by issuing a *fatwa* condemning all Muslims who had obtained French citizenship by renouncing the *sharia*.[71] The issuance of Sheikh Ben Badis' *fatwa* revealed that the Association had finally abandoned its belief that the French government would bargain in good faith on the issues of colonialism. Ben Badis and his colleagues abandoned negotiation and moved towards policies of resistance and independence. By June 1939, the Association of the Ulema officially broke with the Young Algerians and the Blum government. In its newspaper, *Al Shihab,* it said,

The Blum-Viollette proposal is dead and definitely buried. It has fallen, the victim of violent campaigns arranged against it here in Algeria by the rejectionists and by the press and the political parties in France. We now declare that this proposal is dead and we underline the word dead.[72]

Sheikh Ben Badis died on 16 April 1940, causing disarray among the Association's remaining corps of leaders. Bashir al-Ibrahimi replaced Ben Badis as president of the Association. After Ben Badis' death, however, the Association lost much of its influence and dynamism.

The most critical political contribution of the Association of the Ulema to the Algerian nationalist project was its resurrection and restoration of the notion of the nation of Algeria. According to the Association, this nation was established upon the foundations of Islam and Arabic, which would become the two enduring bases of Algerian nationalism. As late as 1976, the FLN officially affirmed that Arabic and Islam were the cultural bases of the Algerian nation.[73]

The Association did outstanding work in political culture. Its foundation of schools and newspapers, its promotion of the use of Arabic, and its propagation of the practice of orthodox Islam helped recreate the Algerian nation that French colonialism had submerged. By enabling Algerians to redefine themselves as separate and culturally different from their oppressor, the French colonialist, the Association empowered Algerians psychologically and politically. They provided a cultural basis for Algerian nationalism that found armed expression in the *Guerre d'Algérie* of 1954 to 1962.

The *Jeunes Algériens:* Liberals Searching for a Mass Constituency

In contrast to the partisans of the *Étoile nord-africaine* (The North African Star) and the Association of the Ulema, the *Jeunes Algériens* (or Young Algerians), although adherents of political reform, were the most moderate and francophilic of the three groups. Using a class or an occupational analysis, one would find that most of the Young Algerians were engaged in the following professions: elementary and high school teachers, court officers, government bureaucrats, lawyers, doctors, pharmacists, and small businessmen.[74] The Young Algerians dressed like Frenchmen, they were trained mostly at French schools, they primarily spoke and wrote in French and, for these reasons, they were the most culturally distant from the masses of Algerian people. The Algerian masses simply had not been offered the same educational or occupational opportunities that had been made available to the Young Algerians.

The Young Algerians never successfully attached themselves to the Algerian masses (i.e., the peasantry) for three reasons. First, their cultural orientation towards francophilia reinforced their cultural liaison with the colonial French oppressor; in contrast, their political rivals, the PPA-MTLD and the Association of the Ulema, were successfully redefining their programs as Arab, religious, and Muslim rather than as French, secular, and Christian. Second, their preference for colonial reform rather than militant resistance eventually became *dépassé* in light of France's failure to reform. And, third, as a class of liberals, they were numerically small. The French in Algeria, unlike their other colonies, never successfully encouraged the creation of a numerically significant, indigenous bourgeoisie class that invested itself in liberal democracy.

The political program of the Young Algerians was first expressed clearly in 1911 and 1912 during discussions concerning the conscription of Muslims into the French army. At that time, the Young Algerians were pressing the colonial administration for political reforms that would have given the *évolués* or "evolved" Muslims the right to vote for *Conseillers généraux*. They were also seeking reform of the discriminatory taxes called the *impôts arabes*.[75] In 1911 and 1912, the Young Algerians could not have been characterized as a party trying to build a mass constituency. Rather, they were a group interested in advancing the interests of a narrow elite of well-educated, assimilationist-oriented Muslims.

Although the Young Algerians were the most francophilic of the three groups discussed in this chapter, they, too, like the North African Star and the Association of the Ulema, would episodically refer to Islam and Arabic in their speeches and declarations. Here is an example:

In this . . . context, you can find everywhere the work done by
our ancestors and the monuments they left us proof of the
sublime, outstanding, and intelligent work of Muslim civilization. What a perpetual memento! The grandeur of our ancestors' work requires us to examine the great deterioration that
has befallen us because of the misfortune of the centuries.
Alas! We are far from their splendor and we should feel humil-
iated in the eyes of our ancestors, whose language few of us
even speak now![76]

Ferhat Abbas, who became the leader of the Young Algerian
movement in the inter-war period and who was among the most
francophilic of the Muslim educated class, despite his love of France
and French culture, would quote the Hadiths and the Qur'an to
support his assimilationist policies:

Work like you will live forever and prepare yourself like a man
who will die tomorrow. Education is obligatory for all Muslim
men and Muslim women.. . . .

People hear my words and engrave them in your memory.
Know that every Muslim is the brother of every other Muslim
and that Muslims are brothers among themselves, and that
you are a family of brothers. . . .

God cannot change the conditions of a people who are unwilling to change themselves.[77]

The first two quotations are from the Hadith and the third is a
quotation from the Qur'an.

While the Young Algerians were not interested in complete rupture with the French colonial system, they were adamant about
fighting for equality and respect within the system. Lamine Lamoudi, who wrote for both the Association of the Ulema and the
Young Algerians, had to say in the Young Algerian journal *Ikdam*:

As a matter of principle we are not hostile to the administration. At the same time a number of us are not blind admirers,
without reservations, of the system. We do not say "amen" to
all its acts and works, and we dare to criticize some of its
actions. We want equality in the law, respect for our Muslim
religion, and the end of discrimination. The European,
whether colon or otherwise, cannot regard the Muslim as his

perpetual and natural inferior. The indigenous Muslim must be taught and progressively initiated into contemporary life. Justice must be strictly applied to all.[78]

The Jonnart electoral reforms of 1919, discussed in the previous chapter, did not grant Muslims the right to vote for legislators to an Algerian parliament. The Jonnart reforms did, however, increase the size of the Muslim electorate (to 425,000 persons) that could vote for the *Conseillers généraux* and the *Délégués financiers*. These *conseillers généraux* and *délégués financiers* were not full-fledged legislators. They could, however, articulate the demands of the Muslim community to the Governor General.

The elections of 1920 enabled several Young Algerians including Khaled Abdelkader, Kaïd Hammoud, El Kohli Ahmed, and Ben Rahal to be elected to these offices. Of these elected officials, Khalid Abdelkader, the grandson of the nineteenth century resistance fighter Emir Abdel Qadir discussed in Chapter II, emerged as their leader.

Khaled Abdelkader must be given credit for being the first Algerian to communicate successfully the postwar demands of the Muslim people to the President of the French republic. Throughout 1924, Khaled rearticulated the demands of the Young Algerian movement. Here is a summary:

(1) Equality of representation in Parliament between Muslim Algerians and European Algerians;

(2) Invalidation of discriminatory laws, repressive tribunals, criminal courts, and the use of house arrests;

(3) Equality of rights and obligations for both Muslims and Europeans in the military service;

(4) The end of discrimination against Muslims in the civil service;

(5) Compulsory education for Muslims, accompanied by freedom of teaching and learning;

(6) Freedom of press and association;

(7) Application of France's law separating Religion and the State to the Muslim religion in Algeria;

(8) General amnesty;

(9) Application of France's social and labor laws to Muslim Algerians;

(10) Absolute freedom of movement of Muslim workers to work in France.[80]

To reinforce their arguments, Abdelkader and the Young Algerians urged that France grant to Algerian Muslims the same political rights that had already conceded to the black people of Martinique, Guadeloupe, and French West Africa by France's law of 29 September 1916.[81]

Newly elected African and Caribbean colonial delegates to the French Chamber of Deputies rallied to the Algerian cause for equal rights. Blaise Diagne, the first black deputy elected from Senegal, urged his fellow legislators to extend the franchise to Muslim Algerians. He said:

> We must involve the indigenous Algerian in French political life. We must encourage indigenous Algerians to turn towards the metropole as their natural arbitrator . . . . The hour has come to be more liberal. It is not wise to wait until Algeria extracts these reforms from us. It is better to implement them when the time is opportune.[82]

Because his political activities upset the colonial order, Abdelkader provoked the wrath of the *colons* and the colonial authorities. Frightened by his activities, the colonial authorities offered Abdelkader two choices: he could either choose house arrest in the deep south of Saharan Algeria or leave the country. Abdelkader chose exile in Damascus.

With the exile of its leader, the Young Algerians lost its most articulate and charismatic leader. The movement, although weakened, pressed on. Without Abdelkader, however, it became more moderate in its goals. Its political program became abbreviated. It focussed on freedom of movement for Algerian workers between Algeria and France, on the repeal of the *code de l'indigènat*, and expanded parliamentary representation for Muslims.[83]

With the departure of Khaled, Ferhat Abbas emerged as the leader of the reorganized Young Algerians. Abbas pursued the politics of rapprochement and assimilation between the Muslim and

European communities. His objectives tended to focus upon obtaining equal rights for Muslims under French law. He was also interested in the complete political merger of Algeria into France rather than independence.[84]

Abbas and other Young Algerians met on 11 September 1927 to form the *Fédération des Élus Indigènes d'Algérie* (Federation of the Elected). This group, which in name replaced the Young Algerians, pressed for reform of the colonial system. This was their program in 1927:

(1) Representation of Muslims in Parliament;

(2) Equality between Muslims and Europeans in military service:

(3) Equality in pay and conditions for both Europeans and Muslims in civil service positions;

(4) The elimination of restrictions for Muslim workers wishing to work in France;

(5) Abolition of the *code de l'indigènat;*

(6) Development of instruction and professional education for Muslims;

(7) Application of French social laws to Algeria; and,

(8) Reform of the electoral laws of 1910 that limited political participation for Muslims to the *Conseils généraux* and the *Délégations financières.*

The *Fédération des Élus* decided to remain a party allied to France. It did not press for independence. It developed amicable relationships with progressive persons within the *colon* community but it did not work during the 1930's to develop a mass following among disenfranchised Muslim Algerians. It remained a party of elites with a narrow base of support.

Throughout the turbulent years of the 1930's, Ferhat Abbas and the *Fédération des Élus* remained loyal to France. They did not preach independence. Even this group of moderate Muslims, however, became tired of having their political representation limited to participation in the *Conseils généraux* and the *Délégations financières;* they wanted legal and political parity with European legislators.

Because of the *colon* community's consistent and intransigent opposition to political reform, the *Federation des Élus* decided that it needed to change its strategy and tactics to enhance its political success. In 1935, Ferhat Abbas decided that the *Federation des Élus* should expand its political base of support by moving from being a party of elites to forming a coalition with other parties. Sheikh Ben Badis, the leader of the Association of the Ulema, endorsed Abbas' proposal for merger in the pages of the *Federation's* newspaper, *La Défense*.[85] This coalition of parties was called the *Congrès des Musulmans Algériens* or the Congress of Algerian Muslims.

The proposition for a coalition of parties organized into one Algerian Muslim Congress was almost derailed when the famous debate emerged between Ferhat Abbas and Ben Badis concerning the existence of the Algerian nation.[86] Despite Ben Badis' extended critique of Abbas' denial of an Algerian nation in the pages of his newspaper, *Al Shihab,* Ben Badis and his colleagues decided to forgive Abbas for his intellectual indiscretion. The creation of the Congress of Algerian Muslims was more important than dwelling upon intellectual differences, even if those differences involved the essential question of whether an Algerian nation even existed.

The Congress of Muslim Algerians met for the first time in Algiers on 7 June 1936.[87] The Congress principally brought together the *Fédération des Élus* and the Association of the Ulema. Members of the North African Star, who did not support the political program of this new yet still assimilationist Congress, did not speak at this meeting or entirely support its results. At the end of the meeting, the Congress produced these demands, which have been summarized:

(1) The repeal of discriminatory laws;

(2) The political integration of Algeria into France and the abolition of the *Conseils généraux* and the *Délégations financières;*

(3) The maintenance of the jurisdiction of Muslim law for Muslims;

(4) The reorganization of the Muslim judicial system;

(5) Separation of religion and the state;

(6) Return of religious buildings from the colonial authorities to the Muslim community;

(7) Return of religious properties to the Muslim community;

(8) Declassification of Arabic as a foreign language;

(9) Freedom to teach Arabic; freedom for the Arabic press;

(10) Compulsory education for Muslims of both sexes;

(11) Integration of educational facilities for Europeans and Muslims;

(12) Equal pay for equal work;

(13) Creation of agricultural cooperatives and agricultural credits for peasants;

(14) Amnesty for political prisoners;

(15) Universal suffrage;

(16) Representation in Parliament.[88]

On 23 July 1936, members of the new Congress, including Doctor Bendjelloul of Constantine, Ferhat Abbas, and Ben Badis went to Paris where they met with Léon Blum to present their demands. Several days later the same party met with Messali Hadj who chastised them for their assimilationist policies.[89] The creation of the Congress of Muslim Algerians was, from Ferhat Abbas' viewpoint, both a strategy for expanding the base of support for the *Fédération des Élus* and a tactical maneuver to mobilize Algerians in favor of the French government's Blum-Viollette political reform bill.

The French Chamber of Deputies proposed the Blum-Viollette bill on 1 January 1937. It was officially endorsed by Abbas' *Fédération des Élus* on 12 January. The *colon* community, which was interested in maintaining its colonial privileges, became increasingly alarmed about the Muslim community's efforts to move either for independence or towards reform of the colonial system. The *colons* decided to mount their own political counteroffensive. Under the leadership of conservative parties including the *Action française,* the anti-Judaic *Front français,* the quasi-fascist *Croix-de-feu,* and the truly fascist *Parti populaire français,* they expressed their rejection of the Blum-Viollette proposal to the Blum government. The Federation of Mayors, which represented the Mayors of Algeria, threatened to resign en masse if the Blum-Viollette proposal were enacted.[90]

The Blum government could have implemented the Blum-Viollette proposal unilaterally. It did not, however, do so. Internal and international factors explain the hesitation of the Blum government. First, we must remember that the disproportionate size of the *colon* community within Algeria distinguished this community from France's other colonial communities around the world. Algeria's colonists functioned as a very effective political force impeding any political reform. Second, in the mind of the *colon* and the colonial administrators, Algeria was not a classic colony but rather was an integral and legal part, a *département*, of France. Third, internationally, outside the orbit of Algerian-French affairs, Blum's government had become concerned about the maneuvers of Adolf Hitler, Benito Mussolini, and Francisco Franco in Europe.

On 10 May 1940, Hitler invaded France. On 25 June 1940 France and Germany signed an armistice that permitted Germany to occupy directly the north of France while Marshall Pétain would direct southern French and colonial affairs from the town of Vichy. Pétain's government also had jurisdiction for Algeria. During the Vichy period, Ferhat Abbas continued to press France for political reform. On 27 August 1942, Abbas and Doctor Bendjelloul wrote a letter to Marshall Pétain and Prime Minister Laval asking them to abolish all forms of discrimination against Muslims and requesting the "complete integration" of Algeria into France.[91] Pétain responded noncommittally to Abbas' letter.[92] No changes were made in colonial policy.

The liberation of Algeria by American troops in November 1942 reanimated Algerian hopes that they would be free of colonial oppression. President Franklin Delano Roosevelt's anti-colonialist views as articulated in the *Atlantic Charter* were well known among Algerians.[93] His representative in Algiers, Robert Murphy, met with Ferhat Abbas and encouraged him in his nationalist efforts.[94] Encouraged by Murphy, Abbas decided to press the Americans for reforms. On 20 December 1942, in a letter addressed to President Roosevelt, he formally asked that Muslims be fully integrated into the war effort to liberate France and that equality in the law be granted to Muslim Algerians.[95] The Americans referred his letter to General Charles de Gaulle's deputy, Admiral Darlan, who dismissed the Algerian request.

Disappointed at this rebuff, Abbas assembled his supporters, members of the PPA, and the Association of the Ulema to support him on a new proposal. On 12 February 1943, he drafted a new proposition that would be known as the Manifesto of 12 February 1943. The Manifesto included the following claims:

(1) The abolition of colonialism in Algeria;

(2) The right of the Algerian people to self-determination;

(3) The demand for a new Algerian constitution that would guarantee:

   (a) Liberty and equality for all inhabitants of Algeria without regard to race or religion;

   (b) agrarian reform;

   (c) parity between Arabic and French as the national language;

   (d) freedom of religion and the separation between religion and the state;

(4) the immediate participation of Muslims in the government of the country; and,

(5) the liberation of all political prisoners.

On 26 May 1943, Ferhat Abbas and his colleagues drafted a corollary protocol to the *Manifeste* known as the *Additif* that went further than the original *Manifeste*. In this *Additif*, Abbas called for the creation of an autonomous Algeria. Ferhat Abbas, the quintessential liberal assimilationist reformer, who had once in his life even denied the existence of the Algerian nation and had claimed that he, too, was French, had tired of French colonial policies. The long years of struggle and waiting had radicalized Abbas. Although he was not willing to endorse the PPA's call for independence, he abandoned his dream of the complete political "integration" of Algeria into France. He now, in a significant change of policy, supported autonomy for Algeria.

The Manifesto was submitted to General de Gaulle on 10 June 1943. On the next day, de Gaulle referred the Manifesto and the management of all Algerian affairs to General Catroux. Catroux's first response to the Manifesto was to place under house arrest two of its principal advocates: Ferhat Abbas and Salah Abdelkader. These arrests provoked demonstrations in the streets of Algiers, which caused Catroux to reverse his decision and free the two political prisoners in December 1943.

Given Catroux's mishandling of the political agenda in Algeria, De Gaulle decided to intervene directly. On 12 December 1943 he announced in Constantine that " . . . the Committee of Liberation has decided to grant immediately to several tens of thousands of French Muslims of Algeria all their rights of citizenship, without permitting that the exercise of those rights be impeded, and without requiring that rights be limited because of objections related to the statute of personal jurisdiction." De Gaulle then, despite the objections of the *colon* community and his own advisors, recommended the following reforms of the colonial system:

(1) The granting of French citizenship to all Muslims, age 21 or older who fell into any of the following categories:

  a) former officers of the military;

  b) holders of elementary school certificates of education;

  c) government employees or former government employees;

  d) members of the Chamber of Commerce or Agriculture;

  e) indigenous leaders *(bachagas, aghas,* or honorary *caïds);*

(2) The granting of French citizenship without the requirement that the candidate renounce the jurisdiction of Muslim law;

(3 The granting of eligibility to Muslims to participate in local political bodies; and,

(4) The admission of a greater number of Muslims into governmental service.[96]

De Gaulle's plan was more ambitious than the Blum-Viollette plan that had been proposed before the war. The reform commission that analyzed his proposals estimated that the de Gaulle reforms would result in the political enfranchisement of 1.5 million Muslims. We should underline, however, that, despite these proposed reforms, the French were not interested in changing the fundamental colonial relationship between Algeria and France. Whereas at the Conference of Brazzaville in January 1944 General de Gaulle had suggested that France might be moving in the direction of independence for Lebanon, Morocco, French West Africa, and Madagascar, France had not made the same decision for its two prized possessions: Viet Nam and Algeria. Rather, by promoting the de Gaulle reforms, the French were adopting a strategy of granting political rights to an expanded electorate of Muslim Algerians in an effort to encourage a closer union between Algeria and France. By bringing more Muslims into the political system they hoped to stave off what they feared most: a movement for autonomy or, worse, independence.

By the time that de Gaulle responded with his reform proposal in 1943, however, the political community within Muslim Algeria had moved from being content with reform to demanding a fundamental transformation in the relationship between France and Algeria. By the time de Gaulle submitted his reform proposals, they had become insufficient. In response to de Gaulle's proposal, Ferhat Abbas united his own supporters with the Association of the Ulema and the PPA into the Les *Amis du Manifeste et la liberté* or the Friends of the Manifesto and Liberty (AML). The AML, which was founded on 14 March 1944, fought for an autonomous Algeria federated with France. Sheikh al-Ibrahimi of the Association of the Ulema, who had replaced the deceased Ben Badis, endorsed the proposal. Messali Hadj, from his residence in Reibell, Algeria, where the French were holding him in preventive detention, supported Abbas although he did not believe that France would negotiate in good faith or cooperate with Abbas.[97]

After the demonstrations and the failed PPA-led rebellion of May 1945,[98] the French again arrested and jailed Ferhat Abbas.[99] Now two of the most prominent leaders on the Algerian political scene, Ferhat Abbas and Messali Hadj, were both in prison. French officials changed their policy in 1945. They moved from a policy of dialogue to one of repression. It decided to jail its opponents rather than negotiate with them. Dialogue, discussions, and negotiations had borne unsatisfactory fruit for both the French and the Algerians. The war of words would soon be over; the war of firearms would soon begin.

While in jail, Abbas decided to break the AML's association with the Messali Hadj's PPA. Abbas believed that the PPA's failed organization of a mass rebellion in 1945 and the bloody French repression that cost thousands of Muslim lives were developments from which he wanted to distance himself. The human carnage that had resulted from the direct confrontation between the PPA and the French led Abbas to conclude that only a moderate political program, operating entirely within the confines of French law and disassociated from the PPA, would be successful. To accomplish these new objectives, Abbas created a new political party: *l'Union Démocratique du Manifeste Algérien* or the Democratic Union of the Algerian Manifesto (UDMA), which replaced the AML. They dismantled the AML's coalition of forces uniting Abbas's bourgeois liberals, Hadj's proletarian nationalists, and al-Ibrahimi's *ulema*. From 1945 through the beginning of the Algerian war for independence in 1954, Ferhat Abbas, through a variety of political parties, dedicated himself to the creation of an autonomous — although not independent — Algeria. The National Liberation Front (FLN), which we will discuss in the next chapter, would lead the armed movement for independence and national liberation.

Conclusion

Between World War I and World War II three groups led the indigenous people of Algeria to resist colonialism. These three groups were the North African Star, the Association of the Ulema, and the Young Algerians. All these factions, in varying ways, referred to Islam to obtain religious validation for their political programs and to encourage mass support. Of these parties, the North African Star and the Association of the Ulema more regularly relied upon the language, the ideas, and the rituals of Islam to encourage support from the masses. The Young Algerians, while not denying their religious identity, were culturally closer to France than the members of the North African Star and the Association of the Ulema. They were less inclined to invoke Islam to validate their political programs. They also, because of their francophilia, were more inclined to invoke the traditions of French republicanism. These differences in cultural orientation accounted substantially for the failure of the Young Algerians to engender mass support and for the greater popularity of the North African Star and the Association of the Ulema.

The political success of the North African Star and the Association of the Ulema and the political failure of the Young Algerians during the interwar period had long term consequences for Algerian politics. The success of the North African Star and the Association of the Ulema accounts for the successful foundation of language-based and religious-based nationalism in Algeria. The failure of the Young Algerians helps explain how bourgeois-based liberal democracy obtained such a weak introduction within the politics of the country.

The conditions of colonialism imposed by France in Algeria encouraged the indigenous people of Algeria to channel their political energy towards two cultural icons, Islam and Arabic, rather than any other set of politico-cultural affiliations. It was by adhering to a different language and to a different religion that Algerians were able to preserve their identities and to define themselves in terms that were different from their colonial oppressors. Because of French colonial strictures, Islam and Arabic would become inextricably woven into the definition of the Algerian identity and into the formulation of Algerian politics. The ineluctable fusion of religion and politics that emerged during this interwar period endured throughout the remainder of this century.

Beginning in 1954 Algerians launched a war of national liberation that eventually obtained success in 1962. This war was led by the National Liberation Front (FLN). The next chapter will reveal how the Front, which welcomed nationalist Algerians of all ideological persuasions, was dominated and guided by leaders whose intellectual formation and world view was formed by the most dynamic political movements of the 1930's and 1940's: the Association of the Ulema and the North African Star.

Chapter V

⁂

The Ideological Revolution within the Armed Revolution (1954–1965)

Introduction

In this chapter we examine the evolution of ideology within the Algerian National Liberation Front (FLN) leadership. Two essential questions arose during and just after the revolution against France — the *Guerre d'Algérie*. We discuss first the relationship between the military and civilian wings of the FLN. During the 1950's and 1960's, civilian leaders within the FLN tried to bring the military establishment under their control. They failed. Their failure affected Algerian politics from the 1960's through the 1990's. Second, we consider the precise role of Islam within the ideology of the FLN during and just after the *Guerre d'Algérie*. We will find that the FLN divided into two essential ideological camps. One group, which we will call the "Islamic socialists," tried to merge Islam into Algerian socialism. Ahmed Ben Bella was the principal leader of this group. The other group we will call "secular socialists." They tried to create a form of socialism that would not emphasize a prominent role for religion within their politics. This group was led principally by Abbane Ramdane.

From its very first communiqué, the FLN proclaimed that its objective was ". . . the restoration of a sovereign Algerian state, democratically social [sic] within the framework of Islamic principles."[1] The FLN was led by nationalists committed to the destruction of French colonialism, to the socioeconomic and political empowerment of disenfranchised Muslim Algerians, to the creation of a just and egalitarian society, and to the promotion of some role for Islam within their polity. As the revolution developed, the revolutionaries regularly referred to but never systematically explained the specific role that Islam would play within their politics. To them Islam was reflexively important. Did the role of Islam within politics, however, ever need explicit clarification?

What is perplexing in the analysis and understanding of the nationalists' commitment to socialism and to Islam is that the merger of these two systems of belief both simplifies and complicates the matter. Islam and socialism share values of egalitarianism and the desire to improve the living conditions of the poor. In these areas, Islam and socialism have parallel objectives. What complicates our analysis, however, is that Islam and socialism diverge on other critical points. Islam specifically recognizes the right to private property.[2] Socialism may and communism does not. Second, according to how it is interpreted, Islam can command the application of democratic principles[3] or it can become the expression of traditional, clerically led, patriarchal political structures.[4] Socialism has had democratic,[5] authoritarian,[6] and totalitarian expressions.[7] Third, Islam is a religion that places worship of God or Allah as the first obligation within life. It tends to fuse religion and politics. By contrast socialism in its traditional Marxist version is secular. Communism goes even further, denying the existence of God all together.

The Algerian nationalists' commitment to both the destruction of colonialism and the improvement of the living conditions of Muslim Algerians, along with their intellectual or ideological formation within either the Association of the Ulema schools or within the PPA-MTLD, stimulated their attempt to unite Islam and socialism. Militants who came to the FLN, while attempting to merge

Islam with socialism, never systematically examined or explained the implications of this merger.

The first essential fact to keep in mind while trying to understand the politics of the FLN between 1954 and 1965 is that the "Islamic Socialists" and the "Secular Socialists" dominated ideological debates within the FLN. The proponents of traditional Islamic politics (as expressed by the Association of the Ulema during the 1930's through the 1960's) did not play central roles. Similarly, proponents of political liberalism, such as Ferhat Abbas and Ahmed Francis of the AML, did not play influential roles either.

This left the Islamic socialists and the secular socialists as the two critical groups. These two groups differed in their views on the role of Islam in politics. Just after independence in 1962, Islamic socialists defeated the secular socialists in the battle for political power. They then claimed the exclusive right to articulate the role of Islam in politics. From 1962 to 1992 the Islamic socialists continued to attempt to create a merger, whether it was symbolic or substantive, between their Islam and their form of socialism. Their attempts at a creative merger eventually failed, to be challenged in the 1980's and 1990's by traditional Islamic parties.

The Revolution within the Revolution

On 1 November 1954 Algerian nationalists began the armed phase of the Algerian revolution by launching seventy simultaneous attacks on French military facilities throughout the country. Eight persons died and eight were wounded on the first day of the war.[8]
[8]When this colonial conflict ended more than eight years later, more than one million Algerians had died in the struggle against France. France's bloodiest colonial war finally ended on 3 July 1962 with Algeria's independence.[9]

Between the beginning and the end of this war, the three branches of politicized Islam described in the previous chapter — the liberals, the proletarian nationalists, and the clerics — temporarily put aside their ideological differences to fight in one united front (the *Front de libération nationale* or FLN) against the French.

Upon the conclusion of the war, these three forces again divided. This chapter examines the diverse ideological factions within the FLN that fought what amounted to an ideological revolution within the armed revolution. This chapter does not examine the Algerians' armed struggle against France. That has been well documented elsewhere.[10] Rather, we examine the ideological debates within the heart of the liberation struggle and show how the three strains of politicized Islam subdivided into yet smaller ideological groupings. These smaller *cliques,* or circles of thought, grappled among themselves about ideology, power, and the role of Islam in politics.

We end our discussion with the adoption of the Algiers Charter in 1964 and the seizure of political power by Colonel Houari Boumedienne in 1965. It was within the Algiers Charter that Algeria officially dedicated itself to becoming an "Arabo-Islamic" nation. The publication of this National Charter must be considered as a crucial moment in the formation of Algerian political ideology because within it the Algerian state formally adopted a policy that claimed to unite Islam with socialism. The seizure of power by Colonel Houari Boumedienne one year later further reinforced the state's ongoing orientation toward merging Islam with socialism.

The stories behind these political and ideological decisions were complex, revealing conflicts and contradictions in the formation of Algerian political ideology. These conflicts and contradictions had their origins in ideological, personal, and cultural differences among the leaders of the FLN. Both the process and the outcome of this ideological struggle revealed that the FLN's decision to incorporate Islam into politics was a gradual process that vacillated between secularism and the integration of Islam. In the end, the integrationists won the political struggle.

In examining the Algerian political leadership during the revolution, three areas of confrontation, beginning from the most important to the least important, emerge: ideology, personality, and cultural orientation. In our examination of cleavages within the FLN, ideology will be the most relevant for our analysis. The leadership of the FLN was composed of different cliques with distinctive ideological orientations. They placed their ideological differences in abeyance temporarily to defeat the French. Both during the revolution and after the revolution, tension existed beneath the surface among these factions. After the defeat of the French, submerged ideological tensions resurfaced and worsened. The second basis for cleavage involved personality. This source of dissension was frequently more dynamic than ideology. Although members of the FLN leadership had different ideological viewpoints, and while ideology was often a critical basis for disharmony, bitter disputes frequently arose among men who simply could not get along with one other. Third, cleavages within the leadership evolved from the cultural orientations of the FLN leaders, often resulting from the different educational systems in which the FLN leaders were trained. Those leaders who had been trained in French-language schools tended to be more accommodating to French educational and cultural values. Those who had been trained in Arabic-language schools tended to be somewhat more chauvinist about their separately valuable Arabic and Muslim cultural traditions.

Ideological factions came from the three larger ideological groupings described in the previous chapter. During the Algerian revolution the liberals, the socialists, and the theocratically oriented subdivided into subgroups. To use categories that are broad, valid, but not altogether precise,[11] we can call them Secular Socialists, Islamic Socialists, Liberals, and Traditional Islamists. Using a four-way table, we can devise the following schema:

Islam Prominent in Politics

Socialist	*Yes*	*No*
Yes	IS	SS
No	TI	L

Secular socialists were committed to socialist principles involving a redistribution of social and economic privileges within Algeria. They were oriented towards centralized economic planning and they de-emphasized the role of religion in politics. Within this group could be found Hocine Aït Ahmed, Mohamed Boudiaf, Saad Dahlab, Frantz Fanon, Mostefa Lacheraf, Mohammed Harbi, and Abbane Ramdane.[12] Islamic socialists were also interested in reordering the socioeconomic privileges of Algerian society. In contrast to the secular socialists, however, the Islamic socialists were interested in integrating Islamic social values into politics. Ahmed Ben Bella, Mohammed Khider, and Houari Boumedienne belonged to this group.[13] The liberals had a French republican orientation. They too were less inclined to support state intervention in the economy. While reverent of Islam as a cultural reference point, they de-emphasized the role of Islam in politics. Within the FLN, they were represented by Ferhat Abbas, Ahmed Francis, and Ahmed Boumendjel.[14] Traditional Islamists were interested in a closer integration of Islam with politics. Within the FLN leadership, Tawfiq al-Madani held this point of view. Al-Madani was an important member of the Association of the Ulema and the FLN but he did not have allies from his ideological camp within the FLN leadership. To interpret al-Madani's relative ideological isolation within the FLN as an indication of the lack of Islamist influence within the FLN, however, would be incorrect. We can trace the Islamist influence within the FLN to those leaders who were either educated at schools run by the Association of the Ulema or who were influenced by the Arabic and Muslim renaissance sponsored by the Association of the Ulema during the 1930's and 1940's. Additionally, most FLN leaders and partisans were products of the Islamically inspired *Étoile Nord Africaine*-PPA-MTLD led by Messali Hadj. By recognizing these sources of ideological influence we can understand how an Islamist point of view would inspire ideological formation within the FLN. The following table arrays these principal members of the four ideological factions:

Membership of Ideological Factions

Secular Socialists	Islamic Socialists	Liberals	Traditional Islamists
Aït Ahmed	Ben Bella	Abbas	Al-Madani
Boudiaf	Boumedienne	Francis	
Dahlab	Khider	Boumendjel	
Fanon			
Harbi			
Lacheraf			
Lebjaoui			
Ramdane			

The armed phase of the Algerian revolution was encouraged with vigor in 1954 by a splinter group from Messali Hadj's MTLD. This group was called the CRUA or *Comité Révolutionnaire pour l'Unité et l'Action*. It was founded on 23 March 1954 by Mohamed Boudiaf, Mostefa Ben Boulaïd, Mohammed Dekhli, and Bouchbouba Ramdane.[15] Shortly afterwards Mourad Didouche, Rabah Bitat, and Larbi Ben M'Hidi joined the group.[16] At its core were younger militants from within the PPA-MTLD who had become impatient with Messali Hadj's willingness to postpone the armed phase of the Algerian revolution. In June or July of 1954 this group of five militants expanded to form the "Committee of 22" that launched the Algerian revolution.[17] This group then expanded their number to include Ahmed Ben Bella, who was living first in Geneva and then in Cairo, and Hocine Aït Ahmed and Mohammed Khider, both resident in Cairo.[18] They called this new, expanded group the *Front de libération nationale* or FLN.

At the same time that these men committed themselves to revolution, they began assigning responsibilities for the organization of political and military affairs. Mohamed Boudiaf first asked Mostefa Ben Boulaïd, Larbi Ben M'Hidi, Rabah Bitat, Mourad Didouche, and Krim Belkacem to join him in forming a six member executive *Comité de direction*.[19] These six men plus Ben Bella, Aït Ahmed, and Khider in Cairo formed the directorate of the revolution. Later, Abbane Ramdane joined this executive group. From its inception the revolutionaries who formed the leadership of the FLN decided that they would make their decisions on a collegial basis and only by consensus. No single person would be clearly designated as the "leader." They instituted collegial decision-making to prevent the empowerment of one principal leader and to avoid the creation of a "cult of the personality." For the remainder of the revolution, collegial decision making remained an important organizational principle.

While the FLN was arranging its political leadership, it organized militarily. The FLN divided Algeria into six regions or *wilayas* (Aurès, Constantinois, Kabylie, Algérois, Oranie, and Sahara). Mostefa Ben Boulaïd was placed in charge of the Aurès, Mourad Didouche in North Constantine, Belkacem Krim in Kabylie, Rabah Bitat in Algérois, and Larbi Ben M'Hidi in Oranie. Initially the Sahara was left leaderless. Hocine Aït Ahmed, Ahmed Ben Bella, and Mohammed Khider, from their positions overseas, were responsible respectively for propaganda, foreign relations, and arms acquisitions. Mohamed Boudiaf remained the coordinator for all the militants.

From 1954 to 1955, the French had considerable success in reversing the Algerians in battlefield combat. By 1955, several important leaders who played roles in the establishment of the FLN, including Mourad Didouche, Mostefa Ben Boulaïd, and Bachir Suidani were all dead. Others, including Rabah Bitat and Yacef Saadi, were in jail. These deaths and imprisonments encouraged the emergence of a new cadre of leaders. Among these new leaders were Abbane Ramdane, Abdelhafid Boussouf, and Lakhdar Ben Tobbal. Ramdane became the leader of the civilian branch of the FLN while Boussouf and Ben Tobbal formed the core of the future military establishment.

The men at the core of the FLN's leadership had become convinced that only armed revolution would deliver independence for Algeria. Within Algeria, they had political rivals such as the UDMA *(Union Démocratique du Manifeste Algérien)* and the Association of the Ulema who did not believe initially that it was wise to wage war against France. The UDMA and the Association of the Ulema were led, respectively, by Ferhat Abbas and Sheikh Bachir al-Ibrahimi. While both the UDMA and the Association of the Ulema initially resisted the FLN's policies of armed resistance, France's continued prosecution of the war and her continued denial of free and fair elections in Algeria pushed these two groups to align themselves with the FLN.[20] As early as the middle of 1955 the FLN had begun discussions with both groups about their possible affiliation with the FLN. Abbane Ramdane and Amar Ouamrane, both of whom worked for the FLN, initiated these discussions. As a result of their discussions, by 26 September 1955, a group of 61 Muslim elected officials that became known as the "Group of 61" published a statement in Algiers that, "[t]he politics of integration, which has never been sincerely applied, is presently of no use. . . ." and that "The vast majority of the population is committed to the idea of the Algerian nation." Several months later these elected Muslim officials, who previously had not been formally aligned with the FLN, called for the dissolution of the Muslim camera of the Algerian legislature. This was done by Governor General Jacques Soustelle on 2 December 1955. These elected legislators, who were liberally oriented, ended their cooperation with the French and began aligning themselves behind the politics of armed resistance advocated by the FLN.

Shortly after this public statement by the Group of 61, Ferhat Abbas, Algeria's leading liberal, announced publicly on 22 April 1956 that he was affiliating himself with the FLN. Abbas' affiliation with the FLN in April 1956 was the result of discussions begun in May 1955 by Abbane Ramdane and Amar Ouamrane, who had urged Abbas to support the FLN.[21] While the FLN was successfully courting Abbas and his liberal colleagues, it was also recruiting the leadership of the Association of the Ulema into its ranks. On 22 April 1956, on the same day that Abbas and his liberal colleagues pledged their allegiance to the FLN, Tawfiq al-Madani, who was associated with the Association of the Ulema, did the same. Both Abbas and al-Madani, as astute politicians, had begun to recognize that Muslim public opinion in Algeria had begun to shift. Their constituencies had become unwilling to support their policies of political evolution through elections. The masses of Algerians now seemed willing, given France's intransigence to change, to sacrifice their lives to support armed resistance. Reform politics now seemed outdated.

While the FLN successfully recruited the liberals and the *ulema* into its movement, it was entirely unsuccessful in recruiting another rival, Messali Hadj and his PPA-MTLD. As the FLN expanded its military and political activities, Messali Hadj and his MTLD reacted by forming their own armed movement called the *Mouvement Nationale Algérien,* or MNA. This group battled violently with the FLN both in Algeria and in France. For the duration of the entire war Hadj and his partisans continued to resist the leadership of those who had departed from their ranks to form the FLN. Efforts at negotiation and reconciliation between them failed repeatedly. From 1954 to 1962 they were caught in a bloody internecine struggle for power that resulted in at least 4000 deaths in France alone.[22] In Algeria and France it has been estimated that 10,000 deaths and 25,000 wounded resulted from this intramural conflict.[23]

The successful incorporation of the liberals and the *ulema* into the FLN's leadership stimulated membership growth. By becoming more ideologically diverse within its leadership ranks, the FLN began appealing more broadly to Algerians of diverse ideological orientations. Party membership and support grew. These leadership modifications should not conceal, however, that at the core of the FLN's leadership were Algerian nationalists who were committed to some form of socialism. The essential difference among these social-ist leaders was whether their socialism would take on a secular or an Islamic character.

Although the Algerian revolution had been in progress for almost two years, it had become evident to the leaders of the FLN that they had not defined their ideological and military objectives precisely. Recognizing this as one of their problems, the FLN lead-ership held a conference to resolve these issues in Igbal in the Soum-mam valley in Algeria on 20 August 1956. This conference had three objectives: first, the reorganization of the war effort; second, the articulation of a political platform; and, third, the clarification and settlement of ideological differences.

Sixteen official delegates participated in the Soummam confer-ence: Larbi Ben M'Hidi, Abbane Ramdane, Amar Ouamrane,

Belkacem Krim, Lakhdar Ben Tobbal, Youssef Zighoud, Mostefa Benaouda, Brahim Mezhoudi, Ali Kafi, Hocine Rouibah, Saïd Mohammedi, Colonel Amrouche, Commandant Kaci, Saddek Dehilès, Si M'Hamed Bouguerra, and Ali Mellah. These delegates represented the fighters of the "internal" revolution in Algeria. The "externals," including Mohamed Boudiaf, Ahmed Ben Bella, and Hocine Aït Ahmed were not represented at the conference. The principal authors of the Soummam Conference platform were Abbane Ramdane and Mohammed Lebjaoui.[24] These men were members of the secular socialist faction of the FLN.

The Soummam conference stated that the FLN's principal objective was the acquisition of independence for territorial Algeria, including the Sahara. It also stated that the objective of the Alger ian revolution was the creation of a progressive, "democratic and social republic" in which neither "monarchy nor an antiquated theocracy" would play a role. The 1956 Soummam Platform clearly articulated an essentially secular direction for the future Algerian state. By the August 1957 Cairo meeting of the FLN, the FLN's position on the question of religion changed with FLN militants abandoning secularism and endorsing a "democratic and social Algerian Republic, which is not in contradiction with the principles of Islam." In the following relevant passages the Soummam platform had this to say on the role of religion in politics:

> The Algerian Revolution wishes to conquer national independence in order to establish a democratic and social republic guaranteeing true equality to all citizens in the country, without discrimination. . . .
>
> It is a national struggle to destroy the anarchic regime of colonialism and it is not a religious war. It is a march forward in the historic sense of humanity and not a return towards feudalism.
>
> It is, finally, the struggle for the rebirth of an Algerian state in the form of a democratic and social republic and not the restoration of an absolute monarchy or a return to theocracy.[25]

The Soummam platform was palpably anti-clerical and anti-theocratic. The authors tried to establish distance between their form of socialism and Islam by trying to lead the FLN towards secularism. We should remember that the authors of this platform (Ramdane and Lebjaoui) were both secular socialists who were opposed to enhancing the role of clerics within the revolution. Nevertheless, because they were committed to the success of a socialist revolution within Algeria, they felt it was necessary not to stress their indifference towards some of the more conservative aspects of Islam so as to appeal for the "unity and the cohesion of the Algerian people."

To obtain this unity, the leaders at Soummam decided that their organizational strategy would be revolutionary struggle without overemphasis concerning religion and without reference to class struggle. All opponents to French colonialism would be welcome into the FLN regardless of race, class origins, or religion. Because most Algerians who would be recruited into the revolutionary struggle were Muslim peasants, however, the Soummam Conference's early criticism about "antiquated theocracies" was later revised and softened by the FLN leadership. In Algeria, the largest class that participated in the revolution was the peasantry. This large, predominantly traditional and preponderantly religious group was difficult to recruit into a movement or a party that was openly critical of religion. Nevertheless, despite the exigencies of peasant recruitment into the revolution, we should remember that the Soummam platform was the first document in the written legacy of Algerian nationalism that was openly cautionary about the potentially conservative role of religion in politics.

The Soummam Conference's ideologists, like those before them in the *Étoile Nord-Africaine,* specifically rejected class struggle as a desired strategy of revolutionary organization. Instead, conference delegates urged organization along nationalist lines with references to Islam; the revolution was to be led by the peasant class, "the largest, the poorest, and the most revolutionary of Algerians."26

Besides focussing on organizing the peasantry, the Soummam Conference also concentrated on political and military organization. It created the political arm of the FLN and reorganized the ALN *(Armée de libération nationale).* They designed the political arm of the FLN to have two branches: a legislature of 34 members (17 full members and 17 deputies) called the *Conseil Nationale de la Révolution Algérienne* (CNRA)[27] and an executive branch of five members called the *Comité de Coordination et d'Exécution* (CCE). At the Soummam Conference, Abbane Ramdane, Larbi Ben M'Hidi, Belkacem Krim, Saad Dahlab, and Ben Youssef Ben Khedda (all secularists) were appointed to the executive CCE. At this moment of the revolution, the leadership of the FLN was firmly in the hands of secularists with socialist orientations.

The Soummam Conference platform recommitted itself to the principle that the CNRA and the CCE would reach decisions by consensus and by collegial decision making. The delegates also decided that only the CNRA would have the authority to negotiate for peace with the French.

From the beginning of the revolution, political and military affairs had been intermingled with no clear division or articulation of authority. Under the leadership of Abbane Ramdane, delegates at Soummam tried to sever the civilian and the military areas of responsibility and tried to obtain civilian control over the military branch of the FLN. They published a principle establishing the "primacy of politics over the military," which the CCE at Soummam believed would make it clear to military *wilaya* commanders that they were to be directly accountable to the civilian leadership of the CCE.[28] This was seen as a first step towards the eventual and complete subordination of the military to civilian political control. This plan for subordination failed in the long run.

Besides this attempt to subordinate the military to political control, the FLN at Soummam also reorganized the army. While Algeria was still divided into six *wilayas* [Aurès (I), Nord-Constantinois (II), Kabylie (III), Algérois (IV), Oranie (V), and Sahara (VI)], they then further divided these *wilayas* into *mintaqas* (zones) and *kism* (sectors). A colonel was assigned to each *wilaya*, a captain and three lieutenants to each *mintaqa*, and an adjutant and three sergeant-majors to each *kism*.

The purpose of the Soummam Conference was to give ideological, political, and military coherence to the Algerian revolution. It accomplished its objective of military reorganization but it was less successful in obtaining ideological clarity (especially on the role of religion in politics), political unity among the combatants, or the clear subordination of the military to civilian control. First, on the question of ideology, apart from assigning "national independence" as its objective, the Soummam Conference failed to clarify whether the FLN would be committed to liberalism, secular socialism, some form of Islamic socialism, or a religious *sharia*-based Islamic state. The FLN leadership did not have time to scrutinize these important issues while it was focussing upon its primary goal: the acquisition of independence from France. In 1956, in the throes of a struggle for independence, scrutinizing the precise role of religion in the future Algerian state may have been premature. Most of the FLN's military efforts and political analysis were necessarily directed towards obtaining independence. The failure to examine the role of religion in politics, however, and postponing it to a much later date in the revolutionary process, only further complicated the analysis when the time for that analysis arrived.

Second, decisions were made concerning political assignments both within the CCE and the CNRA that exacerbated misunderstandings within the political leadership. First, by reserving positions on the five-member executive CCE for themselves, Abbane Ramdane, Belkacem Krim, Larbi Ben M'Hidi, Ben Youssef Ben Khedda, and Saad Dahlab antagonized other members of the FLN (including Mohamed Boudiaf and Ahmed Ben Bella) who were working for the revolution outside the country. Further, this group of "interior" leaders led by Ramdane and Krim used its influence to make sure it had eight members on the FLN's thirty-four member legislative body (the CNRA).[29] This attempt at stacking both the CCE and the CNRA in their favor created antagonism between these leaders and other FLN leaders.[30] This enmity lasted throughout the revolution.

In reaction to Abbane Ramdane's efforts to stack the CCE and CNRA at Soummam, and because of his increasing disagreements with members of the FLN's military establishment,[31] the CNRA met in Cairo from 20 to 28 August 1957 to amend his political efforts.[32] The CNRA's first decision was to expand the legislative CNRA from 34 to 54 members. The CNRA then enlarged the executive CCE from five to 14 members. It then further diluted Ramdane's influence by changing the composition of the CCE. First, two of Abbane's friends and appointees to the CCE who supported civilian control of the military, Ben Youssef Ben Khedda and Saad Dahlab (both of whom were secularly oriented), were removed from that body. Second, the five *chefs historiques* of the revolution who were imprisoned in France (Hocine Aït Ahmed, Ahmed Ben Bella, Rabah Bitat, Mohamed Boudiaf, and Mohammed Khider)[33] were made honorary members of the CCE. Third, military leaders who had been in charge of *wilayas* 1, 2, 3, 4, and 5 (Mahmoud Cherif, Lakhdar Ben Tobbal, Belkacem Krim, Amar Ouamrane, and Abdel hafid Boussouf) were appointed to the executive CCE, increasing military influence in FLN executive ranks. This decision undermined Abbane's intention at the Soummam Conference to clarify the subordination of the military to civilian political control. To these five military men and the five *chefs historiques* were added Abbane Ramdane (secular socialist), Ferhat Abbas (liberal) and Dr. Lamine Debaghine (secular socialist) and Abdelhamid Mehri (liberal/Islamic socialist).

Within this reorganization Abbane Ramdane was named President, Ferhat Abbas became Minister of Information, Abdelhamid Mehri took over Social and Cultural Affairs, and Lamine Debaghine assumed responsibility for Foreign Affairs. Belkacem Krim assumed control of the war effort, Amar Ouamrane took charge of armaments and supplies, Lakhdar Ben Tobbal was assigned to the Interior Ministry, Abdelhafid Boussouf took over Liaison and Communications, and Mahmoud Cherif assumed control for Finance. These assignments diminished the political power wielded by Abbane Ramdane at the Soummam Conference and led to the ascendancy of a military group led by Belkacem Krim, Abdelhafid Boussouf, Lakhdar Ben Tobbal, and Amar Ouamrane that wielded significant influence within the CCE leadership. The following table provides ministerial assignments and designates the minister's military status and his position on the religious question.

Cairo Meeting – August 1957 – Ministerial Assignments

Name	Function	Civilian or Military	Affiliation
Ramdane	President	Civilian	Secular Socialist
Aït Ahmed	Honorary Member	Civilian	Secular Socialist
Ben Bella	Honorary Member	Civilian	Islamic Socialist
Bitat	Honorary Member	Civilian	Secular Socialist
Boudiaf	Honorary Member	Civilian	Secular Socialist
Khider	Honorary Member	Civilian	Islamic Socialist
Krim	Defense	Military	Secular Socialist
Ouamrane	Armaments	Military	Secular Socialist
Ben Tobbal	Interior	Military	Secular Socialist
Chérif	Finance	Military	Liberal
Debaghine	Foreign Affairs	Civilian	Secular Socialist
Abbas	Information	Civilian	Liberal
Mehri	Social and Cultural	Civilian	Islamic Socialist

(N.B. All the Honorary Members were in jail in France)

Second, at this Cairo meeting the CNRA inserted a declaration that "The goal of the revolution remains the establishment of a democratic and social Algerian republic, which is not in contradiction with the principles of Islam." The delegates included this statement at the insistence of Ahmed Ben Bella who, from his jail cell in France, had criticized the Soummam Conference and its negative statements about Islamic theocracy.[34] This insertion was to correct the Soummam Conference's allegedly anti-clerical statements. This was done to reassure those whom were troubled by the Soummam Conference's obvious anti-clericalism. By committing itself to democracy, socialism, and the restoration of Islamic values, the FLN tried to assuage the concerns of Muslim Algerians whom the Soummam Conference's anti-clerical rhetoric had surprised.

Shortly after this conference in Cairo, Abbane Ramdane was assassinated on 27 December 1957 in Morocco. Years after his death it is now generally conceded that he was assassinated upon orders of his political enemies within the army.[35] Apparently both his brash political style and his attempt to rein in the military cost him his life. With the assassination of Abbane, ministerial assignments were distributed among the remaining eight members of the CCE. The critical assignments, however, remained with the members of the military. Belkacem Krim remained in control of the war effort, Amar Ouamrane was still in charge of armaments and supplies, Abdelhafid Boussouf was in charge of communications with the interior of Algeria, Mahmoud Chérif controlled Finance, and Lakhdar Ben Tobbal remained at the Interior ministry. In contrast, civilians still remained in control of less strategic responsibilities. Lamine Debaghine was still the Foreign Minister, Abdelhamid Mehri had the Social Affairs dossier, and Ferhat Abbas was still responsible for the press and communications. This arrangement of responsibilities assured that army officers had a preeminent role in directing political affairs.

These decisions, made in April 1958, seemed to make sense in the context of the war effort; military men were directing the war effort. What is recognized in retrospect, however, is that expanding the role of military officers in the management of political affairs opened the way for creating a long-term role by military officers in the direction of Algerian political affairs. From this time on, but beginning formally in 1958, military officers played roles within the political leadership of *primus inter pares.*

Second, at Cairo, the delegates repealed the Soummam Conference's principle subordinating the military to civilian political control.[36] Instead of having military officers under the control of civilians, military officers became the political equals of, or the superiors to, civilian members of the FLN leadership. This must be considered a critical institutional moment in the embryonic Algerian state because it determined the distribution of organizational power after independence. Organizational and political empowerment of military officers in April 1958 created a force of politicized army officers who, from that date, either determined or helped determine political outcomes from 1958 through the present.

Third, the decision to include the statement that the goal of the revolution remained the "establishment of a democratic and social Algerian republic, which is not in contradiction with the principles of Islam" was a clear rejection of the Soummam Program's anti-theocratic and anti-clerical positions. Further, the murder of Abbane Ramdane, (who with Mohammed Lebjaoui was one of the authors of the "anti-theocratic" Soummam Program), signalled a substantial ideological reversal for the secularists within the FLN.

On 1 June 1958 General De Gaulle was called by the French people from his retirement to assume the office of Prime Minister. He became Prime Minister in the wake of a planned coup d'état against President René Coty's government organized by Generals Massu and Salan. Both Massu and Salan were based in Algeria.[37] The officers' corps in Algeria planned the coup because they believed that the Coty administration had inadequately prosecuted the War in Algeria. When threatened with an imminent coup and the potential for real civil unrest in France, the National Assembly called a special session in which De Gaulle was elected Prime Minister. Members of the Assembly voted for De Gaulle because they believed that only someone of his stature had enough prestige among members of the military to avert the schism that was about to grip the French military and government.

The FLN leadership interpreted the arrival of De Gaulle as France's Prime Minister as an opportunity to initiate discussions for a negotiated settlement to the Algerian war. In reaction to this event, the FLN reorganized its political apparatus to prepare for prospective peace negotiations. On 19 September 1958, the executive CCE met in Cairo to create a provisional government called the GPRA *(Gouvernement Provisoire de la République Algérienne).*[38] The GPRA would negotiate for peace with the government of France. As such the GPRA was intended to function as the de facto Algerian government until independence. The newly formed GPRA included all the surviving members of the CCE except for Ouamrane. Ferhat Abbas was named President. Belkacem Krim, as representative of the armed forces, and Ahmed Ben Bella, as representative of the *chefs historiques* imprisoned in France, were named as Vice Presidents. The four other imprisoned *chefs historiques* (Boudiaf, Bitat, Aït Ahmed, and Khider) remained as Honorary Ministers of State.

The presidency of the GPRA was assigned to Ferhat Abbas because of his reputed familiarity with French diplomats. Because he was a known politician to the French, he was considered at the time as the best representative of Algerian affairs in the prospective peace negotiations. Dividing the vice presidency between Belkacem Krim and Ahmed Ben Bella had two immediate negative consequences. First, Colonel Krim was disappointed because, as the coordinator of the war effort, he believed he deserved the presidency. Second, the decision to name Ahmed Ben Bella as Vice President embittered Mohammed Boudiaf and Rabah Bitat. Both of these men had been founders of the Algerian revolution with Ben Bella and they both had been imprisoned in French jails for as long as Ben Bella had been. Therefore, they felt equally entitled to the vice presidency of the GPRA.[39] Their summary exclusion from the vice presidency later created particular rancor between Ben Bella and Boudiaf.

In addition to these appointments, Lamine Debaghine was appointed Foreign Affairs Minister, Abdelhamid Mehri was placed in charge of North African Affairs, Ahmed Francis was given the dossier for Finance, M'Hammed Yazid became Minister of Information, Ben Youssef Ben Khedda took over Social Affairs, and Tawfiq al-Madani was given the Cultural Affairs dossier. Real power for the direction of politics within Algeria proper, however, remained with military officers. Belkacem Krim remained the Minister of Defense, Mahmoud Chérif was now in charge of Armaments and Supplies, Lakhdar Ben Tobbal still was the Minister of Interior, and Abdelhafid Boussouf became the Minister of Liaison and Communication with the interior of Algeria. These military officers, along with interior *wilaya* commanders, remained the most powerful political players within the GPRA.

Cairo Meeting, September 1958, Ministerial Assignments

Name	Function	Civilian or Military	Affiliation
Abbas	President	Civilian	Liberal
Krim	Vice President & Defense	Military	Secular Socialist
Ben Bella*	Vice President	Civilian	Islamic Socialist
Aït Ahmed*	Honorary Minister	Civilian	Secular Socialist
Boudiaf*	Honorary Minister	Civilian	Secular Socialist
Bitat*	Honorary Minister	Civilian	Secular Socialist
Khider*	Honorary Minister	Civilian	Islamic Socialist
Chérif	Armaments	Military	Liberal
Ben Tobbal	Interior	Military	Secular Socialist
Boussouf	Liaison with Interior	Military	Secular Socialist
Francis	Finance	Civilian	Liberal
Debaghine	Foreign Affairs	Civilian	Secular Socialist
Mehri	North African Affairs	Civilian	Islamic Socialist
Yazid	Information	Civilian	Secular Socialist
Ben Khedda	Social Affairs	Civilian	Secular Socialist
Al-Madani	Cultural Affairs	Civilian	Traditional Islamist

*In jail in France.

Within the newly formed GPRA, decision making was difficult because the group was composed of factions that held differing ideological views. Ferhat Abbas, as President, functioned essentially as a referee or mediator among diverse ideological groups who, aside from their opposition to French colonialism, did not agree on other matters. The liberals (Abbas and Ahmed Francis) did not cohere with the secular socialists (e.g., Ben Khedda) or the Islamic socialists (e.g., Ben Bella) or the sole representative of the *ulema* (Tawfiq al-Madani). In the absence of ideological cohesion, the diverse factions opted to distribute governmental responsibilities among themselves. Minor governmental dossiers, (with the exception of Ferhat Abbas as President), were given to civilians. Real power for the direction of politics within Algeria proper, however, remained with military officers. Of these military officers, Belkacem Krim, Abdelhafid Boussouf, and Lakhdar Ben Tobbal were the most powerful, respectively occupying the positions of Minister of Defense, Minister of Communications with the interior, and Interior Minister.[40]

The ministerial assignments, maneuvers, and distributions that characterized the political machinations of the FLN masked the fact that, ideologically, these leaders did not cohere and that, programmatically, aside from their goal of independence, they remained disunited. The following longitudinal chart provides visual evidence of personnel turnover between 1954 and 1958:

Personnel Turnover – FLN – 1954 to 1958

Name	CRUA	FLN	Soummam 1956	Cairo 1957	GPRA 1958
Boudiaf	*	*	*	*	*
Ben Boulaïd	*	*	*		
Bitat	*	*	*	*	*
Ben M'hidi	*	*	*		
Dekhli	*				
Didouche	*	*			
B. Ramdane	*				
Badji		*			
Belouizdad		✝			
Ben Moustafa		*			
Ben Tobbal (m)		*	*	*	*
Bouali		*			
Boudajadj		*			
Bouchaib		*			
Boussouf (m)		*	*	*	*
Habachi		*			
Hadj Ben Alla(m)		*			
Mellah		*			
Mechati		*			
Merzougi		*			
Abdel Ramdane		*			
Suidani		*			
Zighout		*	*	*	
Aït Ahmed		*	*	*	*
Ben Bella		*	*	*	*
Khider		*	*	*	*
F. Abbas			*	*	*
Al-Madani			*	*	*
Ben Khedda			*		*
Benyahia			*		
Cherif (m)				*	*
Dahlab			*		
Debaghine			*	*	*
Dehiles			*		
Francis			*	*	*
Idir			*		
Krim (m)			*	*	*
Lamine			*		

(continued next page)

Personnel Turnover – FLN – 1954 to 1958 (continued)

Name	CRUA	FLN	Soummam 1956	Cairo 1957	GPRA 1958
Lebjaoui			*		
Louanchi			*		
Mehri			*	*	*
Mellah			*		
Mezhoudi			*		
Ouamrane (m)			*	*	
A. Ramdane			*	*	
Saïd (m)			*		
Temam			*		
Thaalbi			*		
Yazid			*	*	*

N.B.: (m) = military

The ministerial game of musical chairs amounted to temporary truces among competing ideological factions. Within this bureaucratic infighting, the most important political development was the continuous assignment of the most important political and military responsibilities to military officers Krim, Boussouf, and Ben Tobbal. These men and the interior *wilaya* commanders substantially controlled the management of military and political developments within Algeria.

After the assignment of Abbas as President of the GPRA, the legislature (the CNRA) held a meeting in Tripoli between 16 December 1959 and 18 January 1960. In this almost month-long meeting, the legislative CNRA tried to reassess the immediate needs of the war effort and tried again to redefine the relationship between the military and itself. During this meeting, delegates again decided to reassign governmental responsibilities among different ministers. They gave some governmental assignments to civilians while they granted others to military officers. The critical issue, that being whether the military would be subjected to civilian political control, remained unresolved. Cabinet reshuffling resulted in the dismissals of Lamine Debaghine, Ben Youssef Ben Khedda, Mahmoud Chérif, and Tawfiq al-Madani. Ben Khedda seems to have left the GPRA after the GPRA rejected his suggestion for the creation of a single political-military authority.[41] As a substitute to Ben Khedda's rejected suggestion for the control of the military, the CNRA created a *Comité Interministeriel de la Guerre* comprising Krim, Boussouf, and Ben Tobbal. The intended mission of the *Comité* was the oversight and control of Algeria's military establishment. This *Comité* ultimately failed in its mission when the military refused to recognize its authority.[42] At this meeting the CNRA also created an *État-major Général* (General Staff) comprising Colonel Houari Boumedienne and Comandants Kaïd Ahmed, Azzedine, and Ali Mendjli. Over the next two years, this *État-major,* because of its success in assembling a large and effective fighting force, acquired the capability to challenge the *Comité Interministeriel de la Guerre,* the CNRA, and the GPRA for political ascendancy.

In the end, one of the principal issues for resolution at this Tripoli meeting, the need to subordinate the military under civilian control, was not successfully resolved. The *État-major* created by the CNRA and led by Houari Boumedienne would became a separate center of military and political power. Ambiguity persisted in the relationship between civilian political authorities and the military. In the midst of this ambiguity, real power was waiting to be seized. A power struggle emerged between the military men of the *État-major* and the civilian leaders of the FLN. The men of the *État-major,* because of their sacrifices on the battlefield, felt that they and not the civilians were entitled to lead Algeria from war to statehood. The civilians, on the other hand, imagined an independent Algeria in which civilians would exert political authority over the military.

Between January 1960 and August 1961 frequent power struggles continued within the FLN about this and other issues. Divisions were rife. Civilian leaders quarrelled among themselves about who should lead the FLN and what its ideological direction should be. Military officers refused to cede authority to civilian politicians who, they felt, were only polemicists willing to wage a war of words but who were unwilling to sacrifice their lives on the battlefield for Algerian independence.[43] The military, in turn, was divided within itself. *Wilaya* commanders in Algeria challenged Krim, Boussouf, Ben Tobbal, and their representatives on the GPRA, regarding both on the management of the war effort and emerging politics within Algeria.

The next opportunity to resolve those internal differences was the next CNRA meeting held in Tripoli between 9 and 27 August 1961. At this meeting Ben Youssef Ben Khedda and Saad Dahlab, both of whom had been operating at the periphery of political decision making ever since January 1960, returned to challenge Ferhat Abbas' presidency of the GPRA. Both men, whom we can identify with the secular socialist branch of the FLN, challenged the liberal Abbas because they believed he would be too compliant towards the French in pending peace negotiations.[44] After obtaining political support from Belkacem Krim, one of the three critically important military leaders within the GPRA, Ben Khedda successfully moved to have Abbas removed as President of the GPRA. With Krim's support, Ben Khedda assumed the presidency of the GPRA. President Ben Khedda then helped Krim in his successful candidacy as chief of negotiations for the pending peace talks with the French, removing Ferhat Abbas from the GPRA presidency and from the pending peace negotiations. These moves wounded Abbas personally. Abbas, however, had his opportunity to extract revenge against these men shortly after independence.

The ideological significance of these political moves was that Ferhat Abbas, leader of the liberals, was now ousted from the FLN leadership. This further marginalized the role of liberals within the revolution and left the remaining struggle for political power between the secular socialists and the Islamic socialists in one arena and between civilian authorities and military officers in the other. In the ensuing years, the real power struggle was left to these groups. Liberals represented by Abbas and Francis, whose position within the FLN had always been marginal, were only represented indirectly on the diplomatic team that negotiated with the French. The liberals became irrelevant to the exercise of real power or influence within the FLN.

With Ben Khedda in control of the GPRA presidency, the civilians tried again to impose their control over the military establishment by first trying to create a schism between eastern-front officers based in Morocco and western-front officers based in Tunisia.[45] Their effort failed. The GPRA then tried to recruit senior officers to break with their peers and submit to civilian authority by offering these officers special positions within the government or the army. This effort also failed.[46]

On 18 March 1962 the terms for the end of the Algerian war were finally concluded. The agreement, which was signed in Evian, France, became known as the Evian Accords. Under the terms of the agreement, the Algerian delegation obtained the right to hold a referendum on the independence of Algeria. It also obtained, contingent to an affirmative vote on the question of independence, the acquisition of territorial sovereignty over all of Algeria, including the Sahara. As concessions to the French, the Algerian negotiators agreed to permit the continuation of French nuclear testing in the Sahara. They also agreed to lease to France its large naval base in Mers El Kebir for 15 years. As for French citizens deciding to remain in Algeria, they were to be guaranteed political protection for three years. After three years, French citizens deciding to remain in Algeria would have to choose between French or Algerian citizenship.

In the midst of these peace negotiations and just one month before the announcement of the Evian accords, Colonel Houari Boumedienne sent his deputy, Abdelaziz Bouteflika, to talk to the five *chefs historiques* imprisoned in France. Bouteflika approached the *chefs historiques* with an offer to create a new group that would challenge both the terms of the prospective Evian Accords and the political authority of the GPRA. Of the five *chefs* solicited by Bouteflika, Ahmed Ben Bella, Mohammed Khider, and Rabah Bitat agreed to join him, Colonel Boumedienne, and the *État-major* to form a group to challenge the GPRA.[47] Mohamed Boudiaf and Hocine Aït Ahmed declined Bouteflika's offer.

After the conclusion of the Evian negotiations, the GPRA convoked the CNRA from 27 May to 7 June of 1962 in Tripoli to ratify the terms of the peace agreement. The CNRA held a vote and they approved the Evian Accords at this meeting. Ominously, however, five members of the military staff (Colonels Boumedienne and Ouamrane and Commandants Mendjli, Slimane, and Azzedine), and Ahmed Ben Bella, (one of the five *chefs historiques* who had only recently been released from imprisonment in France), cast dissenting votes.[48] From this group of dissenters came the next serious challenge to the GPRA.

At Tripoli, Ben Bella urged the rejection of the Evian Accords and denounced the GPRA claiming that the GPRA had granted too many concessions to the French. Ben Bella also urged the dismissal of Ben Khedda as President of the GPRA and the creation of a new government. In these moves Ben Bella had the support of Colonel Boumedienne and the *État-major*. Ben Bella then pressed the CNRA to create a new group to be called the Political Bureau. Ben Bella proposed that this new Bureau rule Algeria in the period between the referendum for independence and the holding of elections for a National Assembly. He proposed that Hocine Aït Ahmed, Mohamed Boudiaf, Ahmed Ben Bella, Rabah Bitat, Mohammed Khider, Mohammedi Saïd, and Colonel Hadj Ben Alla be made the members of this Political Bureau. Shortly after the announcement of their nominations, Aït Ahmed and Boudiaf declined participation in the group. The CNRA, however, never officially voted upon Ben Bella's recommendation to form the Political Bureau. The meeting was adjourned without a clear decision concerning who was in charge of the FLN.[49] During these debates in Tripoli, intrigue was rife. Besides all the intrigue, what was slowly becoming evident was that the military establishment was beginning to mobilize to displace the FLN's civilian leadership. During the meetings in Tripoli, the *État-major* apparently even tried to arrest President Ben Khedda and other members of the GPRA. These men, however, escaped to Tunis.

At this 1962 Tripoli meeting the CNRA also ratified the Tripoli Program.[50] The Tripoli Program was intended as an ideological platform to reconcile divergent ideological tendencies within the Algerian leadership and also articulate goals for the future Algerian state. Mohammed Ben Yahyia, Mohammed Harbi, Mostefa Lacheraf, Redha Malek and M'Hammed Yazid (all secular socialists) drafted the Platform with Ahmed Ben Bella (Islamic socialist) who was serving as President of the drafting committee.[51]

The Tripoli Program reasserted that, "[t]he goal of the revolution remains the establishment of a social democratic republic that is not in contradiction with the principles of Islam." The writers included this statement at the insistence of Ahmed Ben Bella. During his imprisonment in France, Ben Bella had repeatedly sought a correction of what he thought were the Soummam Conference's intemperate references to the relationship between "theocracy" and "feudalism." The 1962 Tripoli Program, at his insistence, had clearly and specifically reversed the Soummam Conference's positions. The Tripoli Program also reasserted that Islam was a religion of progress.

The Tripoli program also timorously introduced the notion that class conflict was to play a role in the Algerian revolution. It suggested that, "[n]ational unity was not based upon the bourgeoisie." It also added that although the bourgeoisie could participate in the revolution, ". . . they were the bearers of opportunistic ideologies whose characteristics were defeatism, demagogy, an alarmist spirit, a contempt of principles, and a lack of revolutionary conviction, all things that lead to neo-colonialism."[52] These statements were introduced by the secular socialist branch of the FLN, which controlled the corporate authorship of the Tripoli Program. Either intentionally or unintentionally, the statements directly criticized the liberally oriented members of the FLN leadership. The Tripoli Program insisted that the bourgeoisie was not to be encouraged either to grow or to play a significant future role in the revolution. According to the Tripoli Program, to do so would be to play into the hands of the imperialists. Instead of the bourgeoisie, the Program urged that the revolution rely upon the "peasantry, workers in general, young people, and revolutionary intellectuals" for leadership.[53] Of these groups, the peasantry was considered most important for the advancement of the revolutionary movement.[54]

Within the Tripoli Program the reigning leaders of the Algerian revolution declared that they were committed to the "construction of [a] nation within the framework of socialist principles." According to the Program, economic planning in Algeria would be centralized and placed under state control. Both industry and agriculture would be nationalized and decisions concerning economic management would be handed over to workers and peasants. This concept of management was known as *autogestion*. The nationalization of European owned farm lands and the redistribution of these lands to peasants was also considered a paramount objective.

On matters of ideological diversity, the Tripoli Program was equivocal. The Program envisioned an Algeria in which socialism would be the dominant ideology and in which the FLN would be the dominant political party within what seems to be a multi- party political system. The Tripoli Program was ambiguously worded. One interpretation of the Program has been that the proposed Algerian state would be a multiparty state in which the FLN would be the preponderant but not the exclusive source of political power. In many ways, as a political model for the distribution of power, the FLN within the new Algerian state would wield power in a way similar to the political systems of post-World War II Poland, Czechoslovakia, and East Germany.

The authors of the Tripoli program (Mohammed Ben Yahyia, Mohammed Harbi, M'hammed Yazid, Mostefa Lacheraf, Redha Malek, and Ahmed Ben Bella) were militants who held diverse views on the role of religion in politics. Ben Yahyia, Harbi, Malek, and Yazid were all socialist intellectuals who favored secularism, a one party preponderant state, and the diminution of the role of religion in politics. Lacheraf was a liberal to left-leaning professor of Arabic at the Lycée Henri IV in Paris who argued ardently that the Algerian state needed to sever religion from the practice of politics. The fourth author, Ahmed Ben Bella, urged a more prominent role for Islam within the FLN's ideological program.[55] For Ben Bella, however, the role for Islam within the state, while instinctive, was largely symbolic rather than substantive. His references to Islam were intended largely to distinguish muslim Algerians as being different from the French colonizer. He did not call for the restoration of Islamic law (the *sharia*) or for the prominent participation of clerics within the Algerian state.

At Tripoli, a real ideological conflict on the role of religion in politics arose between Mostefa Lacheraf and Ahmed Ben Bella. Ben Bella argued that Islam was critically relevant to the future ideology of the Algerian state. Like many of his colleagues at Tripoli, Ben

Bella was committed to reordering socioeconomic privileges in Algeria via socialism. Ben Bella believed that Islam's scriptural inclination towards social egalitarianism was compatible with the goals of socialism. In addition, Ben Bella argued that the restoration of Islam to Algerian politics, (especially in the context of rejection of French colonialism), was critical to the formation of an Algerian identity or "authenticité algérienne." As early as 1954 the FLN had asserted that Islam was essential to Algerian politics. In its first proclamation it claimed that the objective of the Algerian revolution was the "restoration of a sovereign, democratic and social Algerian state, within the framework of Islamic principles."[56] Ben Bella and many of his colleagues in the FLN repeatedly referred to the importance of integrating Islam into politics. They never, however, engaged in a systematic discussion or analysis of what this would mean or how this issue would be specifically expressed. Lacheraf, in contrast, argued in favor of the severance of religion from politics. He claimed that the integration of Islam into politics would encourage Algeria to become socially conservative, thereby inhibiting social, economic, and political modernization. He also believed that the formal entry of religion into politics would result in the limitation of women's rights.[57]

The Tripoli Program failed miserably in reconciling the divergent ideological points of view within the FLN leadership. Instead of emerging with a united, coherent ideological program, dissension and disagreements continued to reign. Second, in bare-faced political struggle, new coalitions of forces were realigning to acquire power upon the official announcement of independence. The internal ideological schisms within the FLN were fully exposed at Tripoli, revealing fundamental and ultimately irreconcilable personal and ideological differences among the remaining key political players. In the ensuing months and years these rivals continue to battle until the Islamic socialists defeated all their challengers.

Different factions in the FLN began to maneuver for power shortly after the CNRA vote on the Evian peace accords. The principal antagonists in this political conflict involved the GPRA, led by President Ben Khedda, and the *État-major*-Political Bureau, led by

Colonel Houari Boumedienne and Ahmed Ben Bella. Soon after the referendum on self-determination in Algeria on 1 July 1962, the *État-major* and the remnants of the Political Bureau joined to challenge and defeat the GPRA. As was mentioned earlier, Ben Bella proposed the original Political Bureau as a mechanism to manage Algerian political affairs in the period between the cease-fire and the holding of elections for the National Assembly. The members of this Political Bureau were to have been Ahmed Ben Bella, Hocine Aït Ahmed, Mohammed Boudiaf, Mohammed Khider, Rabah Bitat, Mohammedi Saïd, and Colonel Hadj Ben Alla. Very soon after its constitution, Aït Ahmed and Boudiaf refused to be considered as part of the Bureau. Mohammedi Saïd affiliated himself with the GPRA. This left Ben Bella, Khider, Bitat, and Colonel Ben Alla as members of the Political Bureau.

The war between the *État-major*-Political Bureau and the GPRA began on 26 June 1962. On that day, (five days before the Algerian referendum on independence), interior *wilayas* 2 (Constantine), 3 (Kabylie), and 4 (Algér), asked the GPRA to use its authority to restrain the *État-major* from interfering in their internal affairs. In response to these *wilaya* demands, the GPRA issued a declaration on 30 June 1962 denouncing the *État-major* for criminal activities and ordering the demotions of Colonel Boumedienne and Commandants Ali Mendjli and Kaïd Ahmed (alias Slimane).[58] The *État-major* simply ignored the GPRA's order, claiming it had been created by the CNRA and could be dismissed only by the CNRA.[59] The GPRA's decision to dismiss the *État-major* was a tactical error that provoked the military to escalate retaliation against the GPRA.

The next step in this struggle occurred when Ahmed Ben Bella and Mohammed Khider, who had been overseas, moved to Tlemcen in western Algeria. There, on 22 July 1962, they formally allied themselves with Colonel Boumedienne and the *État-major* against the GPRA.[60] Ben Bella and Boumedienne then recruited Ferhat Abbas and Ahmed Francis (both liberals) who joined Ben Bella, Boumedienne, and the *État-major*-Political Bureau for reasons of vengeance.[61] Abbas and Francis had never forgiven the GPRA and

President Ben Khedda for dismissing Abbas as President of the GPRA on the eve of negotiations with the French. Their affiliation with the *État-major*-Political Bureau seems to have been an act of pure retaliation.

The *État-major* then ordered its troops to move from encampments in Morocco and Tunisia to Algeria where they began organizing in eastern and western *wilayas* 1 (Aurès), 5 (Oranie), and 6 (Sahara). These *wilayas* soon aligned themselves with the *État-major*. Ranged against these men were their opponents: the GPRA and central *wilaya* Colonels Hassan, Mohand Ou El Hadj, and Boubnider. Two other leaders, Mohamed Boudiaf and Hocine Aït Ahmed, were also organizing opposition to the GPRA. These two men, however, functioned as independent politicians, refraining from endorsing either the GPRA or the *État-major*-Political Bureau.

The GPRA's support remained centered geographically in the provinces of Algiers and Kabylie. During the month of July the forces of the *État-major*-Political Bureau gradually surrounded the GPRA forces on the West, the South, and East. By late July their position weakened further when Saad Dahlab, the GPRA's foreign minister, deserted President Ben Khedda and the GPRA for exile overseas. Mohammedi Saïd, a GPRA military officer, then defected from the GPRA to the *État-major*. With these developments the GPRA's pockets of resistance narrowed further to the cities of Algiers and Tizi Ouzou in Kabylie.

On 6 August, GPRA President Ben Khedda, recognizing imminent defeat, offered to turn over political authority to the Political Bureau. Despite the GPRA's offer of surrender, resistance to the authority of the Political Bureau continued in *wilayas* III (Kabylie) and IV (Algérois). Faced with this resistance, on 30 August Ben Bella and Boumedienne ordered the National Liberation Army (ALN) to occupy the city of Algiers at any price. After battles in which at least 1,000 persons were killed, Algiers finally surrendered on 8 September. Twelve days later, on 20 September 1962, independent Algeria held elections in which Ahmed Ben Bella was elected President of the Republic and Ferhat Abbas was elected President of the National Assembly.

The election of 20 September 1962 was not a multi-party election and it was far from being fair. On 3 September 1962, Ahmad Ben Bella, in his capacity as chief of the Political Bureau, prohibited key political adversaries, including Ben Youssef Ben Khedda, Lakhdar Ben Tobbal, Abdelhafid Boussouf, Mohammed Harbi, Redha Malek, and Mustapha Lacheraf, from participating as candidates in the election.[62] The election was structured so that Ben Bella's Political Bureau pre-approved the list of candidates. The electorate was left with the sole option of accepting or rejecting, referendum style, this list. The following table provides the election results:

National Assembly Election Results, 20 September 1962

Alger
Eligible: 825,282
Voting: 528,914
Participation: 64.0%
Yes: 516,666
No: 5,055

Auberville
Eligible: 387,851
Voting: 323,085
Participation: 83.3%
Yes: 322,402
No: 424

Mostaganem
Eligible: 385,979
Voting: 344,125
Participation: 89.1%
Yes: 343,124
No: 632

Tlemcen
Eligible: 231,239
Voting: 194,069
Participation: 83.9%
Yes: 193,273
No: 569

Tiaret
Eligible: 196,098
Voting: 174,538
Participation: 89.0%
Yes: 343,124
No: 632

Tizi-Ouzou
Eligible: 434,548
Voting: 364,384
Participation: 83.8%
Yes: 193,273
No: 569

Bône
Eligible: 447,121
Voting: 412,746
Participation: 92.3%
Yes: 411,546
No: 277
Source: *Le Monde,* 22 septembre 1962

With this election, the government of independent Algeria was legally formed and the legal authority of the GPRA and the CNRA, whatever their status may have been under international law, lapsed.

With the arrival of independence, however, a conundrum arose. Would Algeria be a multi-party democracy (as promised implicitly by the 1962 Tripoli Program) or would it become a one-party state (as preferred by Boumedienne's *État-Major* and Ben Bella's Political Bureau)? By the time of the referendum for independence in July 1962 and the September 1962 elections, both the armed forces and Ben Bella's supporters within the FLN clearly were prepared to impose their one-party vision for Algeria. These military men, who were either secular socialists or Islamic socialists, felt that their successful management of the war entitled them to lead the politics of the future state exclusively with their party. These men had guided the course of the revolution since its inception and they had welcomed the liberals (Abbas, Francis, Boumendjel) and the Islamists (al-Madani, Larbi Terbessi) into their movement on their own terms. Now, having achieved independence, they felt entitled to lead.

In Algeria, the newly elected political leadership began articulating their one party authoritarian preference quite early. Their first step was to outlaw competing political parties. On 29 December 1962 the Algerian Communist Party was declared illegal.[63] Less than a year later, in August 1963, Mohamed Boudiaf's *Parti de la révolution socialiste* (PRS) suffered the same fate. Slowly, the FLN affirmed that it would be the only political party. By 1964, with the publication of the Algiers Charter, the FLN publicly shifted from the implicit multipartyism of the 1962 Tripoli Program to its full endorsement of the one party state. The 1964 Algiers Charter said:

> . . . multipartyism is not a criterion for democracy or liberty,
> It relates to a certain stage in the development of society
> divided into opposing classes and the heterogeneity of each
> class constitutes a response that the society invents to demon-
> strate its contradictions, and, without resolving them, tries to
> attenuate and integrate these differences.[64]

After the publication of the Algiers Charter, the regime enacted the 1964 Constitution that codified its one-party authoritarian control in Articles 23, 24, 25, 26, 27, and 30:

Article 23. The FLN is the single party of the vanguard in Algeria.

Article 24. The FLN makes policy for the nation that the state carries out. It controls the work of the National Assembly and of the government.

Article 25. The FLN reflects the profound aspirations of the people. It educates them and organizes them; its guides them in order to help them realize their aspirations.

Article 26. The FLN puts into effect the objectives of the democratic and popular revolution and builds socialism in Algeria.

In Article 27, the FLN was given the sole right to propose candidates to the National Assembly. In Article 30, the FLN was given the power to deprive a member of the National Assembly of his vote. By the enactment of these Constitutional clauses, the FLN created the legal structures for its position as the sole source of sovereignty within Algeria. The Constitution codified authoritarianism.

Ben Bella fully endorsed the idea of a single-party state.[65] Only two of Ben Bella's co-founders of the FLN, Hocine Aït Ahmed and Mohammed Boudiaf, dissented from the creation of this one party state.[66] Ben Bella claimed, quite correctly, that he and his colleagues had successfully wrested independence from the French. As the military victors, they acted or believed that they were entitled to claim the sole right to the political spoils. Although the FLN had evolved from a small group of 22 revolutionaries in 1954 to a multiparty coalition by 1956, shortly after independence in 1962 the leaders of the FLN denied that the FLN was a multiparty coalition and claimed that it was single, unified party.

The FLN's evolutionary process from a small group of revolutionaries to a coalition of parties to a *parti unique* has been observed in other anti-colonial struggles.[67] Often in anti-colonial struggles it seems that the "National Liberation Front" that is usually a coalition of diverse parties eventually merges into a single party led by its military rather than its civilian wing. Some political theorists in the academic community have endorsed this process. They argue that one-party states might mitigate ethnic and class conflict better than multi-party states. They also claim that one-party states facilitate rapid nation- building, thereby promoting rapid economic development in post-colonial contexts.[68]

The FLN leaders, successful soldiers and revolutionaries, created a political system in which they would dominate. Islam had formed their religious identities; battlefield combat and by the political thought of Karl Marx, Mao Zedong and Frantz Fanon had forged their political identities.[69] After the war with France they worked to produce a creative merger between their religious identification with Islam and their political identification with revolutionary socialism. European and American notions of liberal democracy and the separation of religion and state were ideological references that seemed inappropriate to their experiences. As Lakhdar Ben Tobbal said in March 1960, ". . . the democratic character of the Algerian republic cannot be conceived as it is in western countries . . . democracy does not have any meaning but in the midst of the managing directorate *(organismes dirigeants)* [of the revolution]."[70] The FLN leaders rejected European and American pluralist models of democracy in favor of state socialism under the leadership of a single "vanguard" party. Its models for political and economic development were the Soviet Union, China, and especially Yugoslavia rather than France, England, or the United States. They envisioned a political system in which their party would direct both politics and the economy. They intended to subordinate all autonomous organizations (unions, youth organizations, women's organizations, professional societies) to the control of the state.[71]

In their effort to impose state control, the most important struggle took place between the FLN and the only significant independent trade union, the *Union générale des travailleurs Algériens* (UGTA). On 20 December 1962, the FLN reached an agreement with the UGTA in which the UGTA agreed to come under the control of the FLN.[72] Lakhdar Ben Tobbal's lecture to FLN cadres back in February 1960 underscored the FLN's authoritarian thrust. He said, "Your superiors will enlighten you, will serve you as guides, they will contact you and control your activities, and they will watch over you to make sure you do not fall into error. You owe them, in turn, obedience."[73] The FLN's authoritarian preferences were clear in Ben Tobbal's lecture. He said, "Our revolution must without pity abolish all attempts at opposition — not because it holds grudges against its children — but because it must act this way."[74]

As a way of expanding their popularity with the masses, Algeria's state referred instrumentally to Islam and rejected the cultural definitions imposed upon them by French colonialism. This use of Islam to expand personal popularity was manifested in the immediate post-colonial period when Ahmed Ben Bella engaged in a series of political battles to neutralize or eliminate his political enemies. During his first year of rule, with the help of political references to Islam, he eliminated his most important political rival: Mohammed Khider. Khider, who was Secretary General of the FLN, had also been Ben Bella's prison colleague and his former ally on the Political Bureau. After Ben Bella's election as President, he had Khider appointed as Secretary General of the FLN. Khider was very close to the Muslim Brotherhood based in Egypt and he actively organized within the religious and clerical community in Algeria. From his position as chief of the FLN, he began organizing the party in a way that Ben Bella perceived as a threat to his own rule. First, Khider planned to reorganize the FLN as a "mass" party rather than as an "elite vanguard" party. This recruitment strategy troubled Ben Bella. Ben Bella preferred that the FLN remain an elite, vanguard party whose membership would be probationary rather than automatic. By restricting party membership, Ben Bella believed he would be able to assert ideological control as well as political discipline of party members. Second, in the area of organizational politics, Khider was rapidly building the FLN into a mass party by specifically courting the *ulema* and other members of the religious community.[75] With this recruitment strategy, Khider recruited significant numbers of the religious elite within Algeria who feared that Ben Bella was a closet secularist in Muslim political garb.[76] To counter Khider and the support he was receiving from the *ulema*, Ben Bella systematically used references to Islam as part of an effort to convince the public that his form of socialism was Islamic rather than secular.

To defeat Khider, Ben Bella, whether wittingly or unwittingly, either sincerely or cynically, continued to try to outbid Khider on the question of Islam. In December 1962, in his capacity as President, he issued a decree prohibiting the sale of alcoholic beverages to Muslims, he closed cafés that sold liquor, and he raised taxes on alcoholic beverages.[77] The next month, on 26 January 1963, he declared the compulsory observance of the Ramadan fast for all Muslim believers. He then called upon Tawfiq al-Madani, a member of the Association of the Ulema and his Minister for Religious Foundations, to provide a doctrinal rationale for Islamic socialism. In the new religious journal published by the government called *al-Ma'rifa* (Knowledge), al-Madani complied with Ben Bella's request for scriptural confirmation of socialist policies. Citing the *Qur'an* (Sura 9), he claimed that the Prophet Muhammad was committed to socialism.[78] Writers in the government controlled daily newspaper *Al-Sha'b* (The People) claimed that Islam was "a revolution of the poor against the rich."[79] Throughout his period of rule, Ben Bella employed Islam to promote his policies, to defeat his political enemies, and to fend off traditional Islamists who challenged his government and his ideological orientation.

In independent Algeria, traditional Islamists, recognizing the quasi-official affiliation between the Association of the Ulema and the FLN, reorganized themselves into a new organization called *al-Qiyam* (Values). Its first meeting in Algiers on 5 January 1964 drew three thousand people. This group, which Al-Hachemi Tidjani organized, called for ". . . action by the party of God against the party of Satan" and for the creation of an "Islamic state . . . founded upon Muslim principles." Tidjani criticized Ben Bella's form of Islamic socialism, claiming it was more socialist than Islamic. He also criticized Ben Bella for his association with foreign-born Trotskyists. Tidjani demanded that the state grant a greater role for the *sharia* in jurisprudence. He also called for segregation of the sexes in the schools and the workplace.

As Ben Bella tried to fend off his religious critics by referring to Islam, he neutralized his rivals within the FLN by either isolating them politically or having them arrested. Systematically, he pushed his political antagonists into resignation, retirement, exile, or imprisonment. He eventually pushed Mohammed Khider, his principal political rival, to resign as Secretary General of the FLN on 16 April 1963. On 21 June 1963 he had Mohamed Boudiaf, one of his persistent critics and one of the founders of the FLN, arrested for conspiracy to overthrow the state. Ferhat Abbas, the liberal President of the National Assembly, resigned as President of the Assembly on 14 August after he learned that the FLN had drafted Algeria's constitution outside the purview of the National Assembly. Ben Bella then had Abbas expelled from the party on 16 August 1963. Ahmed Francis, Abbas' liberal colleague, soon moved to Switzerland. Ben Bella's tactics of "divide and conquer" and his constant assertion of Presidential prerogatives pushed Hocine Aït Ahmed to announce on 9 July 1963 that he would lead a rebellion against Ben Bella. Ben Bella retorted by invoking Article 59 of the Constitution that authorized him to rule by Presidential decree. This enabled Ben Bella to assume legislative responsibility and bypass the legislature entirely. Incensed, Krim Belkacem told *Le Monde* on 12 July, "We have the duty to fight again."[80]

Although the Tripoli Program of 1960 envisioned an Algerian state in which the FLN would be the dominant but not the exclusive source of political power, Ben Bella commenced the construction of a one-party state. Throughout 1963 the FLN and the army continued to centralize power while constraining the rights either to express alternative political views or to organize alternative political parties.

This brings us to the final political struggle in Algeria between the Islamic socialists and the secular socialists. This last gasp began in October 1963 and finally ended in September 1964.

In October 1963 the French journal *Les Temps Modernes* published an interview with Mostefa Lacheraf entitled "L'Avenir de la Culture Algérienne."[81] In that interview, and in articles in the Algerian journal *Révolution Africaine,* Lacheraf, by forcefully expressing the need for Algeria to be bilingual in French and Arabic, indirectly criticized what he believed were emerging conservative Arabophone and Muslim elements within Algerian politics and society.[82] Lacheraf's articles provoked a real firestorm of criticism from readers. Several commentators in the pages of *Révolution Africaine* accused him of neo-colonial treachery.[83]

The criticism of Lacheraf was part of a public debate that superficially was about bilingualism. Underneath the debate concerning language was a struggle regarding the future of Algerian socialism. By the winter of 1963–1964 the liberals and the more traditional Islamists had been eliminated from ideological debates within the FLN. Only the secular socialists and the Islamic socialists remained to fight the remaining political battles. By December 1963 and January 1964, struggle was progressing but the outcome was still undecided. By September 1964, this struggle finally came to a decisive end.

The defining moment came in September when Mohammed Harbi (a secular socialist and close advisor to Ben Bella) was dismissed as editor of *Révolution Africaine*.[84] Harbi was a Trotskyist, and, until his dismissal, had been a close advisor to Ben Bella. His replacement, Amar Ouzegane, was much more conservative and was an Islamic socialist. Harbi's replacement by Ouzegane marked the moment when the Islamic socialists finally defeated the secular socialists. From this moment, the Islamic socialists were able to embark on a course to fully merge Islam and socialism. This effort lasted from 1964 to 1989.[85]

After his appointment as editor of *Révolution Africaine*, Amar Ouzegane reaffirmed this Islamic socialist trend. In his first editorial for *Révolution Africaine* on 12 September 1964, he declared,

> The Algerian people are an Arab-Muslim people. In effect, ever since the Eighth Century, Islamization and Arabization have given our country a perspective that has preserved it to the present.[86]

As for the secular socialists (Lacheraf, Harbi, et cetera) Ouzegane had this to say:

> To our left, these "revolutionaries of words" denounced by Lenin, these philosophers detached from the people, who come from France or elsewhere, fight for principles and dogma. They want to apply their theories to Algeria, as we say

in an Algerian proverb, "They want to learn to be barbers on the heads of orphans." Pretending to be more absurd than they wish to be, from their ivory tower, they give us lessons, although they are incapable of waging a revolution of their own.[87]

The Islamic socialists were now fully in charge of the Algerian revolution. They expressed their views in an ideological document called the Algiers Charter that was published in April 1964. This document, which served as Algeria's official declaration of ideological policy until the National Charter of 1976, declared that Algeria and the FLN were committed to Islamic socialism and that henceforward any orientation towards a socialism that had a secular orientation rather than an Islamic orientation would be inconsistent with the realities of Algerian culture. The following is the relevant section of the Algiers Charter that discusses Islam:

Algeria is an Arabo-Islamic country. This definition, however, excludes any reference to ethnic criteria and it is opposed to any underestimation of the contributions prior to the Arab invasion. The division of the Arab world into individualized geographic or economic entities does not push into the background the unifying factors that are forged by history, Islamic culture and a common language.

The Algerian people are profoundly religious and they have fought vigorously to rid Islam of all excrescences and superstitions that have tried to stifle it or alter it. The Algerian people have always reacted against charlatans who have wanted to create doctrines of resignation and they have always demonstrated their willingness to put an end to the exploitation of man by man.

The Algerian revolution is devoted to restoring to the true expression of Islam, an expression of progress.

The essential Arabo-Islamic spirit of the Algerian nation constituted a solid bulwark against its destruction by colonialism. [88]

For the revolutionary leaders, Islam was the basis of national unity and a principle for national liberation. From the perspective of the Islamic socialist leaders of the FLN, the imperatives of socialism and Islam were entirely compatible and mutually reinforcing. From their perspective, secular socialism may have been appropriate for France or for Europe but it was inappropriate for Algeria. After the publication of the National Charter and certainly after the demotion of Mohammed Harbi as editor of *Révolution Africaine,* it had become clear that the Islamic socialists had won the struggle for ideological supremacy.

While Ben Bella was scoring these ideological victories, he was losing control over the element of the government that was most crucial for his political survival: the army. Led by Colonel Houari Boumedienne, the army had remained stubbornly independent of Ben Bella's control. In fact some observers have argued that Boumedienne was the real power, the *éminence grise,* behind the throne and that Ben Bella was only his highly charismatic dependent. While Ben Bella was busy eliminating his political enemies (e.g., Khider, Boudiaf, Abbas, Aït Ahmed, et alia) and maneuvering to have some version of Islamic socialism ensconced in the National Charter, Boumedienne was husbanding real political power in the only institution that really mattered: the army. Having successfully eliminated his political enemies, ironically Ben Bella became more isolated and even more reliant upon the army for the survival of his shaky regime. The army soon abandoned him. On 19 June 1965, at 1:30 A.M., Colonel Houari Boumedienne and the army staged a bloodless *coup d'état,* ousting Ben Bella and installing a leader who initially was committed to a more conservative form of Islamic socialism.

Chapter VI

✳

Boumedienne: Shifting from Islamic Socialism to Authoritarianism (1965–1978)

Introduction

On 19 June 1965 Colonel Houari Boumedienne quickly deposed President Ahmed Ben Bella in a *coup d'état.* Colonel Boumedienne and his colleagues seized power for several reasons. First, they believed that President Ben Bella intended to remove them from their positions within the government.[1] Second, they believed that Ben Bella was incapable of forming a government that could manage either Algeria's politics or the economy.[2] Third, they believed that Ben Bella's brand of "Islamic socialism" was more socialist than Islamic or "Algerian."[3]

Shortly after their *coup,* however, Algeria's military leaders tried to expand their social bases of support. They formed a new political coalition with the *ulema* playing important initial supporting roles in the new government. At the beginning, liaisons between the Boumedienne government and the clerical community were quite strong, especially during the first two to three years of the newly installed regime. Eventually, however, this relationship changed. After Colonel Tahar Zbiri staged an unsuccessful *coup d'état* by in December 1967, Boumedienne pushed to centralize political con-

145

trols even further. During this process of centralization, Boumedienne shifted his political emphases from the themes of "Islamic socialism" to the themes of "competent and efficient" technocratic management. He also rearranged the composition of his political alliances so that he relied less upon the *ulema* for support while seeking the backing of technocrats and bureaucrats.

Concurrently, Boumedienne changed the themes and content of his political rhetoric. When he first assumed power there were frequent references to Islam and *authenticité algérienne* and a *retour aux sources.* Over time, however, he began stressing "competent management," "economic progress," and "efficiency," shifting from drawing resources from religion to focussing almost entirely upon fulfilling economic goals. This de-emphasis of religion in political rhetoric was entirely unnecessary. It cost his successor, Chadli Ben Jadid, valuable symbolic political capital that he could never recover.

While Boumedienne was reinforcing the political structures of authoritarianism and de-emphasizing the role of religion in the construction of Algerian political ideology, a new generation was born in Algeria that would not be recruited into the FLN and could not find jobs within Algeria's "technocratically competent" regime. This generation, born after 1962 (the year of Algeria's independence), comprised more than 70% of Algeria's population by the time of Boumedienne's death. This large group of young people were not recruited into the FLN because of the FLN's exclusionary recruitment policies and they could not find jobs because the Algerian economy was not creating a sufficient number of jobs to meet the demand. Eventually they turned towards dissident Islamic political groups to express their frustrations with the regime.

Examining Boumedienne's shift from his particular brand of "Islamic socialism" to creating a state founded upon the principles of political authoritarianism and state management of the economy will show why, in this strategic shift, he began de-emphasizing religious and cultural issues and overemphasizing themes of competent management and accomplishment of economic objectives. Boumedienne's de-emphasis of religion was entirely unnecessary. Moreover, by doing so, he created an ideological vacuum in which dissident Islamist political groups could organize more easily and criticize him for abandoning the role of religion in politics. His alleged abandonment of religion within Algeria's politics made it more difficult for his successor to reacquire the lost political symbolism of Islam when he would find it politically necessary.

From Islamic Socialism to Authoritarianism

After seizing control of the state in 1965, Boumedienne promised the Algerian people that he would end Ahmed Ben Bella's method and style of government, which he characterized as an endless stream of petty factional manipulations, political gambits, and maneuvers. Boumedienne claimed that Ben Bella's politics amounted to "sordid calculations, political narcissism, and the morbid love of power."[4] Boumedienne thought that Ben Bella and other European-trained Marxists who counseled Ben Bella were trying to deprive the army of an important role in management of the state. They also believed that these men were creating a form of "Islamic socialism" in Algeria that was more socialist than Islamic.[5]

Upon seizing power, Boumedienne and his supporters proceeded to carry out their own ideas concerning socialism and Islam. Their ideas were more socially conservative than Ben Bella's view of Islamic socialism yet, like Ben Bella, their form of Islamic socialism still suffered from lack of specific articulation. Boumedienne labored strenuously to distinguish himself from Ben Bella, claiming that he was only trying to correct and redirect Algerian politics to more solid and more familiar ground after Ben Bella's perplexing Marxist and Trotskyist adventures. Essentially, Boumedienne claimed that he would restore *authenticité* to Algerian politics. Immediately after the *coup*, he had this to say about Ben Bella and his government:

> Algerians did not launch a revolution and sacrifice more than one and a half million martyrs in order to make it possible for Trotskyites and opportunists . . . to run Algeria and to proclaim themselves custodians of the revolution in the name of socialism.[6]

Boumedienne's critique of Ben Bella and his "Trotskyist" advisers reflected his belief that Ben Bella was leading Algeria into a political future that would be inefficiently managed, that was full of political intrigue, and, further, that was overly secular in its content and symbolism. He and his supporters also believed that Ben Bella's views were strangely foreign (and strangely European) to their understanding of what Algeria was and what it should be. Their Algeria was more conservative, more socially conformist, and more outwardly Muslim in political expression than Ben Bella's ever would be.

Boumedienne felt that despite Ben Bella's frequent references and allusions to Islam he was actually a secular leader who referred to Islam for symbolic and opportunistic reasons. Boumedienne believed that Ben Bella's over-reliance on a trio of Marxist advisors including Michel Raptis,[7] Mohammed Harbi, and Suleiman Loftallah only proved that Ben Bella was more a secular Marxist than an "Islamic" Marxist. These three Marxist advisors counseled Ben Bella to create a state founded substantially upon the principles of Trotskyist Marxism. As protagonists of ideas arising from the writings of Leon Trotsky and Rosa Luxembourg, they believed that the Algerian state should empower peasants and workers to organize themselves into self-managing committees that would run farms and enterprises from the grass-roots up rather than from the top-down by a centralized state bureaucracy.[8] They called their state a "workers' state based on self- management."[9] For these Trostkyist advisors, self-management or *autogestion* would be the cornerstone of their political and economic policies. This program of *autogestion* began in March 1963.

Ben Bella followed the Trotskyists' suggestions in economic and political organization and simultaneously tried to expand his popularity among the masses by engaging in the symbolic politics of Islam. Recognizing that his constituents were essentially more conservative and more religious than he was, he tried to expand his personal appeal, for example, by discouraging the sale of alcoholic beverages to Muslims and publicly encouraging the observation of the Ramadan fast.

Boumedienne claimed, however, that despite Ben Bella's efforts at such symbolic politics, he was not creating or practicing a genuine form of Algerian socialism rooted in Islam. Boumedienne asserted that, despite his public attestations of faith, Ben Bella was, fundamentally, a European inspired Trotskyist. Hence Boumedienne's frequent references to "opportunists" and "Trotskyists." Boumedienne claimed that Ben Bella's ideology was foreign and, therefore, not completely authentic. He also hinted publicly that Ben Bella was mentally unstable — or at least that he was an opportunist. Who was this man who at one moment espoused "socialism à la Castro," who at others proposed "Algerian socialism," and at yet others suggested "scientific socialism" and "Arabo-Islamic socialism?" What kind of socialism did Ben Bella truly believe in? Weren't these different forms of socialism contradictory? Boumedienne concluded that Ben Bella's public vacillations between the "four socialisms" indicated that Ben Bella was confused, undecided, or, worse, uncommitted to any firm ideological principles. For Boumedienne, failure either to clarify or to choose an ideology was entirely unacceptable and would not lead to a more truly Algerian form of socialism. A more conservative social direction was required and he moved in this direction with support from the more conservative social sectors of the Muslim community within Algeria: peasants, middle-class property owners, upper-level civil servants or technocrats, the *ulema* and, most importantly, the army.[10]

Of these more conservative social sectors, traditional Islamism initially was expressed best by the Association of the Ulema. This group largely agreed with Boumedienne's assessment of Ben Bella's ideological direction and, soon after his *coup*, they provided the political support that Boumedienne sought. On 21 June 1965, two days after the *coup*, Ulema leader Sheikh Bachir al-Ibrahimi, who had always contested the legitimacy of Ben Bella's rule, issued this statement of support: "The *ulema* of Algeria solemnly proclaim their solidarity with and their absolute support of the Council of the Revolution. They exhort the Algerian people, Arab and Muslim, men, women, young and old, to close ranks and unite as one man behind the Council of the Revolution."[11] The *ulema* solidly backed Boumedienne whose vision for integrating a more conservative form of Islam with politics reassured them. To the *ulema*, who had become disquieted by Ben Bella's Nehru jackets, his Trostkyist economics, his Pan-African foreign policies, and his intermittent secularism, Ben Bella must have truly seemed bizarre.[12]

During the first two years of his regime, Boumedienne's initial ideological choice was a socialism emphasizing social conservatism and personal discipline which pleased the *ulema* and their supporters. Whereas Ben Bella referred to Islam largely for symbolic purposes, (e.g., trying to restrict the sale of alcoholic beverages and encouraging the observation of the Ramadan fast), and whereas Ben Bella never assiduously courted the *ulema*, Boumedienne, by contrast, promised the *ulema* that he would give Algerian politics a more conservative and traditional orientation. While Ben Bella maintained high-profile relationships with secular Marxists such as Raptis, Harbi, and Loftallah, Boumedienne surrounded himself with advisors who truly believed they could integrate a socially conservative form of Islam with the aspirations of economic egalitarianism under socialism. Whereas Ben Bella seemed committed to *autogestion,* Trotskyist economics, and a highly visible revolutionary and Pan-African foreign policy, Boumedienne, with his austere mien, promised to temper this zealotry, promising to return Algeria to the principles of discipline, efficiency, and a more conservative form of Islamic Socialism. Boumedienne called his politics a *retour aux sources.* His *retour* was conservative, authoritarian, and patriarchal.

Perhaps Boumedienne's educational background helps us in understanding why he was, at least initially, more amenable to a more socially conservative expression of Islamic socialism. Boumedienne received his pre-university education at a traditional *medresa* in Constantine *(al-Kittaniya).* He then pursued university studies at the Islamic universities of Al-Zitouna (in Tunis) and Al-Azhar (in Cairo).[13] By his own testimony to his biographers Boumedienne was attracted to the conservatism and egalitarianism of an ascetic form of Islam.[14]

Although Islam profoundly influenced Boumedienne's social and cultural viewpoints, theorists of violence and revolution influenced him as well. He and his military colleagues immersed themselves in the writings of Frantz Fanon, Mao Zedong, and Che Guevara.[15] According to the testimony of most of the FLN revolutionaries, Fanon was the most influential of this trio of writers. Fanon was a psychiatrist from Martinique who arrived in Algeria to work as a physician. He subsequently joined the revolution. Of his works that influenced the thinking of FLN leaders, *A Dying Colonialism* and *The Wretched of the Earth* are the two most cited.[16] In these works, Fanon argued that in Algeria and elsewhere in the colonial world the greatest revolutionary potential rested with the peasant classes rather than the proletariat or the left-leaning bourgeoisie. Largely because of Fanon's writings, Boumedienne, among many others in the ALN military leadership and the FLN civilian leadership, became convinced that the peasantry should play a critical role in fighting the Algerian revolution and in the creation of a socialist society in post-independence Algeria. (We should note, however, that other revolutionaries, especially Vietnamese Communists, disagreed with Fanon's assessment about the revolutionary potential of the peasantry.)[17]

Whereas Boumedienne and his colleagues adopted Fanon's views regarding the revolutionary capacity of the peasantry, they unreservedly rejected his views that tended to depreciate the role of Islam within their revolution. Fanon was an atheist who believed that post-independence Algeria should be secular.[18] He recognized only belatedly that Islam was very important to the thinking of his fellow revolutionaries. Besides embracing Fanon's views on the peasantry's role in the revolution, Boumedienne fully accepted Fanon's ideas about the need for violence to effect political change, and he shared Fanon's suspicion and disdain of the urban bourgeoisie.

Boumedienne sought a close merger between socialism with Islam. While his formulation for Islamic socialism was more conservative than Ben Bella's, he never intended a complete fusion of Islam into politics as attempted in Iran after the revolution in 1979. The Ayatollah Ruhollah Khomeini had written before his emergence to power that he intended to establish an Islamic state in Iran in which a class of clerics would provide political guidance.[19] Unlike the Iranian revolutionary leadership, neither Ben Bella nor Boumedienne nor their companions within the Algerian political elite ever clearly articulated the specific role that Islam would play within the state. Lack of ideological clarity and ambiguity on matters of political theory plagued Ben Bella's, Boumedienne's, and subsequent regimes. Algeria's post-revolutionary leaders — all Muslims and putative socialists — attempted their mergers of Islam with socialism, but in an inchoate and inarticulate way. Their failure to articulate this merger clearly played a critical role in the regime's demise in the 1980's.

The ideological meanderings and mistakes made by Boumedienne and Ben Bella were similar to the contemporaneous zigzags and miscalculations made by the Baath regimes in Syria and Iraq during the 1960's through the 1970's. The Baath leaders in Syria and Iraq (Hafez al-Asad and Saddam Hussein) tried to establish other poorly articulated mergers of Islam with socialist egalitarian ideals. In doing so they employed politically authoritarian methods that required the use of either one-party or one-party dominant regimes. Having one-party states or one-party dominant regimes, however, contradicted an Islamic principle requiring consultation between the ruling classes and the ruled. Muslims call this principle *shura*.[20] Jumping ahead just a bit to January 1979, we see an excellent example of how and Algerian cleric invoked the principle of *shura* to criticize the FLN regime. At the Fourth Congress of the FLN that chose Chadli Ben Jadid as the successor to Houari Boumedienne, Sheikh Hammani, President of the Higher Islamic Council, said this:

> Islam runs in us and we in it. . . . It is the religion of freedom — we only owe submission to God — and democracy; there shall be no government *(hukm)* without consultation *(shura)*. Islam makes us in Algeria one nation *(umma)*, one homogeneous people. . . .
>
> We have not made Islam the religion of the state in the National Charter and in the Constitution as part of a fashion. This act signifies that Islam is rooted in us.[21]

The FLN and the Baath parties ignored *shura*. Nevertheless, *shura* has remained relevant to those within the Muslim community who have remained religiously and politically informed.

The FLN neglected *shura,* consultation was dismissed, and one-party authoritarian revolutionary leadership became the organizational norm. The religious community in Algeria, by resurrecting the Islamic principle of *shura* from the 1960's through the present, raised criticism of these one-party leaders and their politically authoritarian drift. *Shura* creates a religious basis for challenging elite principles of political rule. The failure of the one-party oriented socialists to recognize the importance of consultation or the relevance of *shura* was both a tactical and strategic political mistake.

Very early in the establishment of the new state, Algeria's leaders tried to assert state control over religious institutions. From as early as 8 December 1964, while Ben Bella was still President, the Algerian government, through its Ministry of Religious Affairs, arrogated to itself the power to hire and fire religious leaders *(imams).* The state also directed all Quranic schools and Islamic centers and asserted an uncontested monopoly over the publication of religious books and texts.[22] Further, each week the Ministry of Religious Affairs oversaw the selection of appropriate subjects for the Friday sermon *(khotba)* for the entire country.[23] The state clearly intended to establish nearly hegemonic control over religious institutions.

In 1966 Boumedienne reasserted state controls over religious institutions. On 18 February 1966, the government created a *Conseil Supérieur Islamique* (Higher Islamic Council) with authority to name all rectors for all theological institutes in the country.[24] The same Council was also responsible for designating all clerics *(imams)* throughout the country. The state continued its supervision of the clergy. To control religious ideas, the state slowly assumed management of all the *Séminaires sur la pensée islamique* held in the country. At the same time Boumedienne tried to move closer to Islam symbolically. On 16 August 1976 he issued a decree changing the day of rest from Sunday to Friday, the holy day for Muslims. On 12 March 1976, he issued another order forbidding the sale of alcoholic beverages to Muslims.

Boumedienne's authoritarianism and political controls extended to all aspects of Algerian society. These tendencies were reinforced by an attempted *coup d'état* initiated by Colonel Tahar

Zbiri on 14 December 1967. Although the *coup* was not successful, it encouraged Boumedienne to centralize power and focus upon the improvement of economic performance so that the survival of his regime was assured.

Soon after the failed *coup*, Boumedienne, as part of his effort to improve upon the performance of the economy, began shifting his bases of political support from a coalition comprising the army and the conservative and religiously oriented *ulema* to a new coalition comprising the army and the conservative yet not as religiously oriented technocrats. Boumedienne hoped that these technocrats would help propel Algeria into an era of industrialism and prosperity. These men, many of whom may have been privately rather than publicly pious, placed greater emphasis in their politics upon technological competence, efficiency, and results rather than public displays of piety or references to Islam. By empowering the technocrats, however, Boumedienne rearranged the composition of his alliances at the expense of his previously prominent allies: the *ulema*.

Boumedienne's rhetoric for the regime also changed. Instead of "Algerian authenticity" (with references to Islam), themes such as "stability," "order," "efficiency," "discipline," and "results" emerged. Quite tragically and mistakenly, Boumedienne began paying less attention to the symbolic value of Islam, leading his regime in an increasingly authoritarian, technocratic, and apparently secular direction that was wholly preoccupied with economic results while alienating his former allies: the *ulema* and their supporters.

The Economic Context of Authoritarianism

Boumedienne's first open break with Ben Bella's economic legacy was his "official reversal of the *autogestion* experiment" on 19 June 1968, which overturned Ben Bella's Trotskyist theories of workers' self-management.[25] Boumedienne's preference for state direction of the economy by technocrats was in. State economic planning became the rule with publication of the first quadrennial economic plan in 1970. A vigorous program of nationalizations was begun to assert state control of the economy. Boumedienne went on to create a highly structured state apparatus for management of the economy with economic inputs and outputs set by the state. He cast his political fate with the technocrats and bureaucrats rather than with the religious community. Boumedienne hoped that by improving the economy he would be able to both stabilize and popularize his regime.

Faced with the challenge of rapidly improving the performance of the Algerian economy, Boumedienne and his economic advisors decided to expand, exploit, and export Algeria's most valuable resources for hard currency revenue: natural gas and petroleum. Using economic plans derived from the theoretical works of François Perroux and especially Gérard Destanne de Bernis, Algeria's planners adopted a "state capitalist" institutional framework for economic development. The economic planners' long-term goal was Algeria's economic independence by entirely eliminating dependency upon western capitalist economies. They development strategy was based upon a theory of "unbalanced growth," which required extraordinary initial investments in the hydrocarbon industry (even at the expense of other sectors of the economy) to industrialize Algeria rapidly.[26] They believed that extensive and rapid development of the hydrocarbon industry, even at the expense of other sectors, would have ancillary benefits, providing for the creation of new industries including hydrocarbon derivatives (plastics and fertilizers) and steel. A key part of the strategy involved a conscious decision not to invest in agriculture at this early stage of economic development. This aspect of the economic strategy would backfire spectacularly by the 1980's.

In August 1967, the regime began a program to nationalize foreign assets, beginning with Esso and Mobil assets in Algeria. The next year, on 13 May 1968, the government nationalized 14 more foreign-owned petroleum companies. Two years later, in June 1970, they acquired Shell Algérie and Phillips Petroleum. A year later, on 24 February 1971, the government purchased a 51% share of the last remaining private hydrocarbon companies in Algeria: Elf and Compagnie française des pétroles (C.F.P.). As part of this program of nationalizations, SONATRACH (the state firm in charge of hydrocarbons) was given a monopoly over all imports and exports in the hydrocarbon sector. In addition, between 1968 and 1974, the government nationalized more than 500 foreign-owned companies, ranging from metalworks to cement, paint, et cetera.

The purpose of the nationalizations was to weaken foreign control of critical industries, to retard capital flight, and to enhance the government's capacity to retain profits for reinvestment within Algeria. We should underline, however, that these state monopolies within Algeria were operating within a capitalist as opposed to a socialist economic framework. In the strict economic sense of the term, Algeria was not a socialist state. Rather, it was a one-party capitalist state that simply had a very large hydrocarbon driven parastatal sector. In Algeria, the right to private ownership of property and businesses was still legally permitted. Only the large critical industries (e.g., hydrocarbons, steel, textiles, et cetera) had been handed over to the state for management. Smaller firms were left in the hands of private, non-governmental owners. As Jacques Schnetzler said:

> This model of development is only possible in those rare countries in the Third World that have substantial rents for dozens of years. Despite their different ideologies, Algeria is closer to the Iran of the Pahlevis than to popular democracies. What has happened in Iran should make the Iranian leaders reflect upon the risks of not including its people in the economic transformation of the country. We are far [in Algeria] from a method of development that was envisaged by Third World thinkers and economists, whether they were from the East or the West, whether they were Soviet or American. The Algerian discourse is a Third World discourse. As far as its economic plans are concerned, however, Algeria has less in common with the Third World and it is clear it is closer to the capitalist West. [27]

Within this mixed economy, the largest parastatal sector was hydrocarbons. After the 1973 Arab-Israeli war, the price of petroleum skyrocketed due to the coordinated pricing strategies of the OPEC cartel. Boumedienne's decision to nationalize the hydrocarbon industry in 1968 reaped enormous profits when the price of petroleum trebled in 1973.

In 1971, Algeria was the tenth producer of petroleum in the world market and the third producer of natural gas. In terms of relative importance, however, natural gas has been more important than petroleum with Algeria holding 4% of the world's reserves. While these reserves pale in comparison with those of Saudi Arabia, Quwait, Iran, Libya, Iraq, and the United Arab Emirates, they were still substantial and profitable for Algeria when the world price for petroleum and natural gas exploded in 1973. When prices did take off in that year, the Algerian government was poised to exploit this opportunity.

Creation of the state hydrocarbon monopoly (SONATRACH) on 31 December 1963 positioned that government agency to play a large role in managing the Algerian economy.[28] From 1964 to 1968, SONATRACH's participation in the Algerian economy was limited. With the 1968 nationalizations, however, SONATRACH's political and economic role change substantially. As a quantitative index, the production outputs of SONATRACH and its competitors in the Algerian petroleum market for 1970 and 1972 are contrasted:

Algerian Petroleum Production

(Millions of tons)

	1970	Percent	1972	Percent
SONATRACH	14.8	31.0%	37.3	74.5%
C.F.P.	13.8	28.9%	6.9	13.8%
ERAP/Acquitaine	15.0	31.4%	5.9	11.7%
Others	4.2	8.7%		
Totals	47.8	100.0%	50.1	100.0%

Source: Dersa, *L'Algérie en debat* (Paris: Maspero, 1981), p. 70.

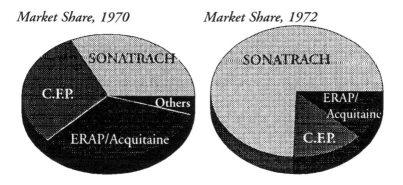

Market Share, 1970   *Market Share, 1972*

Hydrocarbon nationalizations made SONATRACH the principal player in the hydrocarbon industry while diminishing the role of foreign owned companies. When the world price of petroleum began rising geometrically beginning in 1973, the role of SONATRACH similarly became much more important. The unexpectedly high price increases in petroleum enabled Algeria's political leaders to expand their industrial and socioeconomic investments rapidly. The following chart provides figures on petroleum production, petroleum exports, world prices for Algerian Saharan light petroleum, and petroleum revenues from 1971 through 1979:

Petroleum Production, Price per Barrel, Petroleum Revenue

	1971	1972	1973	1974	1975	1976	1977	1978	1979
Petroleum Production (millions of barrels)	287	388	400	368	359	393	420	424	421
Average Spot Price per Barrel of Algerian Saharan Light	3.5	3.5	6.8	16.2	12.2	12.9	14.4	14.2	23.5
Revenue (millions$)	321	613	988	3,299	3,262	3,699	4,255	4,589	7,513

Source: *Annual Statistical Bulletin 1980,* Organization of Petroleum Exporting Countries, Vienna, 1981

Petroleum Production, Millions of Barrels

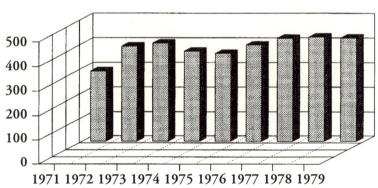

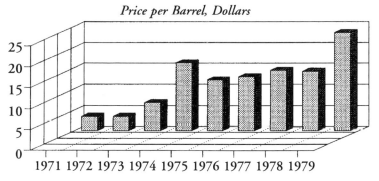

Algerian Saharan Light
Price per Barrel, Dollars

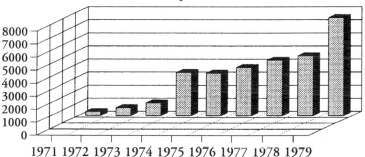

Revenue
Millions of Dollars

In the period between 1971 and 1979, the price of a barrel of Algerian Saharan light petroleum almost septupled and revenues from the overseas sale of petroleum increased by a multiple of twenty-three. The benefits to the regime were obvious. Boumedienne could claim that his policy of nationalizations had made Algeria richer. His gamble of casting his fate with the technocrats had paid off. The conjunction of government nationalization of the hydrocarbon industry with anomalously high world prices for petroleum and natural gas during the 1970's provided substantial rents that stabilized the Boumedienne regime.

While the financial resources of the state expanded geometrically during the 1970's, so, unfortunately, did Algeria's population. With an average growth rate of 3.2% per year, Algeria's population increased from 12.4 million in 1966 to 18.2 million in 1977. With this rate of growth, it was projected that Algeria's population would exceed 30 million persons by the year 2000. Even worse from a political management viewpoint, the urban population was growing at a rate of 5.2% per year because of a rural to urban exodus.[29] The greatest increases in population were in the under-18 cohort, with the most dynamic growth in the 6- to 14-year-old age group. This explosive growth of young Algerians would place increasing demands upon the state to provide employment that the state could not meet during the 1980's.

Demographic Change, 1961–1982

Age Group	1961	%	1966	%	1982	%
1-14	4,284,380	45.8	5,861,160	47.6	9,160,036	46.4
15-29	2,184,520	23.3	2,766,765	22.4	5,383,234	27.2
30-49	1,981,120	21.1	2,199,544	17.8	3,206,906	16.2
50-85+	880,360	9.4	1,454,786	11.8	1,981,729	10.0
Unknown	15,040	.1	21,092	.1	—	
Totals	**9,345,420**	**99.7**	**12,303,347**	**99.7**	**19,731,905**	**99.8**

Sources: *United Nations Demographic Yearbook, 1970; United Nations Demographic Yearbook, 1974; United Nations Demographic Yearbook, 1983*

The structure of the Algerian economy during the 1970's enabled the regime to enjoy formidable hydrocarbon rents, encouraging industrial expansion while providing increased social benefits to a rapidly expanding population. When oil prices began to drop in 1986, the regime suffered a loss of rents, leaving the rapidly increasing population with unsatisfied demands for employment and income. In the 1980's, the government's over-reliance on hydrocarbon rents and its failure to restrain population growth resulted in a severe economic and political crisis. The regime's

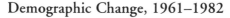

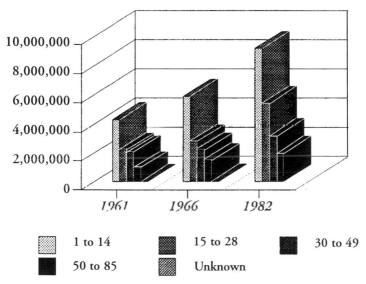

Demographic Change, 1961–1982

	1 to 14		15 to 28		30 to 49
	50 to 85		Unknown		

overemphasis upon positive economic indices and "competent management" as its bases for its political legitimacy coupled with its systematic neglect and devaluation of the symbolic importance of political Islam weakened all its bases for political legitimacy.

By presenting itself to the masses as a technologically and economically competent regime, the government became the victim of its own rhetoric when the economy soured. Relying almost entirely upon competence and economic performance as its bases for political legitimacy, the government created the standard for its rejection by the public. By unnecessarily discarding the political capital of symbolic Islam, it deprived itself of an alternative or supplementary basis of political legitimacy. Boumedienne assured that his successor, Chadli Ben Jadid, would be unable to resurrect religion as basis for providing legitimacy to his faltering regime.

Apart from these issues of legitimacy, the regime created additional problems for itself and for its burgeoning population by its poor management of a critical sector of the economy: agriculture. While the regime was focussing entirely upon the expansion of the state's capacity to reap profits from the extraction and the sale of hydrocarbons, its performance in agriculture was miserable. The following tables and charts display the government's planned investments per sector during the Boumedienne years:

State Investment per Sector (1970–1973)
(in millions of Algerian dinars)

	Total	Percentage
Hydrocarbons	4,573	96
Steel	1,900	15
Mechanical, Electrical	1,275	11
Construction	940	8
Electricity	735	6
Mines	700	6
Miscellaneous	580	5
Textiles	515	5
Chemicals	512	5
Agriculture	470	3
Crafts	140	1
Leather	60	–
Totals	**12,400**	**100**

Source: *Rapport général, Plan quadriennal (1970–1973), Alger, 1970*

State Investment Per Sector (1974-1977)
(in millions of Algerian dinars)

	Total	Percentage
Industry	48,000	43.5
Economic Infrastructure	15,521	14.0
Social Investment	14,610	13.3
Agriculture	12,005	10.9
Education	9,947	9.0
Waterworks	4,600	4.2
Miscellaneous	2,520	2.3
Tourism	1,500	1.4
Administration	1,399	1.3
Fisheries	155	.1
Totals	**110,217**	**100.0**

Source: *Rapport général, deuxième plan quadriennal (1974–1977), Alger, 1974*

Millions of dollars were spent in steel works, petrochemicals, the petroleum industry, and phosphates.[30] Actual investment in agriculture fell from 16.9 % of GDP between 1967 and 1969 to 12.5% between 1970 and 1973 to 7.4% between 1974 and 1977.[31] From 1967 to 1978 the regime invested 38.6% of total GDP in industry, while dedicating 6% to agriculture.[32] Whereas internal production in 1969 met 93% of Algeria's food requirements, by 1980 that proportion slipped to 30%.[33] The failure to invest in agriculture resulted in declining agricultural production. Agricultural exports, especially wine, dropped precipitously, while imports of cereals, meat, dairy products, tea, coffee, and sugar increased markedly, straining the buying power of working Algerians. Whereas before independence Algeria was a net agricultural exporter, by the 1970's, barely ten years later, it was a net importer. Agriculture became the "Achilles Heel" of Algeria's development strategy. The failure to attend to agriculture created real shortfalls in foodstuffs in the 1980's that placed severe pressures upon the regime. The following table documents cereals production in Algeria from 1945 to 1993:

Cereals Production, 1946 to 1993
(in thousands of tons)

	Wheat	Barley
1946	851	514
1955	1306	707
1970	1435	571
1974	1091	331
1982	980	480
1988	614	390
1989	850	870
1990	1005	680
1991	1741	1750
1992	1770	1370
1993	1100	900

Source: *Patrick Eveno, L'Algérie* (Paris: Le Monde, 1994), p. 86.

The conjunction of rapid population growth, overinvestment in hydrocarbons and steel, and underinvestment in agriculture became more apparent in the late 1970's and in the 1980's. Boumedienne's emphasis upon the exploitation of hydrocarbon resources created an economy that provided rents and profitability during the years of extraordinarily high world prices for petroleum (1974–1986). This profitability, however, masked the underlying fact that this strategy, while profitable in the short-term, was creating a society and an economy overly reliant on hydrocarbons, underperforming in agriculture, and failing to create a sufficient number of jobs to meet the demands of an exploding population. Also, because the hydrocarbon industry was capital-intensive rather than labor-intensive, too few jobs were created. According to government figures, in the period between 1966 and 1977, 19% of Algeria's work force was unemployed. According to Algerian experts, however, the figure was much higher. Abdellatif Benachenhou has fixed the figure at 28%[34] and Tahar Benhouria has set it at 46%.[35] Algeria was becoming what Celso Furtado described as an "industrialized, underdeveloped country."

After empowering the technocrats, Boumedienne paid less attention to courting the *ulema* and he exhibited less public reverence in evoking the symbols or the substance of Islam. This decision was a calculated political move. Boumedienne gambled. As he said at the non-aligned conference in Lahore, Pakistan in February 1974:

> . . . human experience in a number of regions of the world has shown that spiritual ties, whether they are Muslim or Christian, cannot endure the blows of poverty and ignorance for the simple reason that men do not want to enter Paradise with an empty stomach . . . . A starving people do not want to listen to [religious] verses.[36]

A clear shift in themes had occurred. The regime became less concerned with being "Islamic" and more concerned with being "technocratically competent." Boumedienne's shift, with its de-emphasis of religio-cultural reference points and his obsession with positive economic results, was a decision for which his successors would pay. While Boumedienne and his colleagues repeatedly proclaimed their commitment that "socialism in Algeria would have no meaning outside of Islamic belief," over time this expression sounded hollow. A dynamic contradiction gradually emerged between Boumedienne's centralization of political power and his *étatist* direction of the economy on the one hand and his increasing devaluation of the political value of religious reference points on the other. This contradiction was neither logically nor analytically imperative. It was also a profound political and cultural mistake that helped undermine the army's and the FLN's power in the 1980's.

The wealth created by anomalous hydrocarbon income of the 1970's created a false sense of security in which the regime thought it could ignore the symbols of Islam. It also ignored the growing appeals of younger Algerians who were not finding employment, who were not being recruited into the FLN, and who were joining Muslim organizations that were beginning to organize against the political status quo. The wealth created by hydrocarbon rents lulled the regime into unresponsive complacency, rendering it less sensitive to the demands of its disadvantaged youth and postponing the latent conflict between older political elites and their younger, disaffected constituencies whom they had excluded from meaningful participation in the political process. For thirteen years (from 1973 to 1986) Algeria profited from anomalous price rises in petroleum and natural gas. These price rises enabled Algeria to function as a Libya-style or Saudi-style rentier state that could buy social compliance to its authoritarian politics as long as the anomalous revenues continued to fill government coffers. When the world price of natural gas began to fall precipitously beginning in 1986, long-deferred political issues relating to sharing political power and the role of Islam in politics began reemerging. In the depressed economy of the 1980's, however, these political issues were expressed with renewed force.

Cultural and Educational Politics, Demographic Change, and Political Resistance

The political and cultural disjuncture between the elites within the FLN and the masses that was largely submerged during the 1960's and 1970's came to full fruition in the 1980's. The political elites who ran Algeria's government during the 1960's and 1970's had been operating in an insulated ideological compartment: they had become disconnected from the masses by their elitist and authoritarian manner of government. Led by Boumedienne, the elites shifted from themes of Islamic socialism of the mid-1960's to the political icons of technocratic competence, efficiency, and authoritarian rule by the 1970's. The masses, excluded from participation in the decision-making processes of the elites, turned away from the FLN and began organizing themselves in anti-political-status-quo groups that increasingly referred to Islam as the basis for cultural and political resistance. In particular, the young turned away from the values of Boumedienne-encouraged technical competence and inverted further towards religious groups and Islam.

The FLN estranged itself even further from the masses of youth by its party recruitment policies which were extraordinarily selective. The party's exclusionary recruitment policies had their origins in 1963 in the debate that had emerged between Mohammed Khider and Ahmed Ben Bella about the criteria for party membership.[37] Khider, as Secretary of the Party at the time, recommended that the FLN become a mass party with relaxed criteria for membership. Ben Bella, as President, preferred that the FLN remain an avant-garde party with members carefully selected and screened. By adhering to strict recruitment standards Ben Bella hoped that he could maintain party loyalty and discipline. The 1964 Algiers Charter articulated Ben Bella's position that the FLN was "an avant-garde party profoundly bound to the masses, drawing its power from that alliance, by the imperatives of the socialist revolution, and its intransigence vis-a-vis its enemies."[38] The FLN was to be the "vanguard of the Algerian people." It was to be a small party, "[deriving] its strength from the masses of peasants and workers and the revolutionary intellectuals; it is the guide of the people for complete

independence, socialism, democracy and peace linked to the peoples' demands for liberation."[39] Rather than creating a mass party as
advocated by his adversary Khider in 1962 and 1963, Ben Bella
insisted that the FLN remain an elite party with a narrow base of
members.[40] Under Ben Bella, membership in the party was open to
any Algerian at least eighteen years old who had taken part in the
war of national liberation and who had pledged "to militate actively
and regularly pay his dues, to conform to the socialist orientation of
the party, and to display moral qualities."[41] Candidates for the party
had to be sponsored by two other party members and submit to one
year of political training before being admitted as a full party member. These membership rules were quite restrictive. In fact, they
were more restrictive than those set up by the Chinese Communist
Party.[42] This difference of opinion between creating an elite party
and a mass party was the essence of the recruitment debate between
Ben Bella and Mohammed Khider in 1963. Their differences concerning this issue led to Khider's resignation as party chief in that
year.[43]

Boumedienne, after ousting Ben Bella, supposedly modified
the criteria for membership in the party. He claimed to have liberalized the criteria, (i.e., "The door is open to all who accept our politics and are willing to work towards its application,")[44] while warning all party members that they would be subject to extreme
scrutiny and discipline by a "tightly screened corps of controllers
who will be in charge of the failings and comportment of the militant."[45] Boumedienne in effect created a police state, with extensive
internal surveillance by the *mukhabarat* or internal police. Surveillance and control of party members by internal security forces reinforced the FLN's orientation towards becoming an elite, exclusive
party that would eventually become cut off from the masses.
Boumedienne repeatedly emphasized that the FLN would be a
small "avant-garde" party whose task would be to "mobilize the
masses" and its "revolutionary capabilities."[46] These party recruitment practices as modified and narrowed by Boumedienne further
alienated the party from the masses. By its very own party membership rules the FLN excluded from participation the very Algerians (the youth) that it needed to grow as a party. The FLN's prefer-

ence for restricted membership and rule by elites isolated it. Elitism in party recruitment also made the party ultimately more responsive to concerns of its elites rather than to concerns of the masses. Its very methods of party recruitment made the construction of responsive political institutions much more difficult. This strategy of limited party membership guaranteed a numerically small base of support for the FLN.

By the mid-1970's, FLN elites and the masses of young people clearly had clearly moved in different ideological directions. Eventually they occupied different worlds that rarely communicated with one another. For members of the FLN and members of the army, either technocratic competence or service in the army became credentials or badges of honor that conferred privileges, personal and political legitimacy, and access to power.[47] For the masses of younger people, their exclusion from politics pushed them towards Islamic groups that were willing to address their concerns and provide them with a means of resistance to elitist rule.

Despite Boumedienne's substantial success in controlling dissident religious groups through legislation and internal surveillance, protests were still heard. The first notable criticism of his regime appeared in 1974 when Cheikh Abdellatif Soltani published a virulent critique of the direction of Algeria's revolution in a book entitled *al-mazdaqiyya hiya asl al-ishtirakiyya* (Socialism is Mazdaqism).[48] In this work Sheikh Soltani criticized the Boumedienne regime for having veered towards secular socialism and away from Islam. Second, although President Boumedienne legally dissolved the dissident Muslim organization *al-Qiyam* on 16 March 1970,[49] the Muslim community found alternatives to continue its criticism of the regime. A magazine called *al-Tadhib al-Islami* (Muslim Education) would continue publication after the dissolution of *al-Qiyam.* This magazine promoted Muslim ideas of political reform ranging from gradualists such as Muhammad Abduh and Jamal al-Din al-Afghani to militants such as Sayyid Qutb. The publication of this magazine and the promotion of these ideas provided a forum for indirect criticism of the regime.

Besides explicit critiques of the government by Sheikh Abdel-

latif Soltani and implicit critiques of *al-Tadhib al-Islami,* Muslims
also organized themselves into armed resistance groups during
Boumedienne's rule. During the 1970's Sheikh Mahfoud Nahnah
established *Ansar Allah,* the first armed Islamic group to appear in
independent Algeria. In 1976, Sheikh Nahnah led Muslim dissidents in directly challenging the regime when it had been leaked to
the public that the country's leaders had intended to draft a new
Constitution and a new National Charter that did not stipulate that
Islam would remain the official religion of the state. Because of
protests organized by Sheikh Nahnah, the FLN reversed itself by
stipulating in the Constitution that "Islam was the religion of the
state" (1976 Constitution, Article 2), that the President of the
Republic must be a Muslim (Article 107), that the state "must
respect and glorify the Muslim religion" (Article 110), and that
"constitutional revisions not restrain the religion of the state" (Article 195).[50] The regime also enacted laws changing the weekly day of
rest from Sunday to Friday (16 August 1976), forbidding the sale of
alcoholic beverages to Muslims (12 March 1976), and prohibiting
the production of pork (27 February 1979). The FLN redrafted the
1976 National Charter so that it would say that:

> . . . socialism in Algeria does not proceed from material meta-
> physics and it does not attach itself to any dogma that is for-
> eign to our national character. It is built and it identifies with
> the flourishing of Islamic values which is a fundamental ele-
> ment of the personality of the Algerian people.[51]

During the 1970's Islamist political movements began reex-
pressing its desire for the modification of Algerian politics so that it
would conform with its vision of political Islam. Boumedienne,
although he for the most part resisted the Islamists through his dra-
conian style of authoritarianism, was still subject to substantial pres-
sure from the Islamist movement. His reversals on the question of
Islam in the Constitution and in the National Charter reflected that
his authoritarian methods had their limitations when faced with
organized resistance from Islamists.

During the 1980's, after a gestational period during the 1970's,
a new generational cohort of Algerians emerged from either the

lycées or the universities. These youths were born after the war for independence and had not been recruited into the FLN. For them, in contrast to the older FLN cadres of the *Guerre d'Algérie* of 1954 to 1962, the relevance of personal service in the war for independence had declining significance. A gap — perhaps an unbridgeable gap — emerged between the *anciens combatants* who were in control of the state and the *jeunes militants* who were born after the war. For the *jeunes militants* service in the anti-colonial war had little meaning. For them, new ideological constructs having their basis in Islam rather than anti-colonial resistance had greater meaning.

The gap between the older FLN cadres and the younger Algerians who had become politicized and religiously inclined was widened not only by the FLN's exclusionary recruitment criteria but also by the FLN's own educational policies, which were aimed at directing the masses towards the understanding and speaking of a form of Arabic known as Modern Standard Arabic. Both during and after the revolution, FLN leaders had hoped that Arabic eventually would fully replace French, the colonial language, as the language of the nation. Algeria's Arabization program, however, was not well thought out. The Arabization program itself created severe social and economic dislocations. What the program failed to appreciate was that, despite the aspirations of its new post-colonial leaders, 132 years of French linguistic colonialism could not be wiped out within a decade or two.[52] The program, which needed to be gradual and consistent, was devised rapidly and was ill-prepared.

We must remember that the French occupied Algeria for 132 years, were present in Tunisia for 77 years (1878–1955), and were in Morocco for only 44 years (1912–1956). The longer French occupation of Algeria enabled the French to emplace French as a *lingua franca*. In Algeria today both French and the Algerian dialect of Arabic are widely spoken. The establishment of French as a working language was eased not only by France's long occupation but also by the presence in Algeria of a proportionally large *colon* community, which comprised approximately 11% of the total population. The proportional size of the *colon* community in Algeria was much larger than in Tunisia or Morocco.

Additionally, Algeria's Arabization program, while necessary from a political, cultural, and a nationalist viewpoint, failed to recognize the linguistic complexity of Algeria, which is a country where French, dialectical Arabic, and Berber languages are spoken. Onto this trilingual linguistic matrix, the state's leaders mistakenly tried to convert the populace to use of a form of Arabic (Modern Standard Arabic) that is close to Classical Arabic. This cultural project, while desirable as a means of reestablishing a linguistic heritage that the French interregnum had submerged, was set up hastily. The educational program created dislocations first among some elements of the youth who were being trained in Arabic for jobs that did not exist, and second among Berberophones and Berberophiles who revered their indigenous languages and who feared that the Arabization program would be insufficiently sensitive to their cultural and linguistic traditions.

The Algerian government began the systematic teaching of Modern Standard Arabic through its educational system in the 1966–1967 academic year.[53] The Arabization program was introduced in the high schools or *lycées* first, with introduction into the university system planned for 1974. The first subjects taught in Arabic in the *lycées* were civics and religion (Islam).[54] When they finally introduced Arabic into the university system in 1979–1980, it was limited to use only in the Faculty of Letters and the Faculty of Law. The Faculty of Science continued its instruction in French. The structure of this system created problems for its students and for the state by creating an essentially two-track university system: they oriented one to studies in the sciences in French and the other to studies in the humanities, social science, and law in Arabic and French. The regime then complicated matters further by providing enhanced economic rewards and better jobs to its French-track science graduates. Some of the Arabophone students derisively identified these Francophone science students as part of the *hizba fransa* or as Francophiles. These Francophone science graduates received the higher paying technical jobs in an economy that rewarded technical competence and that was gearing towards rapid industrialization.

In contrast, the humanities, the social sciences, and law were taught in French and Arabic. This corps of students was predominantly Arabophone. These students pursued studies in areas for which there were few jobs and for which there was less compensation.

Instead of having devised a system that would have provided greater rewards for its Arabophone graduates, the regime, in one of its colossal political-cultural mistakes, created a dual system that granted superior economic and employment rewards to its Francophone graduates.[55] The Francophone students received the plum jobs in government and industry, while the Arabophone students were consigned either to unemployment or underemployment. These Arabophone trained students would participate actively in the Islamic resistance movement of the 1980's and 1990's. Much of the political, economic, and social discontent of the 1980's can be directly traceable to these educational and employment policies that created a ghetto of skilled — yet unemployed — Arabophone students.

The Arabization program complicated matters even further in Algeria because it disaffected large segments of Algeria's indigenous Berber community (the Kabyles, the Chaouias, the Mzabites, and the Touaregs), who speak their own languages. Fearing cultural, social, and economic marginalization because of the government's expanded Arabization program, Berbers in Kabylie, fearing displacement of their own language, began to resist state efforts to enlarge the use of Arabic. In 1980, the first of a series of rebellions broke out in Tizi-Ouzou, the regional capital of the Kabylie.

The government's policy of Arabization was fundamentally flawed in its design and, in its own way, was culturally imperialist. It mistakenly asserted that Algeria was an Arab nation and an Arabic speaking nation when in reality it was and will be an Arab, Berber, and Tuareg nation. The politics of Arabization was both racist and linguistically insensitive. Algeria's political leaders have insisted upon Arabism while remaining insensitive to the need to incorporate and assimilate non-Arabs, particularly the Kabyles, the Chaouias, and the Tuaregs.

Conclusion

One important observation about FLN ideology from the 1950s through the 1990s was that it lacked any essential coherence on the question of Islam. From the 1960s through the 1990s, the Islamic socialists continued to work on a merger of Islam and socialism that, although it was theoretically plausible, was resisted by clerics and their supporters within the religious community. The FLN's political leaders insisted upon the compatibility of Islam and socialism while Algeria's religious leaders insisted that these two ideologies were incompatible. During the period of Boumedienne's rule, given his methods of extensive internal surveillance, his discouragement of dissenting political views, and the prosperity engendered by hydrocarbon-induced wealth, the voices of dissenting Islam were difficult to organize. Nevertheless, despite these factors, the Islamist movement did organize. The group *al-Qiyam* operated from 1964 until 1970. Sheikh Abdellatif Soltani published his criticism of the regime in 1974. Sheikh Mahfoud Nahnah organized his armed group, *Ansar Allah,* in 1976. Voices were finding expression that claimed that the FLN's program of Islamic socialism was impracticable. Muslim political dissidents were saying that Islamic socialism had to be a contradiction because first, Islamic economics is organized on the basis of private property and, second, Islamic politics are based upon the principle of consultation or *shura.* Therefore, according to their argument, the construction of the FLN's ideology of "Islamic socialism" was entirely unsound.

Although the published political programs of the Algerian Islamist movement from the 1970s through the 1990s have been constitutionally ambiguous in many ways, at least their argumentation regarding the question of Islam and politics is more coherent than that of the FLN.[56] One reason the FLN leaders have lacked essential ideological coherence on the religious question has been that the leadership of the FLN, while being dedicated to the rejection of French colonialism, did not have a sufficiently clear ideological or cultural agenda. Despite the publication of the Tripoli Program of 1962, the Algiers Charter of 1964, and the National Charter of 1976, the ideological work of the revolution remained largely unfinished because of the vagueness and excessive rhetorical flourishes of most of the published ideological documents. Grandiloquent rhetoric cannot supplant rigorous and systematic political or ideological analysis. In retrospect, it seems that the *Guerre d'Algérie* was simply an anti-colonial war. It was not a war for socialism or for Islam. Socialism and Islam were simply the ideological and symbolic fuels of the engine of war; they should not be confused with the war itself.

After the war, it became noticeable that despite the rhetoric about "scientific socialism" or "democratic and humanistic socialism" or "Islamic socialism," politics in Algeria had very little to do with ideology; it was more concerned with the partitioning of power, perquisites, and prestige. Politics in Algeria since independence had not really been concerned with ideology; rather ". . . it has been the contest for power among dozens of clans and groups."[57] As one protagonist in the political struggle, Hocine Aït Ahmed, said, "The avant-garde forces are not divided by ideas, but by men."[58]

Chapter VII

The Beginning of the End: Chadli Ben Jadid and the Politics of Disintegration (1978–1992)

The Process of Disintegration

President Boumedienne died after a long illness on 27 December 1978. Shortly after his death, the FLN held a party conference in late January 1979 in Algiers in which the party chose a lesser-known General named Chadli Ben Jadid to run for President. Ben Jadid was chosen as a compromise candidate when the leading candidates for the Presidency, Mohammed Salah Yahiaoui and Abdelaziz Bouteflika, both actively campaigned to be President. This created a schism within the FLN that deprived both from obtaining enough votes to secure the Presidency.[1] On 7 February 1979, Ben Jadid, running as the only candidate for the Presidency, was elected as President of the Democratic and Popular Republic of Algeria.[2]

General Ben Jadid was elected in a political environment that was changing both domestically and internationally. Within Algeria, Muslim militants were continuing to agitate for political change and, outside Algeria, in Iran, in the same month that Ben Jadid was elected President, Muslim militants had just been successful in deposing the Shah of Iran. Ben Jadid observed how Reza Shah had resisted his Islamist opponents by using force, that these measures had failed, and he hoped to avoid the Shah's consequences by adopting more conciliatory measures in Algeria. Keeping these facts in mind, Ben Jadid began carrying out his politics of accommodation with Muslim militants. Meanwhile, the Soviet Union and the rest of Eastern Europe were beginning economic and political transformations, seeing the limitations and inefficiencies of political authoritarianism and state management of economies. These political lessons, played in the Eastern European arena, exerted an impact in Algeria.

While revolutionary political changes were occurring outside Algeria, economic and demographic forces were converging within Algeria in a way that further weakened the regime. The government's over-reliance upon hydrocarbons for revenue backfired in the 1980s when world prices for natural gas and petroleum began a dramatic decade long fall. At the beginning of the decade the average world price for a barrel of petroleum was $30. By 1983, the price slipped to $28. By February 1986 the price fell again to $24 and by the following month it fell to $10! For the rest of the decade the average price for a barrel of oil fluctuated between $12 and $15. The consequences to Algeria's economy were cataclysmic.[3] Revenues from petroleum and natural gas fell from 13 billion dollars in 1985 to 7.7 billion dollars in 1986, a 40% drop in one year alone.[4] In 1990, with inflation spiralling and with economic activity depressed because of the drop in hydrocarbon revenues, more than 100 public and private enterprises failed, sending thousands of workers into unemployment.[5]

While Algeria's economy was worsening, its population was expanding geometrically. The following table documents Algeria's population growth over a 28 year period:

Population Growth — Algeria

Year	Millions
1965	12.0
1975	17.0
1985	21.6
1988	23.6
1990	25.0
1991	25.7
1992	26.5
1993	26.3

Source: Patrick Eveno, *L'Algerie* (Paris: Le Monde, 1994), p. 92.

Demographic Change, 1966-1987

Age Group	1966	1982	1984	1987
1-14	5,861,160	9,160,036	9,588,000	9,946,100
15-30	2,766,765	5,383,234	5,659,000	6,323,746
30-44	921,278	2,539,711	2,662,000	3,142,105
45-59	515,837	1,644,160	1,734,000	1,887,286
60-85 plus	412,352	1,129,865	1,198,000	1,298,863
Unknown	10,800	0	0	2,857

Sources: *United Nations Demographic Yearbook, 1974; United Nations Demographic Yearbook, 1985; United Nations Demographic Yearbook, 1991; United Nations Demographic Yearbook, 1993*

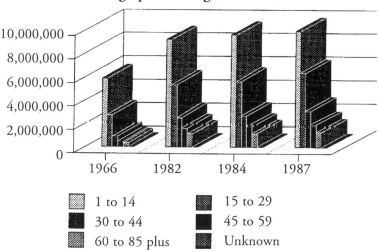

Demographic Change, 1966–1987

From independence in 1962 to 1992, Algeria's population had tripled. Most important, within this explosive population growth, the average rate of growth for the age five to age 24 cohort was 3.4% per year. Of 25 million inhabitants in 1990, 60% were under the age of 20 and 70% were under the age of 30.[6] This age cohort, the largest and most politically important group, was born (and this is the relevant issue) after the Algerian War for Independence (1954-1962). This group had not participated in the war for independence, it had not been recruited into the FLN because of the FLN's exclusionary and elitist recruitment policy,[7] and it felt that it could not participate meaningfully in government or politics. In addition to these concerns, the increased under-30 population group placed enormous burdens upon the state's capacity to provide housing, education, and jobs.

While technically the state was meeting the educational needs of this burgeoning school-age population, its efforts were not effective; many students failed the required qualifying examination known as the *baccalauréat*. Those who failed the *baccalauréat* exam were pushed out of school and into labor markets to search for jobs that did not exist. Unemployment rolls mushroomed. Algeria's youth were turned into the streets with very little hope of ever finding consistent employment. According to official government figures, of the 854,000 unemployed persons in 1989, 66% were in the 15-24 age cohort.[8] Worse, the number of jobs being created by the economy each year (100,000) was not meeting the yearly demand (200,000 to 300,000).[9] The conjunction of these economic and demographic developments created only two viable alternative for those under thirty: resistance to the regime or emigration to France or Spain.

Algeria's degenerating external debt worsened its economic problems. In the period between 1970 and 1992, Algeria's external debt expanded from $1 billion to $27 billion. By 1992, 76% of Algeria's export revenues was being dedicated solely for the payment of that debt. The following table documents the growth of Algeria's foreign debt since 1970.

Foreign Debt — Algeria

	$ US (millions)	Debt Service/Exports Ratio
1970	1.0	
1975	4.6	
1980	19.4	
1985	20.0	
1987	26.7	58.5%
1988	25.5	78.4%
1989	28.9	69.0%
1990	24.0	66.1%
1991	26.0	74.1%
1992	27.0	76.0%

Source: *Le Monde*, 30 novembre 1993

Foreign Debt
(*$ US millions*)

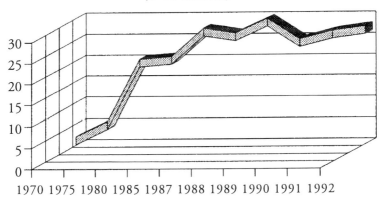

These demographic and economic issues helped provoke a crisis involving religion, culture, and political activism. The FLN had ruled as the *parti unique* for more than two decades yet, in the final analysis, it had failed to manage the economy profitably, it had failed to manage population growth, and it had failed to provide meaningful political participation to its people. These factors provoked a response organized by Muslim organizations.

Economic and political change within Algeria and without Algeria (especially in Iran and the Soviet Union) forced the Ben Jadid regime to reconsider its political and economic strategies. The three tactics of one-party political authoritarianism, repression of dissenting religious and political groups, and government management of the economy could not continue to work successfully in the changing political and economic environments of the 1980's.

At first the regime tinkered and stumbled around the edges of reform, contemplating some economic reform without seriously considering significant political change. Ben Jadid's initial economic reform initiatives were modest, they failed to bring prosperity, and they were inadequate to satisfy the demands of a people who wanted both the restored prosperity of the Boumedienne years and more meaningful participation in government.

In this arena of discontent, effectively organized groups founded with the assistance of Muslim clerics entered the political arena. Aware of the emergence of these clerically led groups, the government tried to deflect them by consciously and systematically trying to reincorporate Islam into its political rhetoric and decrees. By referring to Islam in its official proclamations, the regime hoped to recapture some of the political symbolism of Islam appropriated by dissident Islamic groups. Since the dissidents used the political language of Islam to criticize the regime, the regime countered by using the political language of Islam to deflect its critics. It was a tactic that the regime had employed systematically since the beginning of the Ben Bella regime, believing it would enable them both to fend off their critics and help them to obtain some social compliance to their programs. One example was the 9 February 1980 governmental decree that required that the Ministry of Religious Affairs "remain vigilant in expanding the understanding of Islam, all the while explaining and propagating the socialist principles of the regime." The state from its beginning in 1962 had united the rhetoric of Islam to its allegedly socialist politics. The pre-independence Algerian nationalist movement had done the same. However, the problem for the regime in the 1980's was that it could no longer exercise a monopoly on the political use of the language of Islam.

By the 1980's other Islamic groups had organized themselves as both symbolic and substantive alternatives to the government. These groups effectively invoked the symbolic language of Islam to criticize the regime while simultaneously creating substantive social service programs that challenged the capacity of the regime to deliver same sets of services. Although the regime tried to retaliate with the same language and with some of the same programs that it was confronted with, it could not muster either the same symbolic value in its rhetoric or any real substantive content in its social programs. The regime had exhausted most of its economic, political, symbolic, and economic resources. To put it succinctly, it had become incompetent. The regime had opened the political language of Islam gambit very early in its history. By the 1980s, however, the regime's gambit had reversed itself. Its critics were using the very same language to try to bring down the regime. In effect, the regime had created the symbolic language of its own destruction.

Having inherited the political discourse of Islam from Boumedienne and Ben Bella, Ben Jadid tried to follow the rhetorical strategy of continuing to try to integrate the rhetoric of Islam into the politics of FLN authoritarianism. He did this as part of an ineffective effort to try to deter the Islamist challenge. Besides the decree mentioned above, he tried to codify further the merger of Islam with FLN politics by rewriting the FLN statutes in 1980 saying, "The FLN is dedicated in [its] mission, as part of its basic plan, to the building of socialism within the framework of national and Islamic values, which essentially includes: the consolidation of national independence, the establishment of a society freed of the exploitation of man by man, and the development of the citizen and his Arabo-Islamic personality in the fullest development."[10]

While the FLN was swearing its allegiance to Islam and to the extermination of exploitation, it was also extending its methods of authoritarian control by statute. For example, Article 102 of the new FLN statutes specifically required the placement of party members in all positions of responsibility within the government. Article 120 of the same corpus of statutes stipulated that only party members could serve as leaders of allegedly autonomous social institutions such as the ONM (*Organisation nationale des moudjahidines*), the UNPA *(Union nationale des paysans algériens)*, the UGTA *(Union générale des travailleurs algériens)*, the UNFA *(Union nationale des femmes algériennes)*, the UNJA *(Union nationale de jeunesse algérienne)*, and the OSCP *(Organisation scientifique, culturelle, et professionelle)*. Article 66 of the Electoral law of 1980 declared that the FLN would continue its control of the legislature: "The members of each Popular Assembly are elected from a list established by the FLN. . . . Voters can only vote for the candidates from that list provided according to the first paragraph of this article." The FLN had not intended to loosen its political control on the society. Quite to the contrary, its use of the language of Islam was a subterfuge. It really wanted to extend its control, especially among the clerics that it thought were organizing to challenge the regime. For example, on 6 August 1983, the government issued another decree making all imams government officials. This decision was intended to make them subject to government control and discipline.

Given the fact that the regime was not yet ready to loosen political controls, the question in this period of incipient reform became whether the regime would change and, if so, what it would change. The regime's hoped-for long-term goal throughout the 1980's was the maintenance of hegemonic political control for as long as it possibly could.[11] Its initial "reform" program was to liberalize first the economic regime and to give the impression of some political reform. The regime hoped that this mix of moderate economic reform and minimal political reform would restore some of the prosperity lost when the price of natural gas and petroleum fell in world markets. It also believed that the restoration of prosperity would both quiet domestic discontent and reverse the Islamist challenge. If the economic liberalization program were successful, the FLN hoped to postpone political reform for as long as possible.

The program of economic liberalization began officially on 6 April 1980 when the government declared in the *Journal officiel* that it would subdivide the state petroleum company, SONATRACH, into four enterprises (to encourage greater efficiency) and that it would encourage foreign investment in the hydrocarbon industry. This was the first opening to foreign investment in the hydrocarbon industry since the Boumedienne inspired nationalizations of the 1970's. On 21 May 1980, Standard Oil and the Compagnie Française des Pétroles were the first foreign companies to reinvest in the Algerian hydrocarbon industry. In the years to follow, French, Italian, Japanese, Spanish, and American petroleum and natural gas concerns all reinvested in the Algerian hydrocarbon market.[12] The regime then reorganized fifty state owned "mega-enterprises" in November 1980. It subdivided these fifty businesses into 450 smaller, distinct units.[13] It then reorganized the housing sector to encourage private rather than public investment.[14] To revive agriculture, the government in 1983 and 1987 enacted laws favoring private investment.[15] The regime took these measures to encourage productivity in sectors of the economy that had noticeably foundered under state management. As part of an ongoing program of economic liberalization, on 4 September 1983, the government announced the "financial restructuring" of twenty-one public enterprises. These economic reform measures were intended to encourage investment in Algeria from overseas investors, to resuscitate agricultural productivity, and to increase efficiency in the management of state industries. The investors came (notably from France, Italy, Japan, Spain, and the United States) but they did not come in sufficient numbers to revive the Algerian economy quickly. The economy was simply not growing fast enough, it was not producing enough jobs to meet labor market demands (an average of 250,000 jobs were required each year), and the agricultural sector in the 1980's was still not producing enough food to meet domestic requirements. The structure of Algeria's economy was, despite these reforms, still almost entirely reliant upon the sale of hydrocarbons.

More substantive economic reform had to wait until 12 July 1988 when the regime passed law No. 88–25 specifically encouraging the growth of privately owned businesses in Algeria. This law also provided specific legal remedies and guarantees to foreign investors investing in Algeria. In July 1989, the prices of many products that had been set by the state were gradually lifted. Free market pricing was introduced. With the enactment of these measures, a more realistic dismantling of the parastatal sector of the economy began. The regime enacted these measures to provide a radical stimulus to an economy that simply could no longer be supported the state and its stagnant hydrocarbon rents. The regime hoped that after 25 years of having the state run the economy it could somehow revive entrepreneurialism in Algeria. It staked its political chances on the gamble that there existed in Algeria both a bourgeoisie that was willing to invest in enterprises for profit and that there were financial institutions and structures available in Algeria to make capitalist initiatives possible.

The economic liberalization program was initiated with real structural impediments. First, society at large and entrepreneurs in particular had to switch gears in the mid-1980's from believing that the state with its hydrocarbon rents could continue to deliver real and substantial social benefits, to coming to an understanding that the hydrocarbon boom was over and that real economic and social adjustments were necessary. After thirteen years of economic growth (from 1973 to 1986), a very difficult shift in expectations vis-à-vis the benefits delivered by the state was required. This switch was difficult for large sectors of the population to accept. Second, although the regime partially liberalized financial markets in 1984, 1989, and 1990, there was an insufficient pool of credit available to investors and entrepreneurs alike to invest in the Algerian economy. While entrepreneurial interest was not lacking, there did not exist in Algeria either accumulated savings for investment or the presence of viable financial institutions that could support capitalism. Those most likely to get access to credit from the newly liberalized existing financial institutions were those who had political connections to those in charge of the financial institutions. Third, once access to credit was made available, it was frequently diverted for consumption (i.e., consumer durables or luxury goods) rather than for investment. Consumption rather than investment was logical because of high rates of inflation throughout the 1980's.[16] Inflation encouraged those with cash to consume (to beat future price increases) rather than invest. This combination of economic restructuring, dismantling of the parastatal industries, and high rates of inflation provoked an acceleration of unemployment, making public resentment of the regime even more inevitable. As all of this was happening, Algeria's external debt to foreign banks continued to expand, with the total debt in 1992 increasing to $26.5 billion. This mix of economic factors made the success of the economic liberalization program highly unlikely. The program's failure to stimulate prosperity had political consequences that were negative for the regime and positive for Islamist groups that were organizing political dissident.

The Emergence of the Islamist Opposition

The consistent morbidity of Algeria's economy created an environment that helped dissidents organize against the regime. Into this environment three groups inspired by Islam moved in to organize politically. These three groups were *al-Irshad wa al-Islah* (Guidance and Reform), *al-Nahda* (Renaissance), and the *Front Islamique du Salut* (Islamic Salvation Front) or FIS. Throughout the 1980's these groups proved themselves capable of addressing and resolving the most immediate needs of the masses (temporary employment, health care, physical security, and the hoped-for restoration of Islamic values) while the government found itself incapable of doing so. By being able to satisfy competently the masses' material (and perhaps spiritual) needs, the militants were able to persuade the masses that a political change of direction was needed for Algeria. They argued that this change required the rejection of the FLN and the army and their authoritarian, allegedly socialist, one-party state and its replacement by a government inspired by the Qur'an and Islamic law. Of these three groups, the FIS eventually became the largest and the best organized.

While Ben Jadid tried to pursue the politics of accommodation with the Islamist movement, Muslim militants of the group who became the organizational nucleus of the political party that became the FIS envisioned a plan for the gradual acquisition of power. These militants believed that they would build the new Islamic Algeria very gradually, beginning first with the religious and political training of political leaders at the University of Algiers.[17]

Although the FIS registered as an official political party in February 1989, the organizational leadership of the FIS had asserted that they created its predecessor under another name in 1968, calling it *al-Jamiat al-Islamiyya* (the Islamic Group). They created it at the University of Algiers at the behest of Malek Bennabi, a religious and political thinker best known for his work in French, *Vocation d'Islam*.[18] From 1968 until the official establishment of the FIS in 1989, this group, *al-Jamiat al-Islamiyya*, provided most of the organizational, intellectual, and ideological leadership within the Islamist movement. The Algerian press later renamed this group *al-Djaz'ara* or Algerianization.

According to the founders of this group, Malek Bennabi, (who was also President of the University of Algiers), invited several people into his home in the fall of 1968 to suggest that they create an Islamic organization at the University of Algiers that would be dedicated to the "Islamization of the intelligentsia" and the "development of grass roots support."[19] Bennabi and the other founders of *al-Jamiat al-Islamiyya* believed that the first phase of the revolution in Algeria required the intellectual and religious formation of a cadre of leaders from the University of Algiers who, upon their graduation from the university, would fan out to the provinces of Algeria where they would teach in the elementary and secondary schools to spread the message of the need for spiritual revival and political change.

The new organization got off to an inauspicious start. At its first meeting at the University of Algiers, the organization was unable to obtain a quorum of 11 students for the call to prayer as required by Maliki Islamic law. Members of *al-jamiat al-islamiyya* corralled surprised and perhaps unwitting volunteers from the hallways of the university to provide the quorum.

From 1968 to 1979 the organization dedicated itself largely to religious, cultural, and charitable affairs. It focussed upon publishing newspapers and journals, educating its leadership cadre and the public at large, and building an effective network of charitable institutions. As part of its public education efforts, it held its first annual *Séminaire de la Pensée Islamique* in 1970. The government's Ministry of Religious Affairs cosponsored this event. This seminar was held yearly, organized and led by *al-Jamiat al-Islamiyya* members until it was fully coopted by the government in 1974. *Al-Jamiat al-Islamiyya* also organized an annual *Exposition des Livres Islamiques.*

One way that *al-Jamiat al-Islamiyya* and its allies began extending their popularity and building a network of constituents with the public at large was through its extensive network of charitable activities. The organizations within the Islamist movement quietly and indirectly began challenging the effectiveness of the FLN-run state by creating a system of charities that at first rivaled and then surpassed the social service programs provided by the state. Their alternate social service system effectively responded to the needs of its constituents better than the system provided by the FLN. This effective delivery of social services by these groups undermined the capacity and authority of the state, which because of corruption, inefficiency, and lack of financial resources, could not possibly compete with its honest, competent, and resource rich Islamic counterpart. The Islamist movement's charitable endeavors extended, for example, to providing security to merchants in the *medina*,[20] to maintaining free or low cost medical services to the poor, to supporting the unemployed with temporary work, to securing scholarships for needy students. As a glaring example of their effectiveness, when an earthquake struck in the town of Tipasa on 29 October 1989, they responded with emergency medical services before the FLN-run state organizations arrived at the scene.[21] These charitable endeavors, financed largely by the Saudi government through a charitable trust known as the Islamic Conference Organization,[22] proved the effectiveness of the increasingly politicized Muslim community and the incompetence of the government.

Besides these educational and charitable efforts, however, the FIS believed that building "free mosques" operating outside governmental control was necessary. This effort, while religious, also was patently political. For the first time in many years, Muslims established mosques in Algeria without the government's permission. This first "free mosque" was established in 1971. It was called the *Masjid al-Arkam* and was placed under the direction of Sheikh Ahmed Sahnoun.

The Islamist movement shifted from purely educational and charitable efforts to open political action one month before President Boumedienne's death in November 1979. In that month Muslim militants demonstrated at the University of Algiers, demanding the total Arabization of the structure of government and dismissal of Mostefa Lacheraf as Cultural Affairs Minister. As mentioned in Chapter V, Lacheraf had always soft-pedalled Arabization. Throughout his tenure as a government official he favored a bilingual French and Arabic educational and a linguistic policy for Algeria rather than the exclusive use of Arabic. His program would have emulated the bilingual educational programs of Morocco and Tunisia. The militants rejected this approach, preferring a fully Arabized curriculum. President Ben Jadid, elected President of Algeria two months after the presentation of the strikers' demands, acceded to their requests. He dismissed Lacheraf as Cultural Affairs Minister and replaced him with Mohamed Kharroubi, a proponent of full Arabization.

Shortly after the resolution of the Algiers University strike, the Ben Jadid government encountered a full-scale revolt in Tizi Ouzou in the Kabylie that began on 16 April 1980.[23] The revolt in the Kabylie began after the *wali,* or prefect of Tizi Ouzou, prevented a well-known Kabyle author named Mouloud Maameri from presenting a lecture on ancient Berber poetry at the University of Tizi Ouzou. The cancellation of this lecture provoked a revolt by linguistic and cultural militants in the Kabylie. Berber speakers in the Kabylie had felt for some time that the government had been gradually acceding to the Islamist movement's persistent demands for expansion of Arabic while ignoring their own requests for governmental recognition of their own linguistic traditions. The linguistic nationalists started their insurrection shortly after the regime's shift towards fuller Arabization, fearing that their own linguistic traditions were being subordinated by the regime. The nationalists in the Kabylie had been working for some time upon the preservation of their own indigenous language, *Tamazight.* In their rebellion, partisans from Hocine Aït Ahmed's *Front des Forces Socialistes* (FFS) supported the Berber nationalists. In contrast to the regime's capitulation to the demands of Muslim militants in Algiers, however, the reaction in the Kabylie was altogether different. The regime met force with force. More than thirty students were killed and several dozens were injured.[24]

After its success in obtaining expanded Arabization in January 1980, the Islamist movement again challenged the regime from February 1982 onwards by staging protests on the question of the Family Code being considered in the National Assembly. The Family Code, which the National Assembly would not enact until 29 May 1984, eventually amounted to a huge political victory for the Islamist movement. The Family Code had broad implications beyond the family law issues immediately addressed by the legislation. With the enactment of this law, for the first time in post-colonial Algeria, the state officially adopted Muslim holy law or the *sharia* as a legitimate source for Algerian law. The 1984 Family Code specifically provided for the application of the *sharia* to legal questions not specifically addressed by the code itself.[26] The new law legally recognized polygamy (polygyny),[27] despite requests from Algeria's *Union Nationale des Femmes Algériennes* for the adoption of Tunisia's monogamy statutes. The law prohibited marriages between a Muslim woman and a non-Muslim man.[28] The law also required that all women obtain authorization from their husbands or the oldest responsible male in the household to enter into contracts, to sign legal documents, or to obtain a passport.[29] (This provision specifically contradicted the 1976 Constitution that guaranteed equality before the law.)[30] The law also repealed the previous requirement that delivered divorce by mutual consent and replaced it with a provision making divorce the unqualified prerogative of the husband and a qualified right for the wife.[31] Besides these changes in the substantive provisions of marital law, the Family Code of 1984 was most politically significant because, for the first time since the Emir Abdel Qadir's regime in the nineteenth century, the *sharia* or Islamic law was officially and specifically reintegrated into the corpus of Algerian law. These concessions by Ben Jadid on the Family Code encouraged the Islamist movement to demand yet further concessions from the government.

While one group of Islamists was challenging the state on the Family Code and while it was beginning to organize public and peaceful demonstrations for political change, yet another group, led by Moustapha Bouyali, was being organized within Algeria that was called the *Mouvement Islamiste Algérien* (MIA). This organization, which Bouyali organized in October 1981, was separate from other Islamist movements in Algeria. It had a different objective; it intended to challenge the state by force. Because of their armed activities, which involved attacks on police officers and the stealing of governmental ammunition, Bouyali and 134 members of his group were tried and sentenced on charges of belonging to clandestine organization.[32] Their trial took place in April 1985. The court sentenced Bouyali in absentia. He eluded capture until 3 January 1987 when the police killed him.

After the Arabization program and Family Law legislation challenges, members of the Islamist movement entered electoral politics for the first time in November 1982 when a group of militants presented themselves as candidates for elected positions at the Cité Universitaire de Ben Aknoun. In that university election, they challenged a slate of competing candidates from the *Parti Avant Garde Socialiste* (PAGS). During the electioneering, a fracas ensued between them and the PAGS. One PAGS student was killed, leading the university authorities to decide to close all the mosques at the university. This provoked a large demonstration on 12 November 1982 at which more than 10,000 persons protested at the University of Algiers. The quick organization of such a large demonstration was an open signal to the authorities that the Islamist movement was very well organized. At this demonstration, well-known leaders such as Sheikhs Abdellatif Soltani and Ahmed Sahnoun spoke.[33] Also, for the first time in a public setting two new leaders emerged: Abassi Madani and Ali Belhadj. These two speakers eventually became the nominal leaders of the FIS.

During the 12 November demonstration, Sheikhs Soltani, Sahnoun, and Madani presented a fourteen-point manifesto for political change, calling for:

(1) recognition that there were antireligious factions in the government;

(2) reform of the judicial system;

(3) full implementation of the *sharia*;

(4) freedom to exercise fully the Muslim religion;

(5) reformation of the economic regime so that it would comply with Islamic law;

(6) rejection of French foreign policy which had obstructed the reform of the Family Code;

(7) the abolition of gender mixing in educational and workplace settings;

(8) the end of corruption in the educational system;

(9) the end of false "cultural criticism" in the educational system;

(10) the end of ridicule of Islamic education and Islamic culture;

(11) the end of public relations campaigns in the international and domestic press whose intent was to impede the Muslim revival in Algeria;

(12) the liberation of Muslim political prisoners;

(13) the reopening of mosques, wherever they may be; and,

(14) the punishment of those who attacked the dignity, the beliefs, and the morals of the nation as defined in the *sharia*.[34]

Because of the presentation of this manifesto and because of the organization of this large demonstration, the Interior Ministry ordered the arrests of Sheikhs Soltani, Sahnoun, and Madani and Imam Belhadj. The regime released Sheikhs Soltani and Sahnoun two weeks later because of their advanced age. Sheikh Madani and Imam Belhadj remained in jail until 1984.

The next significant event was the eruption of riots that began in the city of Constantine on 12 November 1986. University students and young underemployed and unemployed persons in Constantine started the riots. The university students were angry about the quality of life at the university (i.e., food, housing, quality of libraries and laboratories) and the young working class rioters were concerned about their dismal job prospects in the Constantine labor market.[35] The Constantine riots were quite serious. They lasted for a week (from 8–16 November) until the army forcibly put them down. According to varying media sources, the army killed two to eighteen persons and arrested more than 200.

The riots in Constantine preceded larger nationwide riots that occurred across Algeria in October 1988. These riots began on 5 October and, by the time they were over, inflicted damages in excess of $20 million. On 6 October the regime sent the army in to restore order. Groups within the Islamist movement did not start these riots. Rather, it has been asserted that these riots were either spontaneous or that President Ben Jadid's enemies within the military instigated them.[36] Whether these riots were spontaneous or whether they were the product of a conspiracy, the underlying reasons for civil unrest could be found readily in the public's needs for better housing, better employment opportunities, and more meaningful participation in government. The nationwide scope, violence, and ferocity of these riots and the ensuing repression by the army that caused more than 500 deaths forced President Ben Jadid to begin the process of real political reform.[37] Boumedienne's policies of authoritarianism, political repression of enemies, and state management of the economy could no longer endure for various reasons. First, Ben Jadid was temperamentally different from Boumedienne. He was more inclined to compromise with his political enemies than to engage in repression. Second, Ben Jadid was apparently convinced that Algeria's economy needed liberalization for economic growth. Third, political change in Algeria was taking place within an international political environment where liberalization and democratization were taking place all across the socialist world, notably in Poland, Czechoslovakia, East Germany, Rumania, Yugoslavia, and the Soviet Union. These countries, (especially East Germany, the Soviet Union, and Yugoslavia), had been Algeria's economic tutors. If change was taking place in the countries that had served as Algeria's economic models, it seemed logical that change would also be required eventually in Algeria. For these internal and external reasons, the Boumedienne model of authoritarianism could not be sustained. Single-party authoritarianism and the putative socialism of the army and the FLN had run its course.

After the October 1988 riots, Algeria veered towards political instability, fragmenting social and political structures, a stumbling
attempt at political liberalization, and the pronounced resurgence of
Islamic cultural, political, and economic themes.

Political Reform

Political pressures created by the October riots pushed President Ben Jadid to initiate substantive political reforms for the first
time. On 25 October 1988, he suggested revisions to the Algerian
constitution, eventually proposing the end of the FLN's status as the
single party of the state. The 25-year reign of the FLN, which had
begun with the 1963 Constitution, was about to come to its constitutional end. The new constitution also dropped the historical
reference that Algeria was a socialist state.[38] Article 40 of the 23
February 1989 Constitution and the electoral law of 5 July 1989
specifically permitted the creation of alternate political parties in
Algeria. A new law enacted on 21 July 1989 provided legal autonomy for mass organizations such as professional associations and
youth groups. Articles 53 and 54 of the constitution reestablished
the right to strike and the right to form independent trade unions.
Article 39 granted the right of freedom of expression and freedom
of association. Ben Jadid's constitutional suggestions were first
approved by referendum on 3 November 1988.[39] The new constitution itself was voted upon and approved, again by referendum, on
23 February 1989.[40] Between these two referendums, Ben Jadid ran
again ironically as the only candidate for the presidency, and was
"reelected" on 22 December 1988.[41]

While Ben Jadid was pushing through these reforms, however,
he was also expanding his presidential power within the new constitution. Articles 129 and 130 made judges specifically subordinate
to the President through the institution known as the *Conseil
Supérieur de la Magistrature* (Superior Judiciary Council). Article 78
stipulated that the President could dissolve the legislature at his
pleasure if the legislature, after two votes, failed to ratify the Prime
Minister's legislative program. Because of these three articles in
the Constitution, separation of powers was not guaranteed and

the Algerian president continued to enjoy extreme presidential power.

The new constitution also provided for the exercise of extraordinary constitutional authority by the President and by the state in cases of emergency. The creation of these emergency powers, as we will see later, eventually made most of these "political reforms" largely illusory. As these constitutional changes were taking place, the state again formally incorporated Islam into Algerian constitutional law by requiring in Article 2 that Islam remain the official religion of the state.

With the enactment of the constitutional provision and the law permitting the formation of political parties, 56 political parties eventually registered. The more significant of these parties were

FIS — Front Islamique du Salut. The principal Islamic Party.

FLN — Front de libération nationale.

FFS — Front des Forces Socialistes. A party led by Hocine Aït Ahmed with strong support in the Kabylie.

RCD — Rassemblement pour la culture et la démocratie. A party led by Saïd Saadi with strong support in Kabylie.

MDA — Mouvement pour la démocratie en Algérie. A small party led by ex-President Ben Bella.

PRA — Parti pour le renouveau algérien. A small liberal party.

HAMAS — A small Islamic party.

MNI — Mouvement de la Nahda Islamique. Another small Islamic party.

PSD — Parti Social Démocrate. A small social democratic party.

MAJD — Mouvement Algérien pour la justice et la démocratie. A small party led by former Military Security Chief Kasdi Merbah.

PAGS — Parti de l'avant-garde socialiste. The former Communist Party.

While the state was pushing forward political reform, it is also important to recognize that a counter-current of factions within the FLN and the army actually opposed the Ben Jadid reforms. The FLN as a party had never been entirely united in its support of political reform. Important factions of the FLN, with substantial support from elements of the army and from the very important Military Security branch, were either concerned about or actually opposed to Ben Jadid's reforms. Despite Ben Jadid's efforts to repress them, these dissident groups mobilized continuously within the government to reverse Ben Jadid's initiatives. In the final analysis, he was unsuccessful in defeating them.

Algeria's attempt at a transition to democracy seems most similar structurally to the successful transition to democracy that took place in the German Democratic Republic (GDR). Like the GDR, Algeria was an authoritarian state led by elites inclined to the use of internal surveillance, intimidation, and repression to obtain social compliance to its policies. In the GDR, however, when social revolts threatened the authoritarian regime in 1989, its leaders within both the civilian and military leadership eventually decided to concede to the social forces demanding political change.[42] In 1990 and 1991 in Algeria we observed a different reaction by elites. Instead of conceding, the leadership of the state split into two groups: one group of civilian and military leaders continued to support democratization; the other group, which was eventually successful, began maneuvering to stop the process of democratization.

While these machinations exposed the divisions within the FLN, at the same time it is also important to recognize that different groups with different viewpoints comprised the Islamist movement in Algeria. The three principal groups within the Algerian Islamist movement were *Al-Irshad wa al-Islah* (Guidance and Reform), *al-Nahda* (Renaissance), and the *Front Islamique du Salut* (FIS). Sheikh Mahfoud Nahnah founded *Al-Irshad wa al-Islah* (Guidance and Reform).[43] Imam Abdallah Djaballah led *Al-Nahda* (Renaissance). Abassi Madani and Ali Belhadj eventually led the FIS.[44]

These three groups had varied ideological interpretations of political Islam. Mahfoud Nahnah and his *Al-Irshad wa al-Islah*, (which was founded in 1988 and became HAMAS in 1990), clearly tried to distinguish themselves from the Madani-Belhadj conservative wing of the FIS. Nahnah declared his group's commitment to

(1) the equality of the genders; (2) the right of women to work out-side the home; and (3) multiparty political pluralism.[45] Sheikh Nahnah also envisioned the gradual application of the *sharia* over a nine to fifteen-year period.[46]

Al-Nahda was founded in December 1988 by Imam Abdallah Djaballah. Politically, *Al-Nahda* has positioned itself somewhat between HAMAS and the conservative wing of the FIS. Djaballah has sought establishment of an Islamic state and application of the *sharia* but he has seemed less willing to endorse the use of armed force to obtain that objective. Unlike Nahnah and the HAMAS, however, he has ascribed to a more conservative vision vis-à-vis women. His organization encouraged women to stay at home rather than participate in the larger economy and society.

The FIS itself has several ideological currents within it. One group has been rather conservative. Sheikh Abbasi Madani and Imam Ali Belhadj led a faction within the FIS preoccupied with the application of Islamic law and the full application of the *sharia*. This group has provided the charismatic leadership of the FIS. Yet another group within the FIS has been interested in carrying out the *sharia* but has also been very concerned with technological, devel-opmental, and economic issues. Within this group are many mem-bers with university degrees in the physical sciences. During the 1980's Mohammed Saïd led this group that has also been known as *al-Djaz'ara*. This group also provided the organizational leadership of the FIS. A third group within the FIS has been disinclined to endorse the use of violence for political change. We can call this group the "nonviolent" branch of the FIS. Saïd Guechi led this group during the 1980's and 1990's. After the annulment of the December 1991 national election results Guechi even participated as a minister in Prime Minister Sid Ahmed Ghozali's government. This description reveals that the Islamist movement in Algeria is decidedly complex with real disagreements about the precise and proper role of political Islam.

The Islamists have attempted to obtain unity among these diverse ideological groups. Unity, however, has been difficult to sus-tain because of real differences in policies and principles. One prominent attempt at solidarity occurred after the October 1988 riots when an Islamic Council of League of the Call *(Rabitat al-Dawa al-Islamiyya)* was formed under the leadership of Sheikh Ahmed Sahnoun. Sahnoun was elected President of the Council, Mohammed Saïd was elected as spokesperson, and Abbasi Madani, Ali Belhadj, Mahfoud Nahnah, and Abdallah Djaballah were all elected as leaders.

After this league's organization, Imam Belhadj proposed to the group the formation of an Islamic political party to be called the *Front Islamique Unifié* (FIU). Abdallah Djaballah and Mahfoud Nahnah refused to agree to the creation of an Islamic political party at the time. Abassi Madani, however, agreed with Belhadj's suggestion but he proposed that the name of the party be changed from the *Front Islamique Unifié* to the *Front Islamique du Salut* (FIS). With the name change, Madani and Belhadj officially declared the establishment of the FIS as a political party at the Bab al-Oued Mosque in Algiers on 18 February 1989. On 16 September 1989, the Ministry of Interior officially registered the FIS as a political party. This was done despite the Constitution's explicit stipulation that the establishment of a political party based on religion was not permissible. The recognition of the FIS as a political party explicitly based on religion enabled the FIS to secure immediate ideological and political legitimacy in a state and a society that were based upon the traditions of Islam. Given the state's recognition of the FIS as political party, Sheikhs Djaballah and Nahnah had no real political alternative other than forming their own political parties. In December 1990, Djaballah formed *Al-Nahda* (Renaissance). In the same month Nahnah returned to his own organization called *al-irshad wa al-islah* (Guidance and Reform). He then changed the name of his organization to HAMAS.

Multiparty Elections and the Attempted Transition to Democracy

On 12 June 1990 Algeria held multiparty elections for the first time. These elections were held for electing candidates to municipal offices (*Assemblées populaires communales* or APC) and provincial offices (*Assemblées populaires du wilaya,* or APW). In the June 1990 elections the FIS won an overwhelming victory, defeating the FLN handily. The following table provides the results.

June 1990 Election Results
Municipal Elections

	Number of Votes	*Percentage*	*Number of Communes Won*	*Percentage*
FIS	4,331,472	54.3%	853	55.4%
FLN	2,245,472	28.1%	487	31.6%
RCD	166,104	2.1%	87	5.7%
Independents	931,278	11.7%	110	7.1%
Totals	*7,674,326*	*96.2%*	*1537*	*99.8%*

Regional Elections

	Number of Votes	*Percentage*
FIS	4,520,668	57.4%
FLN	2,166,887	27.5%
Independents & RCD	1,182,445	15.0%
Totals	*7,870,000*	*99.9%*

Sources: *Le Monde,* 16 juin 1990; *Le Monde,* 22 juin 1990

The victory by the FIS and the solid defeat of the FLN reflected how well entrenched and popular the FIS had become and how estranged the FLN had become from the electorate. The party that was the alleged "vanguard of the people" in "democratic and popular" Algeria had become, because of their elitist and authoritarian manner of government, largely disconnected from the aspirations of their people and largely unresponsive to their concerns. Their ability to capture only 28% and 16.9% of the vote, while notable, displayed the erosion of support for the FLN. On the other hand, the FIS won in every province of the country except Tizi Ouzou in the Kabylie (where the RCD won) and in the extreme south of Algeria (where the FLN had strong support). The success of the FIS across the country showed how well organized and how popular they were.[48] Of the 48 *wilayas* or provinces, the FIS won 32. The FLN won in 14 provinces. An independent candidate won in one wilaya and the RCD also won in one. Of a total of 12.8 million eligible voters, 8.4 million, or 65.1%, actually voted.

After the electoral victory of the FIS in June 1990 municipal and regional elections, maneuvering among the FIS, the FLN, and the army became quite serious. The political actors entered a new, critical, and sensitive stage of negotiations in the transition to democracy in which all relevant parties needed reassurance that their interests would not be damaged or sacrificed. The summer of 1991 became a critical period for the brokering of political interests and the creation of historic compromises among the FIS, the FLN, and the army. In most successful transitions to democracy, from Spain in 1977 to South Africa in 1994, compromises have been made among the relevant political actors about power sharing in the future democratically elected government. Guillermo O'Donnell and Phillipe C. Schmitter have claimed that a "cartel of party elites" that has more or less negotiated the specific terms of the transition to democracy is required for a successful transition.[49] In the summer of 1991, the time for historic compromise had come to Algeria, yet the political actors did not realize that they were in the midst of a critical period that required compromise. Instead of compromise, the actors continued to raise the political stakes, trying to outbid each other, thereby creating an environment where "zero-sum" competition for power rather than compromise was the rule of political engagement.

The FLN on 1 April 1991 began the bidding for group advantage first when, in the wake of their June 1990 electoral defeat, it tried to change both the electoral laws and the boundaries of the electoral districts for the national elections scheduled for June 1992.[50] With this new law, the FLN created "weighted" electoral districts in the south of Algeria which, although sparsely populated, voted for the FLN in the 1990 municipal and provincial elections. They gerrymandered these changes to enhance their success in the national elections. In response to these manipulations, the leaders of the FIS decided to call a "Holy Strike" on 25 May 1991. On 27 May, 30,000 demonstrators marched in the streets of Algiers demanding the immediate creation of an Islamic state.[51] In response to the FIS' strikes and demonstrations, the army ordered a "state of siege" on 5 June 1991.[52] On 28 June, Abassi Madani promised a "holy war" if the government did not lift the state of siege within 48 hours. Two days later, on 30 June, the army arrested Abassi Madani and Ali Belhadj on charges of inciting Algerians to arm themselves to overthrow the government. Over the next few days the government arrested more than 2,600 suspected members of the FIS, including 25 members of the FIS' thirty-five member managing council or *Majlis as-shoura*.

In the midst of this state of siege, on 6 June, Chadli Ben Jadid's preference for Prime Minister, Mouloud Hamrouche, was replaced by Sid Ahmed Ghozali. The army and certain factions within the FLN preferred Ghozali as Prime Minister because they had greater confidence in his ability to deal with the Islamists. The FIS' "Holy Strike" was eventually resolved when Prime Minister Ghozali and the representatives of the FIS reached a compromise regarding the boundaries of the electoral districts. This compromise, finally obtained on 15 September, nonetheless was resolved in favor of the FLN. Instead of a "one-man one-vote" formulation for the electoral districts, they cut Algeria into two zones so that the formula was one for every 80,000 citizens in the north of Algeria and one for every 30,000 inhabitants in the south.[53]

In the month that the FIS and the government resolved the strike, the army also opened five internment camps in the south of Algeria. Since July 1991 these camps have remained open with up to 9,000 dissidents being held there, many without the benefit of trial.[54] State authorities also began escalating military encounters with armed Islamists, with at least 10,000 killed between 1991 and 1994.

The "Holy Strike" of May and June 1991 served the FIS' short-term political interests because it confronted the FLN's efforts to revise the electoral laws and electoral boundaries and because it forced the FLN to include non-FLN persons in its administration for the first time. As far as the long-term political interests of the FIS were concerned, however, the FIS' call for a strike further hardened antagonism of certain factions of the army towards the FIS and their growing power. The army was threatened by the FIS' increasing influence, and they disagreed with Chadli Ben Jadid's tactics of compromise rather than confrontation with the Islamist movement. The evidence has indicated that as early as March 1990 two prominent generals had signalled that the army would intervene in politics to abort the transition to democracy if it felt that the republic was in danger.[55] As far as the army was concerned, the Holy Strike of the summer of 1991 seems to have been the turning point. From that moment, prominent army officers began preparing contingency plans for the annulment of the December 1991 national election results and the forced resignation of Chadli Ben Jadid in case of a FIS electoral victory.

After the troubled summer of 1991, Algeria held the first round of multiparty national elections on 26 December 1991. In the first round, the FIS scored a crushing electoral victory. Of a total of 430 National Assembly seats, with 232 seats available in the first round of voting, the FIS won 188 seats, or 81.0%. The FFS won 25 seats (10.8%), the FLN won 16 (6.8%) and independents won another three. The following table provides the results.

December 1991 National Assembly Election Results
First Round

	Number of Votes	Percentage	Seats Won	Percentage
FIS	3,260,359	49.8	188	81.0
FLN	1,613,507	24.6	16	6.8
FFS	510,661	7.8	25	10.8
HAMAS	368,697	5.6		
Independents	309,964	4.7	3	1.2
RCD	200,267	3.0		
MNI	150,093	2.2		
MDA	135,882	2.0		
Totals	*6,549,430*	*99.7*	*232*	*99.8*

Source: *Algérie-Actualité*, 2-8 janvier 1992

The results in this election were amazing. With 49.7% of the vote in the first round of the elections, the FIS won 81% of the seats in the national legislature. Why this skewed result? The answer lies in the electoral law of 3 April 1991.[56] According to this law, candidates who obtained more than 50% of the vote were elected to the national legislature. Candidates who obtained less than 50% of the vote were required to participate in a run-off election (a *second tour*) to determine the winner. If the FLN had insisted upon an electoral law requiring proportional representation rather than this majority vote requirement they would have been able to maximize their representation in the national legislature.[57] Instead, by adhering to this majority vote formula, they obtained only 6.8% of the seats in the national legislature, despite winning 24.6% of the vote.

The election results were tainted by the somewhat lower voter participation rate (58.5%) than the regional elections of June 1990 (65.1%). Also, many voters went to the polls but submitted abstention ballots (924,906).[58] The number of blank ballots actually exceeded the votes attained by the FFS and approached the number of votes attained by the FLN. The lower voter participation rates and the inordinately high number of abstention votes should not be used as a rationale or a justification for having the election results annulled as some anti-democrats within both the FLN and the RCD have tried to claim. The elections were, under the circumstances and under the rules in place in Algeria, arguably fair. If the FLN had won the elections, they would not have complained post facto of alleged defects either in the construction of the election procedures or in the execution of the elections.

In the wake of the FIS' electoral victory in the first round of the elections, some parties that performed poorly and that were dissatisfied with the results of this democratically held election, notably the RCD, the MAJD, and the PAGS, began openly appealing to the army to intercede and annul the second round of the elections scheduled for 16 January.[59] Some women's groups also joined in this appeal for army intervention. On 3 January 1992, 341 petitions claiming voting irregularities were filed with the Constitutional Council. The FLN filed 174 of these petitions, the FFS filed 30, and the FIS filed 17.[60] Nine days later, on 11 January, the army interceded, annulling the election results and forcing President Ben Jadid to resign. On 4 March 1992, the government legally dissolved the FIS. Algeria's two-year experiment with multiparty democracy ended.

The attempt by the army to follow legal procedure as a means of keeping control of the state was observable in the way that it forced President Ben Jadid to resign, all done in legal conformity with the Constitution. First the army secretly pressured President Ben Jadid to resign. Article 84 (Paragraphs 4, 5, and 6) of the Constitution of 23 February 1989 was then invoked. This article provided for the assumption of control of the Executive Branch of government by the President of the National Assembly in the cases of either the death or the resignation of the President. With the call for national elections and with adjournment of the National Assembly in December 1991, however, there was no President of the National Assembly to assume Executive powers after the resignation of President Ben Jadid. According to Paragraphs 9 and 10 of the same Article 84, the President of the Constitutional Council should then have been the next in line to assume the powers of the presidency. The Constitutional Council met and ruled that Paragraph 9 of the Constitution never foresaw the event of the absence of both the President of the Republic and the President of the National Assembly. They therefore ruled that an *Haut Comité d'État* (Supreme Council of the State) could be formed according to Article 162 of the Constitution.

This *Haut Comité* assumed executive power on 12 January 1992. This *Haut Comité* included Khaled Nezzar (Army General), Ali Kafi (Head of the Veterans' Organization), Tidjani Haddam (Rector of the Paris Mosque), Ali Haroun (former Human Rights Minister), and Mohammed Boudiaf. Boudiaf was one of the original founders of the FLN who returned from exile in Morocco to assume the presidency of the *Haut Comité*.

The *coup d'état* initiated by the army was legalized by their colleagues on the Constitutional Council. The legalization of this *coup d'état* and the setting aside of the election results was inconsistent

204 ** Islam and the Politics of Resistance in Algeria

with democratic processes and it was unfair to those democrats, (both Islamists and non-Islamists alike), who, in good faith, participated in the electoral process. Further, within Algeria, the army's annulment of the elections weakened public confidence in the institution of elections themselves because it reinforced the notion that the army would ratify only those election results that it favored. On another level, the legalization of the *coup d'état* was largely put in place by the army as part of an effort to attempt to silence overseas critics of the military regime.

The Algerian attempt at a transition to democracy was hobbled from its very beginnings. Because the transition was, from an organizational viewpoint, ill-conceived and hastily prepared, it had a very small probability for success. First, the transition to democracy was unlikely to succeed because the elite leadership of the FLN and the army was divided on the question of whether liberalization and democratization were even advisable. One group of leaders led by President Ben Jadid and Prime Minister Mouloud Hamrouche advocated liberalization and democratization; another group led by Generals Nezzar and Lamari opposed this process either overtly or covertly.

Second, the interval of time between the legalization of political parties in the February 1989 constitution and the first elections of June 1990 provided only 17 months for the creation of viable political parties. In this period only the FIS and the FLN had the preexisting resources to organize politically on a mass basis. Algeria quickly evolved from a one-party system dominated by the FLN into an essentially two-party political system in which the FLN and the FIS were the only real competitors. The leaders of the FLN gambled that this would be the result: that given the short period allocated for political organization only the FLN and the FIS would be able to organize effectively. Where the FLN miscalculated was in their belief that the FIS would get only 40% or less of the vote. In their scenario, some FLN leaders envisioned a situation in which they would negotiate with the FIS in discussions that would lead eventually to the creation of a coalition government. The FIS surprised the FLN and upset its calculus of political expectations by obtaining 54% of the vote in municipal elections and 35% of the vote in regional elections, thereby canceling the possibility of a coalition government.

Third, this process had little probability for success because it was conceived and executed entirely by members of the FLN and their supporters within the military. If the FLN and the military had been really serious about liberalization and democratization, they would have consulted with other interested political actors and parties to build a consensus for the process of political reform.[61] This process, however, was not really about fundamental political reform; it was essentially a series of tactics without a strategy to preserve a prominent role in Algerian politics and economics for FLN functionaries and their military supporters. Hence all that we had in Algeria were tactics for political survival rather than a strategy for political reform.

Fourth, the Algerian attempt at a transition to democracy provides further evidence that it may be difficult and destablizing to attempt liberalization and democratization in the political domain and liberalization in the economic realm simultaneously. The attempt to reform both the polity and the economy concurrently can overload the systems of change. Dual political and economic transition was successful in Poland, Czechoslovakia, East Germany and, to some extent, in Hungary. The same approach has had notably mixed or disastrous results in Russia, Roumania, and, of course, Algeria. China's approach for sequential rather than concurrent reform of the economy and the polity may, arguably, be more stable.

The FIS' Positions on Constitutional Issues

The political and constitutional positions held by the FIS are outlined in Abassi Madani's *Azmat al-fikr al-hadith wa mubarrirat al-hall al-islami* (The Crisis of Modern Thought and the Justifications for an Islamic Solution),[62] in the party newspaper, *El Mounquid* (The Savior), and a photocopied political program entitled "Front Islamique du Salut" dated 7 March 1989.

Madani's book is largely a critique of what he describes as the exploitive and decadent nature of European and North American societies. Madani's political philosophy begins with the precept that a moral renaissance is required within the citizen before a just society can be established. To this end he urges an Islamic education and the early training of students in the Qur'an and the *sharia* so that a more moral person may be formed. Regarding the status of women, Madani stresses the physical segregation of the genders and he denounces the relaxation of sexual mores in non-Muslim societies. Besides this critique of non-Muslim societies, however, Madani has little to say about the actual construction, formation, and operation of institutions within an Islamic government.

Imam Ali Belhadj, in the pages of the newspaper *El-Mounquid* was more explicit than Sheikh Madani in his denunciation of non-Muslim societies. He essentially sees non-Muslim societies as perverted and retrograde. Sexual themes dominate his discourse with his railing against the "putrid gender mixing" and "debauchery" of the West. He urges the seclusion of women to the home where they should not leave "except under conditions provided by law."[63] He also strongly denounces the idea and the institution of "positive (i.e., written) laws,"[64] claiming that they "distort the life of the community."[65] He urges Muslims to fight against positive law "because they are the official face of *jahiliyya*."[66] He also has denounced the idea of democracy, claiming that it is inconsistent with Arab culture.[67] Here is what he said in *Al-Mounquid*, No. 23:

> The concept of democracy is strange to Arab language and culture. These systems are the clear enemies of Islam.
>
> The democratic idea is one of a number of pernicious intellectual innovations that has obsessed the consciousness of some people.
>
> To the contrary, for us, in Islam, freedom is tied to obedience to the *sharia* and not to the law.

Further, Belhadj has endorsed the use of violence as a means of fighting for an Islamic state.[68] Belhadj identifies the following groups as obstacles to the creation of just government (and, given the progression of his logic, as targets for aggression):

(1) Journalists;

(2) Authors;

(3) Artists;

(4) Members of the *ulema* associated with the state;

(5) Secular political parties;

(6) The state in Algeria;

(7) The members of the security services.[69]

The document entitled "Front Islamique du Salut," dated 7 March 1989, details many of the FIS' social and economic objectives. Yet, apart from asserting that the *sharia* will be the basis of law, it is hardly specific on the questions of constitutional government or the structure of government. As for law, the document insists that legislation in Algeria will be based upon the *sharia*. The document fails to detail, however, whether a legislature would exist or who would be responsible for the creation of legislation. Would the FIS guarantee a legislature? If so, who would be eligible to participate in this legislature? Also, what would be the procedure for election to the legislature? Second, would a judiciary exist? Would it be independent of the legislature? Who would be able to serve on the judiciary? Third, would an executive branch exist? Who would serve in that capacity? Would that person be elected, appointed, or acclaimed? The FIS' political documents address none of the critical issues that concern the actual construction of government.

Ideological positions taken by Mahfoud Nahnah and Abdallah Djaballah differ from the positions taken by Madani and Belhadj. As leader of HAMAS, Nahnah has been considerably more pluralist in his ideological orientation, explicitly accepting the need to accept and cooperate with non-Islamist parties in the future Algerian state.[70] He has also been more unequivocal in his support of a woman's right to work and for their protection under a more expansive Family Code.

Abdallah Djaballah's views are substantially similar to Madani's and Belhadj's. Their point of separation involves issues of the liberalization of the economy. Madani and Belhadj ambiguously support liberalization efforts while Djaballah has denounced them.[71]

What the documents do express, however, is an intention to reform Algerian society. Through its written documents, the FIS alleged (correctly) that the FLN mismanaged the economy and that the regime needs replacement. The FIS pledges to end corruption, graft, monopolies, waste, and usury. It promises to restore agricultural production. It claims its intention to guarantee work to the father in each family. It announces its dedication to caring for the women of the society and its children, recognizing the importance of stable families in the creation of a just society. Regarding women, it claims that it will impose separation of the genders in the schools and the workplace. The FIS promises to fight against evil. In this regard, it intends to control and manage television programming, radio programming, libraries, theaters, cinemas, et cetera. The documents reveal that the FIS has given a great deal of thought to outlining their social, educational, cultural, and economic objectives. What the documents also reveal, however, is that they provide few specifics on questions of the construction of constitutional government.[72] Although the FIS' constitutional program is imprecise, its founding principle for constitutional government is the implementation of the *sharia*. The *sharia*, in toto, would have to be included in the creation of a legal code.

If the *sharia* is to be the law of the land, the next legal and constitutional question becomes whether a legislature may create additional laws to address questions and situations that the *sharia* may not specifically address. On this point there are divisions in interpretation within the Muslim political community. One group of believers claims that the *sharia* is complete, that it does not need amendment, and that qualified scholars can resolve questionable areas by using *qiyas,* or analogical reasoning. This group also often claims that only the *ulema* or the legal class (the *qadis*) are trained to be competent in the examination and elaboration of *qiyas*. A second group within the Muslim community is prone to suggest that amendment of the *sharia* is possible, that legal elaboration is not solely limited to *qiyas,* and that new legislation is possible if the legislation conforms with Islamic principles. The legislators would create these laws in conformity with the principles of *shura* (consultation) and *ijma* (consensus). By logical implication, this second group would also endorse the expanded use of *ijtihad* (analytical reasoning) in the examination and resolution of legal questions.

The foregoing establishes two new questions regarding the construction of constitutional government: first, who would be eligible to participate in *shura,* and, second, what would the process be for decision-making? The first question requires an examination of who could participate in the *shura* of decision-making. Will the *shura* comprise men and exclude women? (It is historically verifiable that two of the Prophet Muhammad's wives, Khadija and Aisha, were among his most prominent political advisors. Therefore, a precedent does exist for the inclusion of women in the decision-making process.) Second, if the *shura* or *majlis* is to include only men, may all men participate or will participation be limited only to those learned in the holy law (the *ulema* and the *qadis*)? These are questions that divide the members of the FIS, with different groups holding different positions on these important issues. These important constitutional questions have not been resolved.

Conclusion

Eventually, ideas and ideologies really do matter. The FLN's initially sincere attempt to marry socialism and Islam provided the ideological basis of its own political destruction. The merger of Islam and socialism as attempted by FLN activists seemed to make sense to them; the union was holistic, indigenous, and Algerian. Any other attempts to construct socialism on a materialist or secular basis would have seemed to them both unnatural and unpopular with the masses.

In the final analysis, however, only Ramdane Abbane or Sheikh Abdelatif Soltani could possibly be right. Socialism must eventually be secular (Abbane's position) and Islam must reject either the atheism or the secular progression of socialist thought (Soltani's belief). Islamic socialism, as an experiment to merge the egalitarian aspirations of both creeds, did not fail because of irreconcilable contradictions between the two systems of thought. Rather, Islamic socialism failed because of consistent resistance from Muslims within the community of politicized Islam.

The FLN's attempt to marry socialism and Islam officially in its ideology lasted for twenty–five years. (From the 1964 Algiers Charter to the 1989 Constitution that dropped the reference to socialism as one of the goals of the Algerian state.) Even after the discontinuation of the goal of socialism in 1989, FLN partisans continued to discuss the compatibility of Islam and socialism. This group of true believers, however, was quite small. Most Muslims who voted for the FIS in Algeria in the 1990s had become convinced, because of the evolution of Muslim political ideology, that Islam and socialism were entirely incompatible.[73] Additionally, many members of the FLN, in the waste of the wreckage of Eastern European and Russian socialism, wondered aloud whether they had incorrectly invested their belief and faith in socialism. Islamic socialism died and with it died the FLN.

Islamic socialism also perished because Houari Boumedienne decided to cast aside the symbolic importance of Islam within his politics. By denigrating the importance of both the content and the symbolism of Islam and by elevating the values of technocratic competence and the accomplishment of economic goals, he made it impossible for his successor, Chadli Ben Jadid, to reincorporate religious values into his regime. In the minds of many Algerian Muslims, the regime had become materialist and impure; it had strayed from spiritual and religious values. In Muslim countries, this can be a grand political mistake.

Ben Jadid really did try to re-Islamize his regime after Boumedienne had seemingly walked away from Islam. He negotiated with the Islamists, he compromised with the Islamists, and they demanded more. Compromises were only the first stages toward the accomplishment of their real goal: the rejection of authoritarian socialism and its replacement with an Islamic state based upon the *sharia* and Islamic law. Ben Jadid believed he could establish a modus vivendi with the Islamist movement. Some elements within the Islamist movement claimed they would politically cohabit with Ben Jadid and the FLN while others within the movement rejected any arrangements at political "concubinage." Eventually, the decisive factor, at least for the interim in Algeria, became the army. They entered politics decisively, forcing President Ben Jadid to resign and annulling the December 1991 election results that had democratically given the FIS the right to participate in government.

The annulment of the elections and the forced resignation of President Chadli Ben Jadid was a critical mistake made by the army. Ever since the annulment of the elections Algerian society has been ripped in a vortex of violence between the army and the Islamic movement with the Islamists being convinced that, if they play by the rules of the democratic game and win, the army will never allow them to participate in the government. Their lack of confidence in the army is entirely justifiable. The army has been intent upon keeping itself in power, using legal and constitutional subterfuges if necessary, as part of a public relations effort to both convince and silence democratically oriented critics both inside and outside Algeria that it is both operating legally and that it is serious about democratization. When one peels away the legalisms and the rhetoric, however, it becomes quite clear that the army is locked in a bloody power struggle with the Islamist movement for actual control of the government.

Chapter VIII

※

Conclusion

Islam has been present at the center of all Algerian movements of political resistance. Having examined these movements closely we have discovered the operation of political principles inspired by Islam that have stimulated these movements to demand justice in the form of substantial equity. Islam's definition of justice as equity rather than procedure and its ethical direction towards substantive egalitarianism have animated these political movements to reject conditions of social and economic hierarchy wherever they have existed in Algeria. We can observe this anti-hierarchical trend in many other "fundamentalist" Muslim political movements. Anti-hierarchical movements inspired by Islam began in Algeria as early as 1783. Islam's organizations also provided the necessary cultural, ideological, or logistical resources for the eventual success of these resistance movements.

Historical Summary and Theoretical Conclusions for Algeria

During the eighteenth and nineteenth centuries the Sufi brotherhoods organized Algeria's movements of resistance. The Darqawiyya Sufi brotherhood, with its doctrinal principles that emphasized radical social egalitarianism, was the first group to organize a revolt against Ottoman social and economic hierarchy. This brotherhood's esoteric principles emphasized radical egalitarianism; these principles impelled them to reject the Ottomans' ethnically hierarchical social regime. The Darqawiyya's first revolt began in 1783 in the western province of Oran and lasted until 1805. Their second revolt, which began in 1804 and lasted through 1809, took place in the Kabylie mountains. This second rebellion was a cooperative effort, involving the Darqawiyya and the Rahmaniyya Sufi brotherhoods. Thirteen years later the Tijaniyya Sufi brotherhood rebelled in western and southwestern Algeria. Their resistance effort had two phases: they first launched a tax resistance campaign in 1822; they then mounted an armed revolt that began in 1827. For fifty years during the eighteenth and nineteenth centuries Sufis organized to resist Ottoman rule.

With the arrival of the French in 1830, the Sufis shifted their focus of resistance from the Ottomans to the French. From an indigenous viewpoint, oppression was simply oppression, whether practiced by a Muslim or a Christian governor.

Political and military resistance against the French eventually reached higher levels of organization thanks to the efforts of Algeria's most sophisticated Sufi brotherhood and its leader, the Emir Abdel Qadir. The five principal Sufi brotherhoods (the Rahmaniyya, the Tayibiyya, the Qadiriyya, the Tijaniyya, and the Darqawiyya) all participated in resistance against the French. From the viewpoint of organization, however, the Qadiriyya became the most sophisticated of these brotherhoods. This brotherhood's doctrinal principles commanded them to focus upon the provision of charity and education, obliging them to construct a network of *zawiyas*. From their well-developed network of *zawiyas,* the Qadiriyya developed a logistical network first used for charitable and educational purposes, then converted these *zawiyas* to propagandize and organize for war. The Qadiriyya brotherhood's network of *zawiyas* enabled them to wage war systematically. In contrast, their rival brotherhoods could not.

The Qadiriyya's leader, the Emir Abdel Qadir, was also the first indigenous leader to articulate a political ideology in Algeria that was firmly based upon Islam. He first promised that his regime would conform with the *sharia*. He also specifically promised his followers that he would create a legal and a political regime that would be more equitable than that which the Ottomans had realized. This second promise of egalitarian treatment conformed with our definition of "justice as equity." Because of these promises, all of which he publicly linked to Islam, he engendered substantial political support.

Abdel Qadir surrendered to the French in 1847. Resistance against French rule continued, however, after his surrender. In 1871 the Rahmaniyya Sufi brotherhood rebelled again in the Kabylie. In 1876, 1879, and from 1881 to 1882 the Sufis organized and participated in smaller revolts against the French regime.

During the successful installation of the French colonial regime in the last three decades of the nineteenth century, indigenous participation in the Muslim religion did not change initially in Algeria. From 1870 to World War I membership in Sufi brotherhoods continued and in fact expanded. Islam in its more mystical, decentralized Sufi expression rather than Islam in its more legalistic, centralized, ulema-led form continued as the established norm of religious expression in Algeria. During the first three decades of real French colonialism (1870-1900) membership in the Sufi brotherhoods increased. Colonial officials, being alarmed at the dynamic growth of the Sufi brotherhoods, developed a plan under the aegis of colonial officer Louis Rinn in 1882 to coopt these Sufi brotherhoods into political compliance. They also developed a plan to create a class of politically compliant *ulema* that would be answerable to France. Their policy had two parts: the first element punished recalcitrant brotherhoods with additional taxes and other penalties while rewarding compliant brotherhoods with political favors; the second element created an "official" Muslim clergy that the French government approved and compensated.

With the beginning of the twentieth century, French policies concerning the Muslim religion in Algeria evolved curiously and would be at a variance with French policy within France. Whereas in 1905 France decided to pursue rigorous secularism by aggressively separating religious and state affairs in metropolitan France, in Algeria it decided that it had to pursue a different policy. Rather than separating religious and state affairs, France continued to monitor and regulate the Muslim religion rigidly and extensively. Christianity and Judaism were exempted from this kind of regulation. Despite the de jure integration of Algeria into France as a *département,* it was clear to government officials in Algeria that they could not apply in Algeria France's laws concerning religion. Algeria had to remain a case apart. France could not apply its policies separating religion and state in Algeria because to have done so would have liberated Islam as a resource for political activity. This different political treatment of Islam in Algeria proved that the French feared Islam as a political resource for organizing resistance. The different legal treatment of Islam in Algeria proved incidentally that Algeria was a de facto colony.

In this context of imperial domination of religion, religion continued to play an influential and sometimes dominant role in politics. As the fourth chapter explained, despite the creation of three distinct political resistance movements in Algeria (the *Étoile nord-africaine,* the Association of the Ulema, and the *Jeunes algériens*), all three movements, to varying extents, invoked Islam to promote and validate their programs and policies among the masses. For the entire first half of the twentieth century, Algeria's population was overwhelmingly rural and profoundly religious. The marketing of successful political ideas in Algeria required their articulation so that they resonated with the beliefs and values of this overwhelmingly rural and religious population. All of the three groups mentioned above, but especially the *Étoile nord-africaine* and the Association of the Ulema, understood this political reality and they developed their political discourse to conform with this political requirement. Because they did so, they were successful politically.

From the viewpoint of changes in social and political structures in Algeria during the first half of the twentieth century, the first important development of the period between World War I and World War II was the outcome of the political struggle for ecclesiastical power between the Association of the Ulema and the Sufi brotherhoods. During the interwar period the Association of the Ulema emerged victorious as a centrally organized center of ecclesiastical power in Algeria. Before the political emergence of the Association of the Ulema, from an ecclesiastical and organizational viewpoint, the Muslim religion in Algeria was organizationally decentralized. Through its efforts the Association of the Ulema reorganized the Muslim clergy in Algeria during the interwar period so that it became both organized and centralized. Before the Association's efforts, the Sufis' organization of ecclesiastical power had been decentralized. The emergence of the Association of the Ulema as a centrally organized and predominant ecclesiastical voice had real and profound political consequences. Because of its ecclesiastical empowerment during the interwar period, the Association emerged as the political voice of an organized clergy. As an organized, centralized clergy, the Association of the Ulema began exercising a political voice in the 1930's that found continuous reexpression through the 1990's. In the early 1960's the more radical organization *al-Qiyam* replaced the Association of the Ulema as the voice of political resistance. When President Houari Boumedienne dissolved *al-Qiyam* in 1970, *al-Jamiat al-Islamiyya* and *Ansar Allah* replaced it. Later, during the 1980's and 1990's, the FIS, HAMAS, and *al-Nahda* supplanted these groups. The centralization of ecclesiastical power by the Association of the Ulema during the interwar period was the key to the future political power of clerically led groups in Algeria. If the clergy in Algeria had remained decentralized and relatively unorganized as they had been under Sufi leadership, it would have been much more difficult for religious groups to organize for political change in the 1960's through the 1990's.

From the viewpoint of formation of national culture and political ideology, the second indispensably significant development of the interwar period was the creation by the Association of the Ulema of their networks of schools. Within these schools they emphasized both Islam and Arabic as the bases of Algerian identity. Their cultural and educational work had a prolonged political effect. Because of the creation of their schools and because of the Association's educational and cultural influence, they left a lasting imprint on the formulation of Algerian political ideology. Due to their educational and cultural work, they firmly based Algerian political ideology upon the twin cultural foundations of Islam and

Arabic rather than any other set of cultural variables. Since the late 1930s, thanks to the cultural work of the Association of the Ulema, all politics and ideologies of resistance in Algeria have been more clearly founded upon or informed by Islam.

During the 1950s and early 1960s a real political struggle emerged within the FLN to define the role of Islam within their politics. This struggle took place between the secular socialists and the Islamic socialists. The secular socialists, led by Abbane Ramdane, tried to steer FLN politics towards secularism while the Islamic socialists, led most of the time by Ahmad Ben Bella, tried to integrate Islam and socialism, albeit unsuccessfully and incoherently. Nevertheless, when from a historical perspective we examine the development of Algerian political ideology, we begin to understand that the antecedent pre-FLN construction of Algerian political ideology by the Association of the Ulema and the *Étoile nord-africaine*/PPA/MTLD would deprive the FLN of alternate choices for the construction of their political ideology. Because of the groundwork undertaken by these groups, the FLN had no real choice other than basing its ideology upon the twin cultural foundations of Islam and Arabic. Because of the formal and successful installation of these cultural variables in Algerian politics in the 1930's, the use of these two cultural devices for the formation of ideology in the 1950's through the 1990's became *de rigueur*. During the 1950's, given the urgent military struggle against France, the FLN's leaders did not have the time to study either the value or the implications of the use of these two cultural sources for the construction of Algerian politics. The delegates at the 1956 Soummam Congress discussed these issues insufficiently. They then were temporarily deferred while Abbane Ramdane tried to lead Algeria on a secularist course, and they were reintegrated, at the insistence of Ahmed Ben Bella, into Algerian ideology at the FLN conference held in Cairo in 1957. From 1957 until the 1990s, Islam remained a mainstay and a central tenet of official FLN ideology.

Upon Algeria's acquisition of independence in 1962, Islam began playing a different, largely instrumental role in politics. From 1962 onwards we observed secular leaders in Algeria using Islam either to legitimate their politics with the masses or to defeat their political enemies. Ahmad Ben Bella consistently tried to "out-Islamize" his political adversaries. He also used Islam to try to acquire political support from sectors of the population that were more socially and religiously conservative than he was. Playing the politics of Islam was his means of trying to obtain popularity with the masses.

During Ben Bella's period of rule we also saw political and constitutional efforts to integrate Islam formally into the politics and ideology of the FLN. Therefore, we observed the prominent discussion and inclusion of Islam in the National Charter and Constitution of 1963. In those documents the FLN declared that Islam was Algeria's official religion and that socialism was its official ideology. Leaders of the new state defined Islam and socialism as mutually supporting and compatible. We saw religious and political declarations in religious journals such as *al-Ma'rifa* asserting the essential compatibility of socialism and Islam.

Ben Bella's successor, Houari Boumedienne, unlike Ben Bella, was more socially conservative and initially was quite close to the more conservative members of the *ulema*. The *ulema*, at least initially, publicly and substantially supported his regime. They welcomed him as someone who would be more conservative and more predictable than Ben Bella. They hoped he would calm Algeria's political climate after the tempestuous unpredictability and instability of Ben Bella's period of rule. During the first two to three years of his rule Algeria evolved from Ben Bella's aggressively pan-African, pro-Third World, pro-Trotskyist, and pro-revolutionary direction to a political orientation, which while still rhetorically revolutionary, was quite conservative on social and family issues, all the while adhering to "socialist" state management of the economy. The *ulema* and other conservatives in the religious community welcomed Boumedienne's conservatism on social and family issues. Critical thinkers in the religious community, however, eventually rejected his endorsement of state management of the economy.

Whereas Boumedienne initially provided a prominent place for the *ulema* in the formation of his original political coalition, after

Colonel Tahar Zbiri's attempted *coup* in December 1967 Boumedienne relegated the *ulema* to an inferior political position. He then
elevated the role of technocrats within his regime. Boumedienne
rearranged the social composition of his political coalition, hoping
that elevating the participation of technocrats would enable them to
have a positive impact upon the performance of the Algerian economy. Boumedienne hoped that economic progress would stabilize
his regime.

Boumedienne's political gamble paid off. The dramatic rise in
petroleum and natural gas prices that began in 1973 and peaked in
1980 helped him fill government coffers. With these revenues his
regime redistributed income in a way that satisfied large sectors of
the Algerian population. With his economic success, however, also
came some political arrogance. Boumedienne increasingly emphasized that his was an "effective" and "competent" regime that could
deliver tangible material results. He began the gradual and systematic devaluation of the symbolic and substantive importance of
Islam within his politics. He eventually proclaimed in his famous
speech in Lahore in 1974 that he had learned that, ". . . men do not
want to enter Paradise on an empty stomach. . . . A starving people
do not want to listen to [religious] verses."

Over time Boumedienne de-emphasized the role of Islam
within his politics while concurrently emphasizing the imputed
technocratic competence of his regime. He indirectly asserted that
Islam was less relevant to Algerian politics than economic performance. By changing the underlying rationale for the legitimacy and
evaluation of his regime, Boumedienne fashioned a standard for the
eventual rejection of the FLN by the Algerian people. He mistakenly and unnecessarily discarded Islam as a political and cultural
resource. By opting for a standard of regime evaluation based almost
solely upon "competence" and economics he created problems for
his successor. When petroleum and natural gas prices started falling
first in 1983 and then more seriously in 1986, the regime suffered
severe fiscal losses that crippled its capacity to redistribute state
profits to the general population. This redistributive capacity had
provided the regime with the economic resources that it needed to

prolong its rule while its political legitimacy was waning. Boumedienne then died in December 1978, leaving his successor, Chadli Ben Jadid, with the real predicament of trying to defend a regime that had anachronistically maintained authoritarian political and economic structures, that had unnecessarily discarded the political use of Islam, and that was rapidly losing millions of dollars per year in petroleum and natural gas revenues.

In this economic and ideological malaise, Islamist groups began organizing for political change. Even while Boumedienne was still alive, political groups began reorganizing under the banner of Islam. By the time Boumedienne banned *al-Qiyam* in 1970, other groups, including *al Jamiat al-Islamiyya* and *Ansar Allah* had already emerged. As this study revealed, the critical leadership group of the Islamist movement from the 1970's through the 1990's was *al-Jamiat al-Islamiyya,* the core group founded at the University of Algiers that was later renamed *al-Djaz'ara.* From the 1970's *al-Jamiat al-Islamiyya* and other Islamist groups emerged as potent political alternatives to an official state that had become dysfunctional. By the 1980s the state that the FLN and the army managed was beginning to run out of the petrodollars that bought social compliance to its authoritarian politics. The collapse of petrodollar revenues provoked a real political crisis that forced a thorough reexamination of the goals, the ideology, and the practice of government of the FLN. We should clarify, however, that Algeria's economic penury during the 1980s was the catalyst for the political crisis; it was not the cause. Before the economic emergency of the 1980's, Islamist groups had already been organizing and agitating for an end to the FLN's and the army's authoritarian and non-participatory practice of government. They had also been agitating for a state that would deliver substantial social and economic justice.

The most important organizational advantage that Islamist groups had over the FLN and the army was that it captured substantial support of the largest demographic group in Algeria that mattered politically: the under-thirty generation. The FLN's leadership had ignored this generational cohort. The FLN aged without including Algeria's youth. As evidence we can observe that the leaders of the FLN in the 1980's and 1990's were the same leaders who were active in the leadership of the party during the 1950's.

By contrast, Islamist groups regularly and systematically recruited among the youth and included them in leadership decisions. Generationally, leadership of the Islamist movement was much younger than that of the FLN. For example, a key leader of the FIS, Imam Belhadj, was 35 years old in 1992. Other important leaders in the FIS, including Abdelkader Hachani and Anwar Haddam, were also in their late 30's and early 40's. Besides including the youth in its politics, the Islamist groups developed the financial capacity to deliver real material benefits to their constituents. They became able to provide benefits including temporary employment, scholarships, and health care. Islamist groups in effect became a de facto alternative state that could compete with the official state both materially and symbolically.

This study documented that Islam has influenced or informed the entire evolution of Algerian politics from 1783 through 1992. All of the political movements that we have studied and all the written ideological documents that have emerged from the Algerian political experience — from the first oration by the Emir Abdel Qadir (Chapter 2) through the inter-war nationalist struggles (Chapter 4) to the 1956 Soummam Platform, the 1962 Tripoli Program, the 1964 Algiers Charter, the 1976 National Charter and Constitution, and the 1989 Constitution — have shown that Islam has been used either for mobilizing the masses for political action or for trying to obtain legitimacy for governmental policies. Islam, whether it has been used instrumentally as a tactic in political maneuvering or whether it has been used substantively as a goal in ethics, has remained an indispensable reality in Algerian political life. Leaders in Algeria who have attempted to either relegate or denigrate the importance of Islam in Algerian political life have usually perished or have been politically unsuccessful.

Broader Theoretical Conclusions

This study of Islam in Algeria has shown that Islam can have diverse political expressions. In the first chapter, we documented that some scholars and policy analysts have asserted that Islam is incompatible with democracy. In this last section, we will examine whether Islam is compatible with liberal definitions of democracy. We have argued in this text, however, that Islam's principles of *shura* (consultation) and *ijma* (consensus) have resonated with liberal notions of democracy. These two principles constrain the exercise of unilateral dictatorial rule and, therefore, enhance the possibility of democratic processes. Islam needs to elaborate these principles into more precise, formal and stable procedures and institutions for the administration of democracy.

Among the procedural and institutional issues that still need to be addressed are (1) the constitution of the legislature or *majlis;* (2) the powers of this legislature and whether it may operate independently of the executive or *khalifa;* (3) the qualifications for membership in the legislature (i.e., whether it will be limited to clerics only and whether it will be limited solely to men); (4) the precise formulation of the judiciary with the specific enumeration of its powers vis-à-vis the executive and the legislature; and, (5) the precise definition of the powers of the executive. To date these issues have not been universally or specifically resolved. If these issues were to be addressed, the relationship between Islam and democracy would be clarified substantially. Muslim scholars can resolve these questions in a manner that would be fully consistent with the Qur'an.

Besides these procedural and institutional issues, Islam's critics have claimed that Islam's failure to create a secular state has rendered it ipso facto undemocratic. This criticism of Islam's politics is illogical and it obscures rather than illuminates the relationship between religion and politics.

Islamic states cannot be secular because the Qur'an denies the possibility that the secular can be separated from the religious in either private or public life.[1] Despite this scriptural interdiction of secularism, separation of the religious from the secular is not essential for the creation of a democracy. Only the United States and France have rigidly attempted to create a strict "wall of separation" between the religious and the secular in governance. Many democracies including Great Britain, Ireland, and Germany have allowed for a prominent public role for religion in politics. Israel goes further, making religious affiliation one of the conditions for citizenship.[2]

The theoretical issue is not the separation of the secular from the religious. The previously mentioned countries provide ample evidence that this "separation" issue is not relevant to the construction of democracy. Rather, the first set of theoretical issues devolves around questions of whether Muslim states need to provide real legal and constitutional protection to persons who are non-Muslims or persons who are nonbelievers within their states. The second theoretical question involves the resolution of the issue of whether non-Muslims or nonbelievers in Muslim states can be fully enfranchised as citizens.[3]

Although democracy has been defined as rule by the majority, rule by the majority does not automatically constitute a democracy; it may indeed constitute tyranny. An essential aspect of real democracy requires the provision of legal and constitutional protection for persons within the polity who may not be members of or who may decide to dissent from the beliefs of the majority. Democracies must provide protection for those members of their polities who are either religious or political dissenters or who are members of minority groups. If Islamic states were not to provide for explicit constitutional and legal protection for dissenting minorities, they could not, from the viewpoint of precise definition, be considered democratic.

Second, real democracies must offer the franchise of citizenship to all persons who reside within their polities. Democratic states make the right of citizenship available to everyone regardless of the gender, race, religion, ethnic group, or the beliefs of the applicant. Further, they must treat all these citizens, regardless of their differences, equally under the law. The theoretical problem for Islam and the question of democracy from the viewpoint of the law arises from the application and interpretation of the *sharia*. Over the centuries, because of the implementation of the *sharia* by the Ottomans and because of its interpretation by Muslim legal scholars, a confessional system of law has arisen in which Muslim law has been applied to Muslims, Christian law has been applied to Christians, and Jewish law has been applied to Jews, et cetera. This monotheistic definition and vision of law has created particular problems for those who are not monotheists. Whose law is applicable to Buddhists, Hindus, agnostics, atheists, or pantheists who reside within an Islamic state? Would these persons be legally and constitutionally unprotected? Can an Islamic state be called democratic if it does not provide explicit legal and constitutional protection to these persons who are either religious dissenters or minority group members?

Other theoretical and pragmatic issues concern power sharing between the clerical community and secular political elites. Although the Qur'an does not recognize a clergy, a de facto clergy often exists in states where Sunni Islam is practiced. (A much stronger de facto clerical tradition exists in Shiism). If we accept the existence of a real and powerful de facto clergy within many Sunni states, we then must recognize that historically a real political struggle has transpired between secular-oriented elites and religious elites concerning the roles for clerics and secular elites in governance. This struggle, as the first chapter showed, formally began with Suleiman the Great's first significant assertion of secular authority over the law in the sixteenth century, A.D. Since then, secular political interests and religious political figures have been locked in a political struggle.

If we accept the political reality of the existence of a clergy in Sunnism we can understand why this class of clergy may organize itself to challenge the prerogatives of secular leaders who may not have been formally trained in the interpretation and application of Islamic law. Here is where our argument in the first chapter concerning law and justice has particular relevance. First, we established in that chapter that the notion of justice in Islam and in Islamic law is based upon equitable rather than procedural notions. That chapter asserted that Islam's definition of justice as an equitable concept and that the mass expectations that exist in Muslim societies concerning justice were qualitatively different from the expectations concerning justice that operate in contemporary Anglo-American and European societies. Within this ethical matrix of justice as equity, real political battles have emerged in which clerics, as leaders of ethical and political communities, decry the existence of hierarchical or inequitable social conditions wherever they may exist.

These clerics claim that Islam does not permit excessive hierarchy or gross inequity. By reemphasizing the underlying notion that Islam demands justice as equity rather than as procedure, these clerics have helped catalyze movements of political resistance to inequity that seem to be triggered faster than social movements that operate within the ethical matrices for the definition of justice that exist in Anglo-American and European societies.

In the struggle for justice as equity, these clerics have emerged as the spokespersons and organizers for movements that are intent upon the eradication of these conditions of unfairness. These clerics have claimed that only the restoration of Islamic values, Islamic law, and Islamic government will provide real justice. They often claim further that they, as clerics and experts in Islamic law, are the ones who are competent and eligible to lead the people towards fairer government. In the interests of democracy, however, should governmental powers be concentrated especially or entirely in the hands of clerics? Or is power-sharing between clerics and secular leaders a better alternative for the creation of democracy? These questions, which have arisen from the first formal assertion of secular authority four centuries ago, remain unresolved.

The final conclusions in this study are that if secular leaders intend to participate in the construction of democracies in Muslim countries, they need to remain sensitive to both the substance and the symbols of the equitable demands of Islam and Islamic law. Second, they need to remain aware of the inevitable need for creative compromise with clerical leaders who participate in politics. Third, they need to recognize that clerically led resistance movements are more likely to be successful where the clerical community is centrally organized as opposed to decentrally dispersed. Where the clergy and other religious and political dissidents have found a way to unite and substantially centralize, they have been more successful in challenging established political regimes.

Appendix
Educational and Political Backgrounds
of Prominent FLN Leaders

Name	Education	Pre-FLN Affiliation
Abbas, Ferhat	Secular	UDMA
Aït Ahmed, Hocine	Religious and Secular	MTLD
Al-Madani, Tawfiq	Religious	Association of Ulema
Ben Bella, Ahmed	Secular	MTLD
Benkhedda, Benyoussef	Secular	MTLD
Bentobbal, Lakhdar	**	MTLD
Ben Yahyia, Mohammed	Secular	MTLD
Bitat, Rabah	**	MTLD
Boudiaf, Mohammed	Secular	MTLD
Boumedienne, Houari	Religious	MTLD
Boussouf, Abdelhafid	**	MTLD
Cherif, Mahmoud	Military	UDMA
Debaghine, Lamine	Secular	MTLD
Francis, Ahmed	Secular	UDMA
Harbi, Mohammed	Secular	MTLD
Khider, Mohammed	*	MTLD
Krim, Belkacem	Secular	MTLD
Lacheraf, Mostefa	Religious and Secular	MTLD
Ouamrane, Amar	Secular	MTLD
Ramdane, Abbane	Secular	MTLD
Yazid, M'Hammed	Secular	MTLD

* = Family too poor to afford school expenses

** = Information not obtained

Endnotes

Chapter I ~ Endnotes

1. Robin Wright, "Islam, Democracy, and the West," *Foreign Affairs* (Summer 1992), pp. 131–145; Judith Miller, "The Challenge of Radical Islam," *Foreign Affairs* (Spring 1993), pp. 43–56: Samuel Huntington, "The Clash of Civilizations?" *Foreign Affairs* (Summer 1993), pp. 22–49; Judith Miller, "Faces of Fundamentalism," *Foreign Affairs* (November/December 1994), pp. 123–143.

2. To name but a few: Nazih Ayubi, *Political Islam* (London: Routledge, 1991); Habib Boularès, *Islam: la peur et l'espérance* (Paris: J.-C. Lattes, 1983); Olivier Carré, *Mystique et politique* (Paris: P.S.N.S.P., 1984); Youssef M. Choueiri, *Islamic Fundamentalism* (Boston, MA: Twayne, 1990); Hamid Enayat, *Modern Islamic Political Thought* (Austin, TX: University of Texas, 1982); John L. Esposito, *The Islamic Threat* (New York, NY: Oxford University Press, 1992); John L. Esposito, *Islam and Politics,* 3rd ed. (Syracuse, NY: Syracuse University Press, 1984); John L. Esposito, ed. *Voice of Resurgent Islam* (New York, NY: Oxford University Press, 1983); Henry Munson, Jr., *Islam and Revolution in the Middle East* (New Haven, CT: Yale University Press, 1988); Olivier Roy, *L'échec de l'Islam politique* (Paris: Seuil, 1992); Emmanuel Sivan, *Radical Islam* (New Haven, CT: Yale University Press, 1985); Mehran Tamadonfar, *The Islamic Polity and Political Leadership* (Boulder, CO: Westview, 1989); Bassam Tibi, *Islam and the Cultural Accommodation of Social Change* (Boulder, CO: Westview, 1991); W. Montgomery Watt, *Islamic Fundamentalism and Modernity* (London: Routledge, 1988); Rafiq Zakaria, *The Struggle within Islam* (New York, NY: Penguin, 1988).

3. I use the term dissident to define those who critique the status quo, whether within the community of Islam or outside of it.

4. The Holy Qur'an defines justice as an equitable concept. See *The Holy Qur'an*, 6:1, 6:151, 25:68, 39:69, 39:75.

5. Max Weber, *Max Weber on Law in Economy and Society*, ed. Max Rheinstein; trans. Edward Shils and Max Rheinstein (Cambridge, MA: Harvard University Press, 1954) p. 213, fn. 48.

6. Dragan Milovanovic, *Weberian and Marxian Analysis of Law* (Brookfield, VT: Gower, 1989), p. 66.

7. Max Weber, *Economy and Society*, ed. By Guenther Roth and Claus Wittich (Berkeley, CA: University of California Press, 1968), pp. 976–978.

8. Milovanovic, *Weberian and Marxian Analysis of Law*, pp. 67–68; See also Weber, *Economy and Society*, p. 657–658.

9. Karl Marx, *A Contribution to the Critique of Political Economy* (Chicago, IL: Charles H. Kerr & Co., 1904), pp. 11–12; See also Karl Marx, *Capital, Vol. 1* (New York, NY: International Publishers, 1967), pp. 37, 40, 49; Karl Marx and Frederich Engels, *The German Ideology* (New York, NY: International Publishers, 1947); and Karl Marx and Frederich Engels, *The Communist Manifesto* (Chicago, IL: Charles H. Kerr & Co., no date).

10. Weber, *Economy and Society*, p. 883. See also page 725.

11. Ibid., p. 847.

12. Ibid., p. 812.

13. David M. Trubek, "Max Weber and the Rise of Capitalism," *Wisconsin Law Review*, Volume 1972, No. 3, p.749.

14. *The Holy Qur'an*, 5:42, 49:9.

15. The European and American law traditions have evolved since the emergence of the post-industrial state after the Great Depression. Both in Europe and the Americas, the systems of law are less formally "rational" than they were before the economic cataclysm of the Great Depression. The end of laissez-faire capitalism and the emergence of a larger governmental sector in the capitalist economy ushered in new legal age that expanded the role of judges in creating equitable solutions. Although both the European and the Anglo-American systems of law are still more "formally rational" than the Islamic system of law, they are less "formal" and less "rational" than they once were. Capitalism — and the legal system that supported it — evolved to survive. See Roberto Unger, *Law in Modern Society* (New York, NY: The Free Press, 1975); Charles Reich, "The New Property," *Yale Law Journal*, Vol.73; Goldberg v. Kelley, 96 S. Ct. 1011 (1970).

16. Antonio Gramsci, *Selections from the Prison Notebooks*, ed. by Q. Hoare (London: Lawrence & Wishart, 1971).

17. Ibid., p. 12.

18. Louis Althusser, "Ideology and Ideological State Apparatuses," in *Lenin and Philosophy and Other Essays,* trans. by Ben Brewster (New York, NY: Monthly Review Press, 1971); Nicos Poulantzas, *Pouvoir politique et classes sociales* (Paris: Maspero, 1970).

19. Jürgen Habermas, *Faktizitat und Geltung* (Frankfurt: Suhrkamp, 1992), p. 141. See also his *The Theory of Communicative Action, Vol. 1, Reason and Rationalization of Society,* trans. T. McCarthy (Boston, MA: Beacon Press, 1975), pp. 273–337.

20. Benjamin Lee Whorf, *Language, Thought, and Reality* (Boston, MA: MIT Press, 1956), p. 221.

21. See, Michael Novak, *Will It Liberate? Questions about Liberation Theology* (Lanham, MD: Madison, 1986); Phillip Berryman, *Liberation Theology* (New York, NY: Pantheon, 1987); Arthur F. McGovern, *Liberation Theology and its Critics* (Maryknoll, NY: Orbis, 1989); Paul E. Sigmund, *Liberation Theology at the Crossroads: Democracy or Revolution?* (New York, NY: Oxford University Press, 1990).

22. Trubek, "Max Weber and the Rise of Capitalism," pp. 729–730.

23. Ann K. Lambton, *State and Government in Medieval Islam* (Oxford: Oxford University Press, 1981); E. I. J. Rosenthal, *Political Thought in Medieval Islam* (Cambridge: Cambridge University Press, 1958).

24. Arthur Goldschmidt, Jr., *A Concise History of the Middle East* (Boulder, CO: Westview Press, 1991); John O. Voll, *Islam: Continuity and Change in the Modern World* (Boulder, CO: Westview Press, 1982), pp. 14–17.

25. Habib Boularès, trans. Lewis Ware, *Islam: The Fear and The Hope* (London: Zed Books, 1990), p. 66.

26. The *ulema* are the religious leaders of the Muslim community.

27. John L. Esposito, *Islam and Politics,* 3rd ed. (Syracuse, NY: Syracuse University Press, 1991), p. 19.

28. Richard Bulliet, *The Patricians of Nishapur* (Cambridge, MA: Harvard University Press, 1972), p. 62; Ira Lapidus, *Muslim Cities in the Latter Middle Ages* (Cambridge, MA: Harvard University Press, 1981), pp. 44–78, 116, 130–131, 188–189; N. Levitzon, *Ancient Ghana and Mali* (London: Methuen, 1973), pp. 206–207; Roger Le Tourneau, *Fez in the Age of the Marinides* (Norman, OK: University of Oklahoma Press, 1961), pp. 40–43; Elias Saad, *Social History of Timbuktu: The Role of Muslim Scholars and Notables* (Cambridge: Cambridge University Press, 1983); Boaz Shoshan, "The Politics of Notables in Islam," *Asian and African Studies* 20 (July 1986): 179–215.

29. Abu Hamid al-Ghazali, *Ihya ulum al-din* (Cairo: 1878–1879); Ali ibn Muhammad al-Mawwardi, *Al-ahkam al-sultaniyya;* Ahmad ibn Taimiyya,

Al-siyasa al-shariyya, 2nd. ed., ed. A. S. Nashshar and A. Z. Atiyya, (Cairo: 1951) Ahmad Ibn Taimiyya, *Le traité de droit d'Ibn Taimiyya,* trans. H. Laoust (Beirut, 1948); John Voll, Islam: *Continuity and Change in the Muslim World* (Boulder, CO: Westview Press, 1982), p. 36.

30. N. J. Coulson, *A History of Islamic Law* (Edinburgh: Edinburgh University Press, 1978), Chapter 14.

31. Rafiq Zakaria, *The Struggle Within Islam* (New York, NY: Penguin Books: 1988), pp. 116–118.

32. *The Holy Qur'an,* 3:159.

33. India was an exception. In India, partial citizenship was available to the indigenous people through the *raj* system of government.

34. Muhammad bin Abd al-Wahhab, *Al-Rasa'il,* Part V (Riyadh: University of al-Imam Muhammad B. Saud al-Islamiyya, 1978); Boularès, *Islam: The Fear and The Hope,* p. 95; Malise Ruthven, *Islam in the World* (New York: Oxford University Press, 1984), p. 282; Bassam Tibi, *Arab Nationalism,* 3rd. ed. (London: MacMillan Press, 1990), pp. 88–90; Bassam Tibi, *Islam and the Cultural Accommodation of Social Change* (Boulder, CO: Westview Press, 1991), pp. 20–21.

35. Albert Hourani, *Arabic Thought in the Liberal Age, 1798–1939* (Cambridge: Cambridge University Press, 1983), pp. 103–160.

36. Hourani, *Arabic Thought in the Liberal Age,* p. 144.

37. Muhammad Iqbal, "The Principle of Movement in Islam," chap. in *The Reconstruction of Religious Thought in Islam* (Lahore: Sh. Muhammad Ahraf,1968).

38. Abu Nasir al-Farabi, *Ara ahl al-madina al-fadila; The Perfect State,* trans. Richard Walzer (Oxford: Oxford University Press, 1985).

39. Al-Ghazali, *Ihya ulum al-din;* Ibn Taimiyya, *Al-siyasa al-shariyya.*

40. There was a fourth school that proposed secularizing Islam. Its most prominent proponent was Kemal Ataturk of Turkey. This school of thought, however, has been the exception rather than the rule in twentieth century Islam.

41. See especially Sayyid Qutb, *Maalim fil Tariq* (Cairo: Dar al-Sharuq, 1989); Syed Qutb, *Milestones* (Lahore: Kazi Publications, n.d.).

42. Abu al-Ala al-Mawdudi, *Islam: Its Meaning and its Message,* trans. Khurshid Ahmad (London: Islamic Council of Europe, 1976), pp. 147–148, 158–161, 163–167; Fazlur Rahman, "Implementation of the Islamic Concept of State in the Pakistani Milieu,' in *Islamic Studies,* pp. 205-224.

43. John L. Esposito, "Islam and Muslim Politics," in *Voices of Resurgent Islam,* ed. John L. Esposito (New York, NY: Cambridge University Press), pp. 8–9.

44. Abdallah Laroui, *La crise des intellectuels arabes;* Frantz Fanon, *Les damnés de la terre* (Paris: Prospero, 1962).

45. Hassan al-Banna, *Al-salam fi al-Islam* (Cairo: Dar al-Fikr al-Islami, 1957); Hassan al-Banna, in *Political and Social Thought in the Contemporary Middle East,* ed. Kemal H. Karpat (New York: Praeger, 1968), pp. 118–122.

46. Voll, Islam, p. 154.

47. Sayyid Qutb, *Maalim fil Tariq,* pp. 165–170; Sayyid Qutb, *Fi Zilal al-Quran,* rev. ed., 6 Vols. (Cairo: Dar al-Shuruq, 1981), pp. 2144–2155; Sayyid Qutb, *Al-Islam wa Mushkilat al-Hadara,* 6th ed. (Cairo: Dar al-Shuruq, 1980), pp. 82–105.

48. Ayatollah Ruhollah Khomeini, *Islamic Government* (New York: Manor Books, 1979); Ayatollah Ruhollah Khomeini, *Islam and Revolution,* trans. and annotated by Hamid Algar (Berkeley, CA: Mizan Press, 1981), pp. 40–54, 79–125.

49. *The Holy Quran,* 49:13.

50. This typology is a reformulation of ideas from various sources including Gabriel L. Almond and G. Bingham Powell, *Comparative Politics: System, Process, and Policy* (Boston, MA: Little, Brown, & Co., 1978); James A. Bill and Robert Springborg, *Politics in the Middle East,* 3rd ed. (San Francisco, CA: HarperCollins, 1990); Samuel P. Huntington, *Political Order in Changing Societies* (New Haven, CT: Yale University Press, 1968); Juan Linz and Alfred Stepan, eds., *The Breakdown of Democratic Regimes* (Baltimore, MD: Johns Hopkins University Press, 1978); Juan Linz, "Totalitarian and Authoritarian Regimes," in F. Greenstein and N. Polsby, eds., *Handbook of Political Science,* Vol. 3 (Reading, PA: Addison-Wesley, 1975); Guillermo O'Donnell, *Modernization and Bureaucratic Authoritarianism* (Berkeley, CA: University of California Press, 1973); Jean-François Seznec, "The Politics of the Financial Markets in Saudi Arabia, Kuwait, and Bahrain" (Ph. D. diss., Yale University, 1994); and Max Weber, *Economy and Society,* Vol. I (Berkeley, CA: University of California Press, 1978).

51. John L. Esposito, *Islam and Politics,* 3rd ed. (Syracuse, NY: Syracuse University Press, 1991), p. 105.

52. Hudson, *Arab Politics,* p. 25.

53. See, Guillermo O'Donnell, *Modernization and Bureaucratic Authoritarianism* (Berkeley, CA: University of California Press, 1986).

Endnotes ~ Chapter II

1. Julian Baldick, *Mystical Islam* (London: I. B. Tauris, 1989); Annemarie Schimmel, *Mystical Dimensions of Islam* (Chapel Hill, NC: University of North Carolina Press, 1975).

2. Jamil Abun-Nasr, *The Tijaniyya* (London: Oxford University Press, 1965); Christian Coulon, *Le Marabout et le Prince* (Paris: Pédone, 1981); D. B. Cruise O'Brien, *The Mourides of Senegal* (Oxford: Oxford University Press, 1971); Clifford Geertz, *Islam Observed* (New Haven, CT: Yale University Press, 1968).

3. Augustin Berque, "Essai d'une bibliographie critique des confréries algériennes," *Bulletin de la société de géographie et d'archéologie de la province d'Oran,* vol. 39 (septembre-décembre 1919): pp. 199–200; Julia Clancy-Smith, "Saints, Mahdis, and Arms: Religion and Resistance in Nineteenth Century North Africa," in *Islam, Politics, and Social Movements,* ed. Edmund Burke, III, and Ira M. Lapidus (London: I. B. Tauris, 1988), pp. 62–63, 76; René Gallisot, "La Guerre d'Abd El Kader," *Hespéris-Tamuda,* vol. 5 (1964): p. 33; Mohamed Cherif Sahli, *Abdelkader, chevalier de la foi* (Alger: Enterprise algérienne de presse, 1984); Peter Von Sivers, "The Realm of justice: Apocalyptic Revolts in Algeria (1849–1879)," *Humanoria Islamica,* vol. 1(1973): p. 60.

4. Charles Henry Churchill, *La vie d'Abd El Kader,* trans. Michel Habart (Alger: Enterprise Nationale du Livre, 1991) (Originally published in English in 1867), p.167; J. S. Trimingham, *The Sufi Orders in Islam* (London: Clarendon Press, 1971), p. 176.

5. The indigenous Algerians were Berbers. After the Arab invasions beginning in the eighth century, C.E., they became Arabo-Berber..

6. Raphael Danziger, *Abd Al-Qadir and the Algerians* (London: Holmes and Meier, 1977), p. 13; René Gallisot, "Abd el-Kader et la nationalité algérienne," *Revue Historique* 233 (avril-juin 1965): 349–350; Ahmed Nadir, "Les ordres religieux et la conquete française," *Revue Algérienne des Sciences Juridiques, Economiques, et Politiques,* vol. 9 (décembre 1972): 820–822.

7. Louis Rinn, *Marabouts et Khaouan* (Alger: Adolphe Jourdan, 1884), pp. 45, 452.

8. Gallisot, "Abd el-Kader," p. 350; Rinn, *Marabouts et Khaouan,* p. 111.

9. *Encyclopedia of Islam,* 1913–1934 ed., s.v. "Kadariya"; Octave Depont and Xavier Coppolani, *Les confréries religieuses* (Alger: Adolphe Jourdan, 1897), p. 293; Rinn, *Marabouts et Khaouan,* p. 30; Trimingham, *Sufi Orders,* pp. 40–44.

10. Depont and Coppolani, *Les confréries religieuses,* pp. 216, 484; Rinn, *Marabouts et Khaouan,* pp. 42, 279, 371.

11. Rinn, *Marabouts et Khaouan,* pp. 43, 374.

12. Pierre Boyer, *L'evolution de l'Algérie médiane,* (Paris: Maisonneuve, 1960), p. 58; Gallisot, "Abd el-Kader," p. 350.

13. Abun-Nasr, *The Tijaniyya; Depont and Coppolani, Les confréries religieuses;* Rinn, *Marabouts et Khaouan,* p. 416; Trimingham, *Sufi Orders,* p. 107.

14. Depont and Copollani, *Les Confréries religieuses,* 416–421.

15. Jamil M. Abun-Nasr, *A History of the Maghrib in the Islamic Period* (Cambridge: Cambridge University Press, 1987), p. 168.

16. Rinn, *Marabouts et Khaouan,* pp. 32, 46.

17. Depont and Coppolani, *Les confréries religieuses,* pp 216, 506.

18. Verses from the Qur'an banning racism can be found at Sura 49, Aya 13 and Sura 43, Ayat 23 and 24.

19. Abun-Nasr, *A History of the Maghrib,* p. 167; Muslim Ibn Abdul-Qadir Al-Wahrani, *Anis al-gharib wa'l musafir* (Algiers, 1974), pp. 72–74; Pierre Boyer, *Algérie médiane,* p. 59; Pierre Boyer, "Contribution à l'étude de la politique religieuse des Turcs dans la Régence d'Alger (16—19 siècles)," *Revue de l'Occident musulman et de la Méditerranée* (1966), pp. 41–44; Al-Mosselem bin Muhammad, "Résumé historique sur le soulèvement des Derkàoua de la province d'Oran," trans. Adrien Depelch, *Revue Africaine,* vol. 18 (1874), pp. 38–58; Walsin Esterhazy, *De la domination turque dans l'ancienne Régence d'Alger* (Paris: Gosselin, 1840), pp. 201–215; Alphonse Rousseau, "Chronique du Beylik d'Oran par un secrétaire du Bey Hassan," *Moniteur algérien,* 30 March, 5 April, 10 April, and 15 April, 1855.

20. Marcel Bodin, trans. "La brève chronique du Bey Hasan: extraite et traduite de Talat-os-Sasis-Sooud de Mazari," *Bulletin de la Société de géographie et d'archéologie de la province d'Oran,* vol. 44 (1924), pp. 23–61; L. Arnaud, "Histoire de l'Ouali Sidi-Ahmad et-Tedjani," *Revue Africaine,* vol. 5 (1861), pp. 468–474; L. Demaeght, "Notice sur la mort de Sidi Mohammed al-Kabir et-Tidjani," *Bulletin de la Société de géographie et d'archéologie de la province d'Oran,* vol. 13 (1893), pp. 150–152; Auguste Cour, *L'établissement des dynasties de Chérifs au Maroc et leur rivalités avec les Turcs de la Régence d'Alger* (Paris: Leroux, 1904), pp. 233–235; Pierre Boyer, "Contribution à l'étude de la politique religieuse des Turcs dans la Régence d'Alger (16–19 siècles)," *Revue de l'Occident musulman et de la Méditerranée* (1966), pp. 45–47.

21. Yves Lacoste, André Nouschi, and André Prenant, *L'Algérie, Passé et Present* (Paris: Sociales, 1960), pp. 239–241.

22. Churchill, *La vie,* p. 57; Nadir, "Les ordres religieux," pp. 836–837.

23. Cf., See discussion of *dar al-makhzen* and *dar al-bled* by Ibn Khaldoun in *The Muqaddimah,* 3 vols., 2d ed., trans. Franz Rosenthal (Princeton, NJ: Princeton University Press, 1967).

24. Paul Azan, *L'Emir Abd el Kader, 1809–1883* (Paris: Hachette, 1925), pp. 38–41; Nadir, "Les ordres religieux," pp. 828–830.

25. Marcel Emerit, *L'Algérie a l'époque d'Abd-El-Kader* (Paris: Larose, 1951), p. 201; Charles Richard, *Etude sur l'insurrection du Dahra* (Alger: A. Besanciez, 1846), pp. 127–141; Rinn, *Marabouts et Khaouan,* p. 352.

26. Muhammad ibn Abdel Qadir al-Jazairi, *Tuhfat al zair fi tarikh al jazair wa-l amir abd alqadir* (Beirut: Dar al yaqadha al arabiyya, 1964), p.116; Rinn, *Marabouts et Khaouan,* p. 381.

27. Azan, *Abd el Kader,* p. 4

28. Azan, *Abd el Kader,* p.5; Danziger, *Abd al-Qadir,* p. 56; Alexandre Daumont, "Abd el-Kader," *L'Afrique Française* (July 1837), pp. 45–50.

29. Aside from the support of Qadiriyya initiates, Muhi al-Din received support from the Hachemand Beni Amer tribal groups.

30. Al-Jazairi , *Tuhfat,* pp. 115–156; Churchill, *La vie,* p. 65; Danziger, *Abd al-Oadir,* p. 51; Gallisot, "Abd el-Kader," p. 351; Sahli, *L'Emir Abdelkader,* p. 30.

31. Azan, *Abd el Kader,* pp. 67, 125–127; Churchill, *La vie,* p. 161; Gallisot, "Abd el-Kader," p. 361.

32. Churchill, *La vie,* p. 162; Gallisot, "Abd el-Kader," p. 366.

33. Churchill, *La vie,* pp. 66, 168–169.

34. Churchill, *La vie,* p. 67; Gallisot, "Abd el-Kader," p. 366.

35. Gallisot, "Abd el-Kader," pp. 361-362; Gallisot, "La Guerre," pp. 122–124.

36. al-Jazairi, *Tuhfat,* p. 162.

37. Rinn, *Marabouts et Khaouan,* pp. 75–78.

38. Ibid., p. 75.

39. Al-Mahdi literally means "the guided one." In the history of Islamic societies, figures have appeared who have been accepted by the masses as persons who will restore righteousness. The mahdi's mission is to restore righteousness just before the end of the world or the day of judgement (yawm al-din). Belief in the role of the mahdi prevails in both Sunnism and Shiism. Although the mahdi 's role is primarily spiritual, it can also be political. Examples of political Mahdis outside of Algeria include Ibn Tumart of the Almohad dynasty (1077–1130, A.D.), Uthman dan Fodio of the Sokoto Caliphate in Nigeria (1809–1816, A.D.), and Muhammad Ahmad ibn Abd Allah of the Sudan (1843–1885, A.D.).

40. Richard, *Dahra,* pp. 13, 15–17, 90.

41. Ibid., pp. 127, 135.

Chapter III ~ Endnotes

1. Alexis de Tocqueville, "Rapport fait par M. de Tocqueville à la chambre des deputés, 24 Mai 1847," in *Journal officiel* (Session de 1847), p. 306.

2. Charles-Robert Ageron, *Les algériens musulmans et la France, 1871–1919* (Paris: Presses Universitaires de France, 1968), p. 95; Mahfoud Bennoune, *The Making of Contemporary Algeria* (Cambridge: Cambridge University Press, 1988), p. 46.

3. John Ruedy, *Modern Algeria* (Bloomington, IN: Indiana University Press, 1992), p. 95.

4. Abdellatif Benachenhou, *Formation du sous-développement en Algérie* (Alger: OPU, 1976), 194; Bennoune, *Contemporary Algeria,* p. 48.

5. Ruedy, *Modern Algeria,* p. 97.

6. Ageron, *Les algériens musulmans,* p. 718; Ruedy, *Modern Algeria,* p. 90.

7. Ruedy, *Modern Algeria,* p. 91.

8. W. Oualid, *Bulletin de la réunion d'études algériennes* (nos. 1 et 2, 1911); See also the article by the same author in *L'Écho d'Alger* (Alger), 18 decembre 1912.

9. Charles-Robert Ageron, *Histoire de l'Algérie contemporaine,* Tome II (Paris: Presses universitaires de France, 1968), p. 98; Ruedy, *Modern Algeria,* p. 98.

10. Ageron, *Les algériens musulmans,* p. 849; Bennoune, *Contemporary Algeria,* p. 57.

11. Ageron, *Les algériens musulmans,* p. 849.

12. Madeleine Trebous, *Migration et développement: le cas de l'Algérie* (Paris: Centre de développement de l'O.C.D.E., 1970), pp. 56, 154.

13. Bennoune, *Contemporary Algeria,* p. 77.

14. Ageron, *Les algériens musulmans,* pp. 157–160; Yves Lacoste, André Nouschi, and André Prenant, *L'Algérie: passé et présent* (Paris: Sociales, 1960), p. 436.

15. Loi du 23 décembre 1875.

16. The *hijrah,* required of all Muslims who can afford it and are in good health, involves a religious pilgrimage to the Holy City of Mecca. It occurs yearly.

17. Ageron, *Les algériens musulmans,* pp. 898–900. Mahfoud Kaddache, *Histoire du nationalisme algérien, 1919–1951,* Tome I (Alger: S. N. E. D., 1980), p. 42.

18. Governor General Jonnart, cited in Ageron, *Les algériens musulmans,* p. 900.

19. Ageron, *Les algériens musulmans,* pp. 298–299.

20. Augustin Berque, "Decadence des chefs héréditaires," *Écrits sur l'Algérie* (Aix-en-Provence: Edisud, 1986), pp. 42–46; Charles-Robert Ageron, *Histoire de l'Algérie Contemporaine,* Tome II, pp. 172–175.

21. The Senoussiya was founded in Cyrenaica, Libya, by an Algerian cherif in 1835. Algerian membership in the brotherhood became significant in the Moab region in the 1880's.

22. Ageron, *Les algériens musulmans,* p. 299.

23. Louis Rinn, *Sur l'instruction politique musulmane* (Alger: 1882).

24. Alexis de Tocqueville, "Rapport fait par M. de Tocqueville à la chambre des députés," pp. 326–327.

25. See E. Formestraux, *L'instruction publique en Algérie (1830–1880)* (Alger: 1880).

26. This policy coincided with France's metropolitan policy with regard to education that emphasized the role of the school in the development of secular culture and civic responsibility.

27. Ageron, *Les algériens musulmans,* p. 950.

28. See report of General Valaze in Ferhat Abbas, *La Nuit Coloniale* (Paris: René Julliard, 1962), p. 50.

29. Ageron, *Les algériens musulmans,* p. 1067.

30. *Dépêche algérienne,* 1 octobre 1908.

31. *Petit Parisien,* 27 septembre 1908.

32. *The Holy Quran,* Sura 4, Ayat:99–100, Sura 8, Aya 73, Sura 73, Sura 75.

33. *Rapport du Gouverneur General,* 4 janvier 1909.

34. The option of exit or defection when the option of contestation has been frustrated has been superbly discussed in Albert O. Hirschman, *Exit, Voice, and Loyalty* (Cambridge, MA: Harvard University Press, 1970).

35. Ageron, *Histoire de l'Algérie contemporaine,* Tome II, p. 230.

36. *L'Exode de Tlemcen en 1911* (Alger: 1914).

37. The Crémieux Decree of 24 October 1870 allowed Jews to become French citizens without requiring them to renounce their religious law.

38. The *Conseillers généraux* were advisors to the Governor General.

39. *Bulletin du comité de l'Afrique française* (1919), p. 121

40. Cited in Ageron, *Les algériens musulmans,* p. 1166.

41. This legal discrimination on the basis of religion had a historical precedent in the French laws of citizenship. Despite the 1791 Constitution's cre-

ation of expansive, liberal criteria for the acquisition of French citizenship, descendants of expatriated Protestants were discriminated against. These Protestants had to take a civic oath declaring publicly their intention to become French citizens whereas their Catholic counterparts did not have the same obligation placed upon them. This distinction on the basis of religion repeated itself in the Jonnart Reforms that required Muslims to renounce the *sharia* whereas Christians and Jews were not required to do the same. See Rogers Brubaker, *Citizenship and Nationhood in France and Germany* (Cambridge, MA: Harvard University Press, 1992), pp. 86–87.

42. Ageron, *Histoire de l'Algérie comtemporaine*, Tome II, p. 274, 279; Kaddache, *Histoire du nationalisme algérien, 1919–1951,* Tome I, p. 44.

43. The *Conseils généraux* (General Councils) were responsible for (1) the appropriation of tax revenues; (2) the auditing of governmental accounts; and (3) the provision of advice to the Governor General. The *Délégations financières* (Financial Delegations) were peculiar to Algeria. They exercised less power than the *Conseils généraux*. They were responsible for the provision of financial advice to the Governor General.

Endnotes ~ Chapter IV

1. Mahfoud Kaddache, *Histoire du nationalisme algérien,* Tome I (Alger, S.N.E.D., 1980), p. 127.

2. *La Lutte Sociale,* 12 novembre 1911.

3. *Demain*, 17 mai 1919, 28 juin 1919.

4. *Demain,* 28 juin 1919.

5. Kaddache, *Histoire du nationalisme algérien,* Tome I, p. 129.

6. A *fatwa* is a published opinion or decision regarding religious doctrine or law made by a religious authority.

7. *Demain*, 22 février 1930.

8. *Demain*, 10 avril 1926, 12 juin 1926, 27 novembre 1926.

9. "Le procès-verbale du Cinquième Congrès du Parti Communiste Français, 1924," In Archives du Parti Communiste Français, Paris, France.

10. See *La Lutte Sociale,* 8 avril 1927, 6 avril 1928, 18 juillet 1928.

11. *La Lutte Sociale,* 30 mars 1928.

12. Ageron, *Histoire de l'Algérie Contemporaine,* Tome II, (Paris: Presses Universitaires de France, 1968), p. 290; Roger LeTourneau, *Evolution politique de l'Afrique du nord musulmane, 1920–1961* (Paris: Armand Colin,

1962), pp. 312–313; André Nouschi, *La naissance du nationalisme algérien* (Paris: Minuit, 1962), p. 61.

13. See Chapter III.

14. Ageron, *Histoire de l'Algérie contemporaine,* Tome II, p. 526; Kaddache, *Histoire du nationalisme algérien,* Tome I, p. 173.

15. Kaddache, *Histoire du nationalisme algérien,* Tome I, pp. 184, 187–188.

16. Ageron, *Histoire de l'Algérie contemporaine,* Tome II, p. 350; Kaddache, *Histoire du nationalisme algérien,* Tome I, p. 192.

17. Program of the *Étoile Nord-Africaine* at the Anti-Imperialist Congress (Brussels), 25 February 1927.

18. *Demain,* 21 octobre 1927.

19. Archives d'Outre-Mer, Aix-en-Provence, France, (Carton 11 h 47); *El Ouma,* octobre 1933.

20. In the twentieth century, centenary celebrations of colonialism or independence frequently provoked responses by dissident intellectuals in the colonies. These intellectuals converted centenaries into protests against colonial rule. See the examples of Indonesia, Viet Nam, the Phillipines, the Congo, Mozambique, and Angola in Benedict Anderson, *Imagined Communities* (London: Verso, 1983), pp. 107–108.

21. Cited in Kaddache, *Histoire du nationalisme algérien,* Tome I, pp. 249–250.

22. Archives d'Outre-Mer, Aix-en-Provence, France, (Carton 15 h 25).

23. *L'Humanité,* 30 janvier 1930, 28 juin 1930, 30 juin 1930.

24. "Les Nord-Africains et la paix," *El Ouma,* septembre 1931.

25. *Annuaire statistique de l'Algérie, 1939–1947,* p. 21.

26. In the period from 1930 to 1938, Algeria became the world's third largest producer of wine, after France and Italy.

27. Kaddache, *Histoire du nationalisme algérien,* Tome I, p. 289.

28. Ageron, *Histoire de l'Algérie contemporaine,* Tome II, pp. 423–424; Kaddache, *Histoire du nationalisme algérien,* Tome I, p. 293; Nouschi, *La naissance du nationalisme algérien,* p. 72.

29. See *La Défense,* 14 septembre 1934.

30. For example, the Crémieux decree granted French citizenship to Jews but not to Muslims.

31. Archives d'Outre-Mer, Aix-en-Provence, France, (Carton 24 x 2); *El Ouma,* août-septembre 1934 and septembre-octobre 1934; *La Lutte Sociale,* 15 au 25 novembre 1934.

32. *Al Shihab,* 11 septembre 1934; *La Défense,* 16 novembre 1934.

33. *El Ouma,* avril 1936.

34. *El Ouma,* mars-avril 1936.

35. Cited in Ageron, *Histoire de l'Algérie contemporaine,* Tome II, p. 354; See also Le Tourneau, *Évolution politique,* p. 327.

36. Kaddache, *Histoire du nationalism algérien,* Tome I, p. 473.

37. Ibid., p. 474.

38. See *La Défense,* 4 décembre 1936, 18 décembre 1936, 29 janvier 1937; 23 juillet 1937.

39. *El Ouma,* 27 mars 1938.

40. *Le Parlement Algérien,* No.1; *Centre d'Information et d'Études du Gouvernement Général,* juin 1940, Archives d'Outre-Mer, Aix-en-Provence, France, (Carton 11 h 49); Ageron, *Histoire de l'Algérie contemporaine,* Tome II, p. 359.

41. Mohammed Harbi, *Le FLN: mirage et réalité* (Paris: Les Editions J.A., 1985), p.23.

42. Harbi, *Le FLN: mirage et réalité,* p. 28; Charles-André Julien, *L'Afrique du nord en marche* (Paris: René Julliard, 1972), p. 241.

43. Ageron, *Histoire de l'Algérie contemporaine,* Tome II, p. 573; Julien, *L'Afrique du nord en marche,* p. 262; Le Tourneau, *Évolution politique,* p. 349.

44. Julien, *L'Afrique du nord en marche,* p. 263; Kaddache, *Histoire du nationalisme algérien,* Tome II, p. 718; "Declaration du Docteur Bendjelloul," *Assemblé Nationale Consultative,* 28 février 1946, p. 507; "Declaration du délégué Belhadi," *Assemblé Nationale Consultative,* 29 juin 1949, p. 507.

45. Julien, *L'Afrique du nord en marche,* pp. 263–264; Kaddache, *Histoire du nationalisme algérien,* Tome II, p. 719–720.

46. Kaddache, *Histoire du nationalisme algérien,* Tome II, pp. 723–728.

47. *Le Monde,* 23 octobre 1947, 24 octobre 1947.

48. *Combat,* 25 juin 1946.

49. Article 12.

50. Article 5.

51. Article 21.

52. Slimane Chikh, *L'Algérie en armes* (Alger: OPU, 1981), p. 73; Harbi, *Le FLN,* p. 70.

53. See F. Chatelet, "Nationalisme et conscience de classe," in *Consciences Algériennes* (décembre 1950), pp. 16–21.

54. See *Liberté,* 16 juin 1949.

55. *Le Monde,* 21 October 1947; Kaddache, *Histoire du nationalisme algérien,* Tome II, p. 788.

56. Kaddache, *Histoire du nationalisme algérien,* Tome II, p. 796.

57. *Alger Républicain,* 27 juillet 1951, 5–6 août 1951.

58. *La République Algérienne,* 28 septembre 1951.

59. See Article 3 of its founding charter; see also *Al Shihab,* mars 1931, p. 197.

60. See Chapter I; see also Ali Merad, *Le réformisme musulman en Algérie de 1925 à 1940* (Paris: Mouton, 1967).

61. Benedict Anderson, *Imagined Communities,* especially Chapter 8.

62. *L'Entente,* 23 février 1936.

63. *Al Shihab,* avril-juin 1936.

64. Anderson, *Imagined Communities,* Chapter 3.

65. *Islah,* 19 septembre 1929.

66. *L'Afrique Française,* 1935, pp. 229–230.

67. Archives d'Outre-Mer, Aix-en-Provence, France (Carton 9 h 14).

68. *Marabout* is a term used in North or West Africa for a Saint. In North and West Africa, *marabouts* can be important actors in spiritual practice. Veneration of saints is discouraged in countries were Wahhabi practice prevails.

69. Merad, *Réformisme musulmane,* pp. 66–67.

70. *Al Shihab,* juin 1936, p. 159.

71. Ageron, *Histoire de l'Algérie contemporaine,* Tome II, p. 335.

72. *Al Bassair,* 14 January 1939.

73. *Al Shihab,* June 1939.

74. See Algerian National Charter, 1976

75. Ageron, *Histoire de l'Algérie contemporaine,* Tome II, pp. 315–318.

76. See their journal *L'Islam,* avril 1911.

77. Taleb Abdessalem, in *Akhbar,* 20 avril 1920.

78. Ferhat Abbas, *Le Jeune Algérien* (Paris: Garnier, 1981), pp. 98–100.

79. *Ikdam,* 23–30 avril 1920.

80. See *Afrique Française,* octobre 1924, pp. 530–531; *l'Humanité,* 3 juillet 1924; *Trait d'Union,* 6 juillet 1924.

81. Emir Khaled, *La situation des Musulmans d'Algérie* (Alger: OPU, 1987), originally published in 1924.

82. *Ikdam,* 7–14 May 1920 and 21–28 May 1920; Emir Khaled, *La situation,* p. 28; See also Julien, *L'Afrique du nord en marche,* p. 250.

83. Cited in Ageron, *Histoire de l'Algérie contemporaine,* Tome II, p. 306.

84. Kaddache, *Histoire du nationalisme algérien,* Tome I, p. 126.

85. Ferhat Abbas, *Le Jeune Algérien,* pp. 92–93.

86. *La Défense*, 3 janvier 1936.

87. See previous section of this chapter.

88. Kaddache, *Histoire du nationalisme algérien*, Tome I, p. 427.

89. See *L'Afrique Française*, 1936, p. 462.

90. The 1936 demands of the Congress of Muslim Algerians regarding separation of church and state, compulsory education for both sexes, and the encouragement of linguistic pluralism in the form of the teaching of Arabic amounted to an agenda that can be called "friendly separation" between church and state. Juan Linz in an unpublished article entitled "The Religious Use of Politics and/or the Political Use of Religion" argued that a critical distinction should be made between the "hostile model" of separation of church and state and "friendly separation." The French Third Republic, which was the colonial power in Algeria, tried to enforce a "hostile model" of separation between church and state in France. The proponents of this model tried to impose a militant form of secularism that was at variance with the goals of the Congress of Muslim Algerians. The Congress, on the other hand, pursued an political agenda of "friendly separation." This agenda envisioned more tolerant policies by the government with regard to religion without creating, however, a privileged or special role for religion in politics. See Juan Linz, "The Religious Use of Politics and/or the Political Use of Religion: Ersatz Ideology versus Ersatz Religion," pp. 7–8.

91. *L'Afrique Française*, 1936, p. 535.

92. Ageron, *Histoire de l'Algérie contemporaine*, Tome II, pp. 463–465; Charles-André Julien, *L'Afrique du nord en marche*, 3rd ed., p. 114.

93. Ageron, *Histoire de l'Algérie contemporaine*, Tome II, pp. 551–552; Julien, *L'Afrique du nord en marche*, pp. 242–243; Kaddache, *Histoire du nationalisme algérien*, Tome II, pp. 609–610.

94. Julien, *L'Afrique du nord en marche*, p. 243.

95. See *The Atlantic Charter*, paragraphs 3 and 4; See also Julien, *L'Afrique du nord en marche*, p. 244.

96. Harbi, *Le FLN: mirage et réalité*, p. 23.

97. Ageron, *Histoire de l'Algérie contemporaine*, Tome II, p. 588; Julien, *L'Afrique du nord en marche*, p. 245; Kaddache, *Histoire du nationalisme algérien*, Tome II, p. 640.

98. See *L'Écho d'Alger*, 13 decembre 1943

99. Harbi, *Le FLN*, p. 27; Kaddache, *Histoire du nationalisme algérien*, Tome II, p. 670.

100. See the second section of this chapter.

101. Ferhat Abbas, *La Nuit Coloniale* (Paris: Julliard, 1962), p. 157.

Endnotes ~ Chapter V

1. "Declaration du comité révolutionnaire d'unité et d'action du 1er novembre 1954," in André Mandouze, *La révolution algérienne par les textes* (Paris: Maspéro, 1961), p. 15.

2. *The Holy Qur'an,* Sura 43, Aya 32 and Sura 16, Aya 71.

3. See discussion of *shura* and *ijma* in Chapter I.

4. See Chapter I.

5. See Labour governments of Britain, Social Democratic governments of Sweden and Norway.

6. E.g., Post-Stalinist Soviet Union, Titoist Yugoslavia, Castroite Cuba.

7. Stalinist Soviet Union.

8. Droz, Bernard and Evelyne Lever, *Histoire de la guerre d'Algérie, 1954–1962* (Paris: Seuil, 1982), p. 60.

9. An interesting contrast can be drawn between the ideological evolution of Algeria's revolutionaries and that of the revolutionaries of France's other large colony at the time: Viet Nam. Why did Viet Nam's revolutionary leadership pursue secularism and why did Algeria's pursue the integration of religion and politics? After all, the founders of both revolutionary movements were colleagues in the Communist Internationale and they both underwent ideological training in Paris in the 1920's. Why these two different results?

   Most importantly, the leaders of Viet Nam's revolution created a political ideology of resistance that was founded upon classical Marxist-Leninist ideas concerning class struggle and the diminution of the role of religion in politics. Although Messali Hadj and Ho Chi Minh were both members of the Communist Internationale and although they both participated in the same Communist sponsored anti-colonial conferences, Messali Hadj did not adopt the Communist Party's policy on the question of religion in politics whereas Ho Chi Minh did. The political leadership of both the *Parti Communiste Indochinois* and the *Viêt-Minh* had very close ties to the Comintern in Moscow because many of their leaders were educated there in the 1920's. As a result of their ideological training in Moscow, the leaders of Viet Nam's revolution espoused traditional Communist Party doctrine. By contrast, by 1926, Messali Hadj had broken with the Communists and he had helped construct a political ideology of resistance that ultimately relied upon religion as a source of inspiration for the mobilization of the masses. The use of religion for political mobilization, which was introduced by Messali Hadj and the Association of the Ulema during the 1920's and 1930's, carried over into FLN politics. For more on Viet Nam, see Jean Chesneaux, "Les fondements historiques du communisme vietnamien," *L'Homme et société,* No. 14 (octobre-décembre 1969):

pp. 83–98; Christine Rageau, "Ho Chi Minh et l'internationale communiste," *Partisans,* No. 48 (juin-août 1969): pp. 44–55; Paul Mus, "Insertion du communisme dans le mouvement nationaliste vietnamien," *Les Temps Modernes,* No. 78 (avril 1952): pp. 1796–1809.

10. See Edgar O'Ballance, *The Algerian Insurrection* (London: Archor Books, 1967); Yves Courrière, *La Guerre d'Algérie,* 4 Vols. (Paris: Fayard, 1968–1971); Alistair Horne, *A Savage War of Peace* (London: Penguin, 1985); Henri Alleg, *Guerre d'Algérie,* 3 Vols. (Paris: Temps Actuels, 1981); Bernard Droz and Evelyne Lever, *Histoire de la Guerre d'Algérie, 1954–1962* (Paris: Seuil, 1982).

11. The problem with this scale is that, depending upon either the political issue or the historical moment in time, some political actors may fit in more than one category.

12. See, intra alia, David C. Gordon, *The Passing of French Algeria* (London: Oxford University Press, 1966), pp. 94–95, 97–98; Peter R. Knauss, *The Persistence of Patriarchy* (New York: Praeger, 1987), p. 92.

13. Mohammed Harbi, Interview by author, 3 September 1994, Paris; Gordon, *The Passing of French Algeria,* pp. 99–106.

14. See William B. Quandt, *Revolution and Political Leadership: Algeria, 1954–1968* (Cambridge, MA: M.I.T. Press, 1969), p. 26.

15. Mohamed Boudiaf, *Où va l'Algérie* (Paris: Librairie d'Étoile, 1964), p. 70; Mohamed Boudiaf, "La preparation de 1er Novembre," *El Jarida;* Slimane Chikh, *L'Algérie en armes* (Alger: OPU, 1981), p. 87.

16. Mohamed Boudiaf, "La preparation de 1er Novembre," Mohammed Harbi, *Le FLN: mirage et réalité* (Paris: Editions Jeune Afrique, 1985), p. 96, 101; Quandt, *Revolution and Political Leadership,* p. 92.

17. The members of this group included Beji Mokhtar, Ahmed Bouchaïd, Outhmane Belouizdad, Ramdane Abdelmalek, Benaouda Ben Mostefa, Mustapha Ben Boulaïd, Larbi Ben M'Hidi, Lakhdar Ben Tobbal, Rabah Bitat, Bouadjadj Zoubir, Said Bouali, Mohamed Boudiaf, Abdlehafid Boussouf, Mourad Didouche, Habachi Abdessalem, Rachid Mellah, Mohamed Merzougui, Mohammed Mechati, Suidani Boudjemaa, Youssef Haddad, Lamoudi Abdelkader, and Youssef Zighout.

18. Harbi, *Le FLN: mirage et réalité,* p. 115; Quandt, *Revolution and Political Leadership,* p. 92.

19. Slimane Chikh, *L'Algérie en armes* (Alger: OPU, 1981), p. 89; Jacques C. Duchemin, *Histoire du FLN* (Paris: La Table Ronde, 1962), p. 41; Quandt, *Revolution and Political Leadership,* p. 93.

20. Henry F. Jackson, *The FLN in Algeria* (Westport, CT: Greenwood Press, 1977), p. 26.

21. Harbi, *Le FLN: mirage et réalité,* p. 133.

22. *Le Monde*, 20 mars 1962.

23. Benjamin Stora, "La guerre FLN/MNA," in *Le drame algérien*, ed. Reporters sans Frontières (Paris: La Découverte, 1994), p. 75.

24. Mohamed Lebjaoui, *Vérités sur la Révolution Algérienne* (Paris: Gallimard, 1970), pp. 112–113.

25. *Plateforme de la Soummam*, Part III.

26. *Plateforme de Soummam*.

27. The seventeen permanent members were Mustapha Ben Boulaïd, Youcef Zighoud, Belkacem Krim, Amar Ouamrane, Larbi Ben M'Hidi, Rabah Bitat, Ramdane Abbane, Ben Youssef Ben Khedda, Aïssat Idir, Mohammed Boudiaf, Hocine Aït Ahmed, Mohammed Khider, Ahmed Ben Bella, Mohammed Lamine, Ferhat Abbas, Tawfiq al-Madani, and M'Hamed Yazid. The seventeen deputies included Lakhdar Ben Tobbal, Saïd Mohammedi, Slimène Dehiles, Abdelhafid Boussouf, Ali Mellah, Benyahia, Mohammed Ledjaoui, Abdelmalek Temam, Saad Dahlab, Salah Louanchi, Tayeb Thalbi, Abdelhamid Mehri, Ahmed Francis, and Brahim Mezhoudi.

28. *Plateforme de la Soummam*, Part III.

29. Harbi, *Le FLN: mirage et réalité*, p. 184.

30. Resistance movements whose leadership is divided between "interior" and "exterior" leaders frequently fracture. Yossi Shain said, "The insiders and outsiders soon [grow] apart, developing into factions with incompatible interests." See Yossi Shain, *The Frontiers of Loyalty: Political Exiles in the Age of the Nation-State* (Middletown, CT: Wesleyan University Press, 1989), p. 82. Shain cited Spain (where divisions were rife among anti-Franco Communist exiles), Germany (where insider-outsider conflicts weakened the anti-Nazi Social Democratic Party), Venezuela (where insiders challenged outsiders within the anti-Pérez Jiménez *Acción Democrática*), Chile (where the Communist party again split between insiders and outsiders), and the Phillippines (where splits between insiders and outsiders were manifested within the anti-Marcos movement) as examples of insider/outsider schisms. Splits often manifest themselves because "the insider world [is] dominated by the exigencies of practical political struggle, and the outside world of abstract political designs . . ." See Shain, p. 83.

31. See Ferhat Abbas, *L'autopsie d'une guerre* (Paris; Garnier Frères, 1980), pp. 210-212.

32. Present at this conference were Abbane, Abbas, Amara, Benaouda, Ben Khedda, Benyahia, Boumedienne, Boussouf, Dahlab, Dhiles, Ben Tobbal, Francis, Krim, Lamouri, Mezhoudi, Ouamrane, Taalbi, al-Madani, Yazid, Lamine, Mehri, and Chérif.

33. These five men were imprisoned in France after their airplane, which was on a flight from Rabat to Tunis, was intercepted on 22 October 1956 by the French air force and forced to land in Algiers.

34. Mohammed Harbi, Interview by author, 3 September 1994, Paris; Mohammed Harbi, *Le FLN: mirage et réalité*, p. 187.

35. See Ferhat Abbas, *L'autopsie d'une guerre*, p. 228; Yves Courrière, *L'heure des colonels* (Paris: Fayard, 1970); Mohammed Lebjaoui, *Vérités sur la révolution algérienne*, pp. 156–158; Ahmed Rouadjia, *Grandeur et décadence de l'état algérien* (Paris: Karthala, 1994), p. 38.

36. Ben Youssef Ben Khedda, "Contribution à l'historique du FLN," in *Les archives de la révolution algérienne*, ed. Mohammed Harbi (Paris: Jeune Afrique, 1981), pp. 312–321.

37. Jean La Couture, *De Gaulle: The Leader, 1945–1970* (New York, NY: Norton, 1992), pp. 164–185; Bernard Ledwidge, *De Gaulle* (London: Weidenfeld and Nicholson, 1982), pp. 228–237.

38. *El Moudjahid*, 19 séptembre 1958.

39. Mohammed Harbi, Interview with author, 3 September 1994, Paris; Mohammed Harbi, *Le FLN: mirage et réalité*, p. 223.

40. See Chikh, *L'Algérie en armes*, p. 116.

41. Quandt, *Revolution and Political Leadership*, p. 140.

42. See "Mémoire de l'État-Major Général de l'ALN à Monsieur le Président du Gouvernement Provisoire de la Republique Algérienne," dated 15 July 1961, signed by Colonel Boumedienne, Commandant Mendjeli, Commandant Azzedine, and Commandant Slimane, in Harbi, *Les archives de la révolution algérienne*, pp. 322–332; Jackson, *The FLN in Algeria*, p. 52.

43. Political struggles within liberation movements do not ineluctably lead to the assertion of political authority by military leaders. Two notable examples of submission of armed military groups to civilian authorities include post-World War II France and Italy. See Jean Lacouture, *Charles de Gaulle, Vol. I* (Paris: Seuil, 1984), pp. 569–592, 701–731, 736 (wherein Jean Moulin as left-wing leader of the French Resistance Movement and the *Front de libération nationale* urged his followers in the Communist Party to submit to the civilian leadership of the French Republic led by General Charles De Gaulle) and Charles F. Delzell, *Mussolini's Enemies* (Princeton, NJ: Princeton University Press, 1961), pp. 343–344 (wherein two armed left-wing parties, the Italian Communist Party and the Italian Socialist Party of Proletarian Unity, echew continued armed resistance and participate in the post-Mussolini civilian government led by Marshal Pietro Badoglio). See also Donald Sassoon, *The Strategy of the Italian Communist Party* (New York, NY: St Martin's Press, 1981), pp. 41–58.

44. Harbi, *Le FLN: mirage et réalité*, p. 283.

45. Ibid., p. 288.

46. Ibid., p. 289.

47. Mohammed Harbi, Interview by author, 3 September 1994, Paris; *Jeune Afrique*, 13 juillet 1964; Chikh, *L'Algérie en armes*, p. 397; Harbi, *Le FLN: mirage et réalité*, p. 296; Arslan Humbaraci, *Algeria: The Revolution that Failed* (New York, NY: Frederick A. Praeger, 1966), p. 225; Jackson, *The FLN in Algeria*, p. 57.

48. Ben Youssef Ben Khedda, "Contribution à l'historique du FLN," April 1964, in Harbi, *Les archives de la révolution algérienne*, pp. 322–332.

49. Harbi, *Le FLN, mirage et realité*, pp. 342-343.

50. "Programme de Front de la libération nationale adopté à Tripoli par le CNRA en juin 1962," in *Annuaire de l'Afrique du Nord, 1962* (Paris: CNRA, 1972), pp. 683–694.

51. Mohammed Harbi, Interview by author, 3 September 1994, Paris.

52. *Programme de Tripoli.*

53. Ibid.

54. The reliance upon the peasantry for leadership was a cardinal principle of the FLN. This principle was promoted forcefully within the FLN by Frantz Fanon, the psychiatrist and ideologist from Martinique, who served as doctor, diplomat, and political theorist for the FLN. Fanon's most influential works in the Algerian revolution were *Les damnés de la terre* (Paris: Maspero, 1982) and *Sociologie d'une révolution* (Paris: Maspero, 1982).

55. Mohammed Harbi in an interview with the author in September 1994 revealed that Ben Yahyia, Harbi, Lacheraf and Malek had written the entire text of the Tripoli Program without significant references to Islam. They then submitted the text to Ben Bella who in his capacity as chairman of the drafting committee demanded insertions recognizing and elevating the role of Islam within the FLN's ideological program.

56. See *El Moudjahid*, no. 4.

57. Harbi, *Le FLN, mirage et réalité*, pp. 333–334.

58. See Appendix I that describes the educational backgrounds of FLN political leaders.

59. *Le Monde*, 3 juillet 1962.

60. Chikh, *L'Algérie en armes*, p. 402.

61. See "Proclamation du Bureau Politique du Front de Liberation Nationale Algérienne," dated 22 juillet 1962, at Tlemcen, Algeria, in Harbi, *Les archives de la révolution algérienne*, pp. 350– 352.

62. See *Le Monde,* 8–9 juillet 1962.

63. *Le Monde,* 14 septembre 1962, 15 septembre 1962.

64. The Algerian Communist Party was suppressed for two reasons: first, Ben Bella did not believe he could assert control or discipline over the organization; second, by rendering the Communist Party illegal Ben Bella was able to appease his critics from the religious community who were calling for the abolition of the Communist Party. From interview with Mohammed Harbi by author, 3 September 1994, Paris.

65. *La Charte d'Alger,* 1964, Part III.

66. *El Moudjahid,* 6 novembre 1962, 23 avril 1964, 27 avril 1964.

67. Rouadjia, *Grandeur et décadence de l'état algérien,* p. 143.

68. Immanuel Wallerstein, "The Decline of the Party in Single Party African States," in *Political Parties and Political Development,* ed. Joseph La Palombara and Myron Wiener (Princeton, NJ: Princeton University Press, 1963).

69. See, for example, Gwendolyn M. Carter, ed., *African One-Party States* (Ithaca, NY: Cornell University Press, 1962).

70. Chikh, *L'Algérie en armes,* p. 393.

71. Lakhdar Bentobbal, *Conférence aux cadres du FLN,* 14 mars 1960, in Harbi, *Les archives de la révolution algérienne,* p. 296.

72. Kaïd Ahmed, *Rapport aux membres de CNRA,* 10 April 1962.

73. "20 decembre 1962 Accord FLN-UGTA," in *Annuaire de l'Afrique du Nord, 1962* (Paris: CNRS, 1972), p. 740.

74. Lakhdar Bentobbal, *Conférence aux cadres du FLN,* 5 février 1960, in Harbi, *Les archives de la révolution algérienne,* p. 283.

75. Ibid.

76. Mohammed Harbi, Interview by author, 3 September 1994, Paris; Gérard Chaliand, *L'Algérie: est-elle socialiste?* (Paris; Maspero, 1964), p.26.

77. Robert B. Revere, "Consensus in Algeria, 1962–1965" (Ph. D. diss., New York University, 1970), p. 166.

78. Peter K. Knauss, *The Persistence of Patriarchy* (New York: Praeger, 1984), p. 102.

79. *al-Ma'rifa,* Vol. 1. Al-Madani quoted from Sura 9: "Those who accumulate wealth and do not spend it in the way of God are to be warned of a painful torture."

80. *Al-Sha'b,* 24 May 1964; See als, Raymond Vallin, "Muslim Socialism in Algeria," in I. William Zartman, ed., *Man, State and Society in the Contemporary Maghreb* (New York: Praeger, 1973), pp. 52–54.

81. *Le Monde,* 12 July 1963.

82. Mostefa Lacheraf, "L'Avenir de la culture algérienne," *Les Temps Modernes* 209 (octobre 1963), pp. 720–745.

83. See *Révolution Africaine* (14 décembre 1963), pp. 22–23; *Révolution Africaine* (11 janvier 1964), pp. 22–23.

84. *Révolution Africaine* (28 décembre 1963), pp. 16–20; *Révolution Africaine* (4 janvier 1964), pp. 18–19.

85. *Révolution Africaine* was the FLN's principal ideological journal.

86. In 1989 Algeria enacted a new constitution that dropped socialism as one of its goals.

87. *Révolution Africaine*, 12 september 1964, p.4.

88. Ibid., p. 5.

89. La Charte d'Alger 1964, Chapter 3, Front de libération nationale.

Endnotes ~ Chapter VI

1. Houari Boumedienne, "Aux officiers de l'Académie Militaire Interarmes de Cherchell," in *Discours du Président Boumediene, 19 juin 1965–19 juin 1970* (Constantine: El-Baath, 1970), pp. 29–30.

2. Houari Boumedienne, "Réunion des cadres de l'est Algérien (Constantine)," (6 mars 1966), in *Discours du Président Boumediene, 19 juin 1965–19 juin 1970* (Constantine: El-Baath, 1970), p. 163.

3. Houari Boumedienne, "Aux officiers de l'Académie Militaire Interarmes de Cherchell," in *Discours du Président Boumediene, 19 juin 1965–19 juin 1970* (Constantine: El-Baath, 1970), pp.29–30; Houari Boumedienne, "1er anniversaire du 19 juin, Alger" (19 juin 1966), in *Discours du Président Boumediene, 19 juin 1965–19 juin 1970* (Constantine: El-Baath, 1970), pp. 275–276, 284.

4. Houari Boumedienne, "Proclamation du Conseil de la Révolution, 19 juin 1965," in *Discours du Président Boumédiène, 19 juin 1965–19 juin 1970, Tome I.* (Constantine: El-Baath, 1970), p. 7.

5. Houari Boumedienne, " Discours fait aux officiers de l'Académie Militaire Interarmes de Cherchell," (10 juillet 1965), ibid., p. 30; Houari Boumedienne, "IIIme anniversaire du 19 juin," (19 juin 1968) in *Discours du Président Boumediene, Tome II,* p. 105.

6. *Al-Ahram,* 8 October 1965.

7. Raptis was an elected leader of the Fourth Communist Internationale.

8. Their ideas for autogestion or self-management evolved from Leon Trotsky's

History of the Russian Revolution (New York, NY: Anchor Found, 1980) and *Results and Prospects* and Rosa Luxembourg's *Accumulation of Capital* (Ann Arbor, MI: Books on Demand, n.d.).

9. Michel Raptis, *Socialism, Democracy, and Self-Management,* trans. Marie-Jo Serrié and Richard Sissons (London: Allison & Busby, 1980), p. 76.

10. John R. Nellis, "Social Management in Algeria," *Journal of Modern African Studies* 15 (December 1977): p. 530.

11. Arslan Humbaraci, *Algeria: A Revolution that Failed* (New York: Praeger, 1964), p. 23.

12. For a historical description and critique of the FLN's Pan-African foreign policy see Guy Pervillé, "Le panafricanisme du FLN algérien," *L'Afrique noire française: l'heure des Indépendances* (Paris:CNRS, 1992), pp. 513–522.

13. Humbaraci, Algeria: *The Revolution that Failed,* p. 228; Juliette Minces, *L'Algérie de Boumedienne* (Paris: Presses de la Cité, 1968), p. 38.

14. Ania Francos and J. P. Séréni, *Un algérien nommé Boumediène* (Paris: Stock, 1976), pp. 39–40.

15. Slimane Chikh, *L'Algérie en armes* (Alger: OPU, 1981), p. 393.

16. Frantz Fanon, *A Dying Colonialism* (New York: Grove Press, 1967); Frantz Fanon, *The Wretched of the Earth* (New York: Grove Press, 1968); in French, *Sociologie d'une revolution* (Paris: Maspero, 1982) and *Les damnés de la terre* (Paris: Maspero, 1982).

17. See Nguyen Nghe, "Frantz Fanon et les problèmes de l'indépendance," *La Pensée,* No. 107 (février 1963), pp. 23–36.

18. See Frantz Fanon, "Algeria's European Minority," in *A Dying Colonialism;* See also, by Fanon, "Appel de la fédération de France du FLN," in *El Moudjahid,* Vol. 2, No. 59 (5 February 1960); Fanon, "Les accords franco-algériens, in *El Moudjahid,* Vol. 3, No. 90 (9 March 1962).

19. See Ayatollah Ruhollah Khomeini, *Kashf al-asrar,* 1941; Ayatollah Ruhollah Khomeini, *Al-Hukuma al-Islamiyya;* Ayatollah Ruhollah Khomeini, *Islamic Government,* trans. Joint Publications Research Service (New York: Manor Books, 1979).

20. See Chapter I; *The Holy Qur'an,* 3:151.

21. Al-Asala, No. 65–66, January-February 1979, pp. 59–67.

22. Décret no. 64–332 du 8 décembre 1964, *Journal officiel de la république algérienne,* 8 décembre 1964, no. 100.

23. See Raymond Vallin, "Muslim Socialism in Algeria," in *Man, State, and Society in the Contemporary Maghrib,* ed. I. William Zartman (New York: Praeger, 1973), pp. 60–61.

24. Décret no. 66–45 du 18 février 1966, *Journal officiel de la république algérienne,* 22 février 1966, no. 15.

25. *Discours du Président Boumédiène, 19 juin 1965–19 juin 1970,* vol. 2, p. 111.

26. See Gérard Destanne de Bernis, *L'Afrique de l'indépendance politique à l'indépendance economique* (Paris: Maspero, 1975); Gérard Destanne de Bernis, "Deux strategies pour l'industrialisation du Tiers Monde. Les industries industrialisantes et les options algériennes." *Revue Tiers Monde* Vol. XII, No. 47 (juillet-septembre 1969): pp. 545–563.

27. Jacques Schnetzler, *Le développement en Algérie* (Paris: Masson, 1981).

28. Mahfoud Bennoune, "The Industrialization of Algeria: An Overview," in *Contemporary North Africa,* ed. Halim Barakat (London: Croom Helm, 1985), p. 243.

29. Bennoune, "The Industrialization of Algeria," p. 186.

30. Mohamed Dahmani, *L'Algérie: légitimité historique et continuité politique* (Paris: Le Sycomore, 1979), p. 179.

31. Driss Dadsi and Lazhari Doukali, *L'Algérie: les années de tous les dangers* (Paris: Présence Africaine, 1994), p. 44; Richard Lawless, "Algeria: The Contradictions of Rapid Industrialization," in *North Africa,* ed. by Richard Lawless and Allan Findlay (London: Croom Helm, 1984), p. 166.

32. Dadsi and Doukali, *L'Algérie: les années de tous les dangers,* p. 44.

33. Smaïl Goumeziane, *Le mal algérien* (Paris: Fayard, 1994), p. 63.

34. Abdellatif Benachenhou, *L' experience algérienne de planification et développement, 1962–1980* (Alger: OPU, 1983), p. 221.

35. Tahar Benhouria, *L'economie d'Algérie* (Paris: Maspero, 1980), p. 363.

36. Boumedienne, *Discours du Président Boumèdiéne, 2 juillet 1973–3 décembre 1974,* Vol. V (Constantine: Ministère de l'information et culture, 1975), p. 144.

37. See Chapter V.

38. *La Charte d'Alger 1964,* Front de libération nationale, p. 107.

39. Ibid., p. 118.

40. Hervé Bourges, *L'Algérie à l'épreuve du pouvoir* (Paris: Éditions Bernard Grasset, 1967), pp. 93–98; P. J. Vatikiotis, "Tradition and Political Leadership: The Case of Algeria," in *Man, State, and Society in the Contemporary Maghreb,* ed. I. William Zartman (New York: Praeger, 1973), pp. 319-320.

41. *La Charte d'Alger 1964,* p. 118.

42. Marnia Lazreg, *The Emergence of Classes in Algeria* (Boulder, CO: Westview

Press, 1976), p. 120; See Franz Schurmann, *Ideology and Organization in Communist China* (Berkeley, CA: University of California Press, 1973).

43. See Chaper V.

44. *Discours du Président Boumédiène, 19 juin 1965–19 juin 1970,* Vol.2, p. 115.

45. See Tariq Maschino and Fadéla M'Rabet, *L'Algérie des Illusions* (Paris: Robert Laffont, 1972), pp. 171–177.

46. *Discours du Président Boumédiène, 19 juin 1965–19 juin 1970,* Vol. I, pp. 88, 99.

47. For a discussion of the role of the Algerian War in the construction of the FLN's unstable political legitimacy see I. William Zartman, "The Algerian Army in Politics," in *Man, State, and Society in the Contemporary Maghreb,* ed. I. William Zartman (New York: Praeger, 1973), pp. 211–224.

48. Mazdak was a 6th century A.D. priest in Persia who became the leader of a religious group within Zoroastrianism. He preached the holding of women and property in common, and advocated Dualism, a system of belief that is ambivalent on the questions of good and evil. Similarities exist between Mazdaquism and Manicheism.

49. For the origins of *al-Qiyam* see Chapter V.

50. The 1976 Constitution was written principally by Mohamed Bedjaoui, a lawyer who was also Algeria's Ambassador to France. He was assisted in his work by Mohamed Ben Ahmed (aka Abdelghani), Belaïd Abdessalem, Ahmed Ben Cherif, Abdelkrim Benmahmoud, Mohammed Seddik Benyahia, Abdelaziz Bouteflika, and Ahmed Taleb Ibrahimi. The Constitution was approved by referendum on 20 November 1976. In that election there were 7,708,954 registered voters and 7,163,007 voters actually voted. Those voting in favor of the constitution amounted to 7,080,904. 57,922 persons voted against its approval. The approval rate was 99.18%. (Source: *Le Monde,* 21 novembre 1976).

One month later, on 10 December, Houari Boumedienne was "elected" as President of the Algerian republic in another referendum. He received more than 99% of the vote. (Source: *Le Monde,* 12–13 decembre 1976).

51. *La Charte Nationale 1979,* p. 23.

52. The principal political antagonists in the "Arabization" debate were Mostefa Lacheraf who proposed gradual Arabization and Abdelhamid Mehri who supported rapid Arabization.

53. Abdallah Mazouni, *Culture et enseignement en Algérie et au Maghreb* (Paris: Maspero, 1969), p. 55.

54. Ibid., p. 55.

55. See Paul Balta and Claudine Rulleau, *L'Algérie des Algériens: vingt ans après* (Paris: Ouvrières: 1981), pp. 175–176.

56. See Chapter VII.

57. David and Marina Ottaway, *Algeria: The Politics of a Socialist Revolution* (Berkeley, CA: University of California Press, 1970), p. 5.

58. Hocine Aït Ahmed, *La guerre et l'après-guerre* (Paris: Minuit, 1964), p. 152.

Endnotes – Chapter VII

1. See *Le Monde Diplomatique,* octobre 1986 and novembre 1988.

2. Ben Jadid obtained 94.2% of the vote. (7,434,118 of a total of 7,470,728 voters voted in favor of his candidacy.) In this election, 5.3% of the electorate (418,147 voters of 7,888,875 who were registered) did not participate. See *Le Monde,* 10 février 1979, p. 3.

3. In 1992, 98% of Algeria's hard currency revenues were derived from hydrocarbons.

4. Abdelkader Djeghloul, "Le défi de la crise," in *Le Monde Diplomatique,* novembre 1986, p. 31.

5. *Collections statistiques no. 36: situation d'emploi 1990* (Alger: ONS, 1992); *Parcours Maghrebins,* 25 novembre-1 décembre 1986, p. 31.

6. Driss Dadsi and Lazhari Doukali, *Algérie: les années de tous les dangers* (Paris: Présence Africaine, 1994), p. 101; Abderrahim Lamchichi, *L'Islamisme en Algérie* (Paris: L'Harmattan,1992), p. 49.

7. See Chapter VI.

8. *Démographie algérienne 1989* (Alger: ONS, 2e trim., 1989), p. 2; *Al-Moudjahid,* 20 février 1990, p. 7.

9. Dadsi and Doukali, *Algérie, les années de tous les dangers,* p. 101; Lamchichi, *L'islamisme en Algérie,* p. 49; Fawzi Rouzeik, "Algérie, 1990–1993: la democratie confisquée," in *L'Algérie incertaine,* ed. Pierre Robert Baduel (Aix-en-Provence: CNRS/IREMAM, 1994), p. 35.

10. *Statuts du parti du FLN,* Articles 7 and 8. (Alger: Ben Boulaïd, 1980).

11. *Jeune Afrique,* No. 963, 20 juin 1979, p. 28; *Jeune Afrique,* No. 1002, 28 juin 1980, pp. 44–45; *Jeune Afrique,* No. 1366, pp. 38–39.

12. *Jeune Afrique,* No. 1137, 20 octobre 1982, p. 30; *Jeune Afrique,* No. 1217, 2 mai 1984, pp. 38–39.

13. Presidential decree of 20 November 1980.

14. Loi 81–01 du 7 février 1981 and loi 86–03 du février 1986.

15. Loi 83–18 du 13 août 1983 and loi 87–19 du novembre 1987.

16. The inflation rate for 1988 was 6%. For 1989 it was 18%. In 1990 it jumped to 23.3% then to 30% in 1991 and to 32% in 1992.

17. Anwar Haddam, FIS representative to the United States, Interview by author, 1 June 1994, Washington,DC.

18. Malek Bennabi, *Vocation d'Islam* (Paris: Seuil, 1954).

19. Haddam interview, 1 June 1994.

20. *The New York Times,* 8 October 1991.

21. *Le Monde,* 16 juin 1990, p. 3.

22. See interview with Saudi Minister of Defense Prince Sultan Ibn Abd al-Aziz in *Al-Sharq al-Awsat* (London), 26 March 1991.

23. *Jeune Afrique,* No. 1008, 30 avril 1980, p.22.

24. Amnesty International Report, 1982; *Jeune Afrique,* No. 1008, 30 avril 1980, p.22.

25. See Hélène Vandevelde, "Où en est le problème du code de la famille en Algérie," *Maghreb-Machrek* (juillet-septembre 1982): pp. 39–54; Hélène Vandevelde, "Le Code algérien de la famille," 107 *Maghreb-Machrek* (janvier-mars 1985): p. 52–64.

26. *Code de la famille, 1984* (Alger: OPU, 1985): Article 222. .

27. Article 8.

28. Article 31.

29. Article 11; Articles 87–98.

30. 1976 Constitution, Article 42: This constitution guarantees all political, economic, social, and cultural rights to the Algerian woman.

31. Article 53: A woman could obtain a divorce for: (a) financial non-support; (b) certain illnesses; (c) imprisonment of the husband; (d) abandonment for a year; (e) failure of the husband to allow visits by her family; (f) failure of the husband to engage in sexual intercourse for more than four months; or (g) "grave moral impediments" on the part of the husband.

32. *Jeune Afrique,* No. 1158, 16 mars 1983, p.29; *Jeune Afrique,* No. 1296, 6 novembre 1985, pp.38–39; *Jeune Afrique,* No. 1301, 11 decembre 1985, pp. 49–53.

33. Sheikh Abdellatif Soltani was born on 8 June 1902 in al-Qantra in the département of Aurès. He was well respected within the Islamist movement both because of his educational training (at Tunisia's mosque-university of al-Zitouna) and because he wrote the first religiously based critique of the Boumedienne government (*Al-mazdaqiyya hiya al-asl al-ishtirakiyya* or "Mazdaquism is the basis of Socialism"). He was an associate of Sheikh Ben Badis (the founder of the Association of the Ulema) and he joined that organization in 1931.

Sheikh Ahmed Sahnoun was born in 1908. Although less prominent than Soltani, he also was well respected. He was also a member of the Association of the Ulema and he was a student of Sheikhs Ben Badis and Uqbi.

34. Mustapha al-Ahnaf, Bernard Botiveau, and Franck Frégosi, *L'Algérie par ses islamistes* (Paris: Karthala, 1991), pp. 47–48.

35. Karim Chergui, "La révolte des jeunes à Constantine," *Hérodote,* Vol. 45 (avril-juin 1987): p. 65; *Jeune Afrique,* No.1351, 26 novembre 1986, pp. 47–49.

36. See Abed Charif, *Octobre* (Alger: Laphomic, 1990); *Le Monde,* 8 octobre 1988, 13 octobre 1988, 15 octobre 1988, 20 octobre 1988, 24 octobre 1988, 25 octobre 1988; *Le Monde Diplomatique,* novembre 1988.

37. See *Le Monde,* 13 and 15 octobre 1988.

38. See Article 1 of 1989 Constitution that stated that Algeria was a "Democratic and Popular Republic" and contrast with Article 1 of the 1976 Constitution that clearly stated that the Algerian state was "socialist."

39. In this referendum, 83.1% of eligible voters actually voted. From this group 92.3% voted in favor of constitutional reform.

40. The constitution was approved by 74.3% of those voting. The number of voters participating in the election (12,961,628) was disappointingly low (78.8% of the electorate). Voter participation dropped 10 points from the December 1988 Presidential election (88.9% voter participation) and 5 points from the November 1988 referendum (83.1% voter participation).

41. In this election, 88.9% of Algerian voters went to the polls. Ben Jadid received 81.2% of the vote in this one-candidate presidential election. This result should be compared with Boumedienne's "election" of 1979 when he received over 99% of the vote.

42. Daniel V. Friedheim, *The Collapse of East Germany,* forthcoming.

43. Sheikh Mafoud Nahnah was born in 1938 at Blida. He was a scholar and a professor of Arabic at the University of Algiers. In 1976 he prominently opposed President Boumedienne's efforts to delete references to Islam in the National Charter. Because of efforts led by Nahnah, Boumedienne reversed himself. In 1988 he formed the group *al-irshad wa'l islah* (Guidance and Reform). In 1990 he changed the name of his group to HAMAS.

44. Sheikh Abbasi Madani was born in Sidi Okba (near Biskra) in 1931. He was a professor of education at the University of Algiers who obtained his license in philosophy from the University of Algiers and his doctorate in education from the University of London. In 1954 he joined the FLN. He then quit that organization in 1966 to join the Muslim dissident organization, *al-Qiyam.*

Imam Ali Belhadj was born in Tunis in 1956 to an Algerian family that had emigrated there during the *Guerre d'Algérie.* He was not a graduate of a renowned center of Muslim education but he did study with Sheikhs Soltani and Sahnoun. He was close to Mustapha Bouyali who formed the armed Islamic group, the *Mouvement Islamiste Algérien* during the 1970's. During the 1980's he was the *imam* at both the Bab al-Oued mosque and the Ben Badis mosque in Algiers.

45. See *Tribune d'Octobre,* 16 janvier 1990. See also, Al-Ahnaf, Botiveau, and Frégosi, *L'Algérie par ses islamistes,* pp. 115–117.

46. *El Watan,* 20 June 1991.

47. Algeria's HAMAS should not be confused with the HAMAS of Palestine which is a separate organization.

48. See *Jeune Afrique,* No. 1539, 27 juin au 3 juillet 1980, p. 18.

49. Guillermo O'Donnell and Phillipe C. Schmitter, *Transitions from Authoritarian Rule,* (Baltimore, MD: Johns Hopkins University Press, 1986), p. 41.

50. *Le Monde,* 28 mai 1991, p. 6. Juan Linz and Alfred Stepan have argued that the sequence of elections in the transition to democracy is critical. They claim that national elections should precede regional elections in the transition. They posit that the holding of regional elections first encourages and exaggerates the articulation of local grievances against the *ancien régime* while inhibiting the formation of nation-wide party systems and a nation-wide political agenda. See Juan J. Linz and Alfred Stepan, *Problems of Democratic Transition and Consolidation,* Chapter 6, forthcoming.

51. *Le Monde,* 29 mai 1991, p. 3.

52. Article 86 of the 1989 Constitution permits a state of siege in cases of "extreme emergency."

53. Rouzeik, "Algérie 1990–1993, la démocratie confisquée." p. 41.

54. "Algeria: Deteriorating Human Rights under the State of Emergency," (London: Amnesty International, March 1993); Human Rights Watch, *World Report 1992* (New York, NY: Human Rights Watch), p. 289–296.

55. See interview by Reuters with General Mustapha Chelloufi, Secretary General of the Ministry of Defense, on 1 February 1990, that appears in *Algérie-Actualité,* 15 March 1990, and September 1990 interview with General Khaled Nezzar in *El Moudjahid* as reported in *Le Monde,* 12 September 1990.

56. See Loi No. 91–06 du 3 avril 1991.

57. For a discussion of the advantages of proportional representation, see Seymour Martin Lipset and Stein Rokkan, *Party Systems and Voter Alignments* (New York, NY: Free Press, 1967).

58. Rouzeik, "Algérie 1990–1993: la démocratie confisquée," p. 45. Of 13.2 million eligible voters, 7.8 million actually voted, representing a partici- pation rate of 59%. 5.4 million voters did not vote.

59. *Le Monde,* 2 janvier 1992, p.4.

60. *Le Monde,* 7 janvier 1992, p. 4.

61. For theoretical and empirical analyses of transitions to democracy see Juan J. Linz and Alfred Stepan, *Problems of Democratic Transition and Consoli- dation: Theoretical Perspectives* (Baltimore, MD: Johns Hopkins Univer- sity Press, forthcoming); Guillermo O'Donnell and Phillipe C. Schmit- ter, *Transitions from Authoritarian Rule: Tentative Conclusions About Uncertain Democracies* (Baltimore, MD: Johns Hopkins University Press, 1986); Adam Prezeworski, *Democracy and the Market: Political and Eco- nomic Reforms in Eastern Europe and Latin America* (New York, NY: Cam- bridge University Press, 1991); Giusseppe Di Palma, *To Craft Democra- cies: An Essay on Democratic Transitions* (Berkeley, CA: University of Cal- ifornia Press, 1990).

62. Abassi Madani, *azmat al-fikr al-hadith wa mubarrirat al-hall al-islami* (Alger: Ameziane, 1989).

63. *Algérie-Actualité,* 4 janvier 1990.

64. *Le Monde,* 20 juin 1991; *Algérie-Actualité,* 20 juin 1991.

65. The reader should note that the position taken by Belhadj on the question of positive law is a minority position within the ideological community of political Islam. The University of Al-Azhar has determined that posi- tive law is justifiable as long as it conforms with the Qur'an and Islamic principles.

66. Literally, pre-Islamic society. In Islamic political discourse, as defined by Sayyid Qutb in *Ma'alim fi-l tariq,* "impure" or "irreligious" society.

67. *Libération,* 1 juillet 1992; *Le Monde,* 17 juin 1990 and 11 juin 1991.

68. *Algérie-Actualité,* 4 juin 1990; *El Mounquid,* No. 23.

69. *El Mounquid,* No. 9.

70. Interview with Mahfoud Nahnah, *Révolution Africaine,* 10 avril 1991.

71. Al-Ahnaf, Boitiveau, and Fregosi, *L'Algérie par ses Islamistes,* p. 94.

72. The FIS' imprecision on constitutional matters can be contrasted with the precision of the Iranian Revolution's ideologists. Note especially the dis- cussion and analysis of the positions taken by Bazargan, Shariati,and Khomeini in H. E. Chehabi, *Iranian Politics and Religious Modernism* (Ithaca, NY: Cornell University Press, 1990), pp. 54–85, 214–220.

73. See especially the seminal work by Sayyid Qutb, *Maalim fi-l tariq* (Cairo: Dar al-shuruq).

Endnotes ~ Chapter VIII

1. *The Holy Qur'an,* Sura 112.
2. Charles Liebman and Eliezer Don-Yehiya, *Religion and Politics in Israel* (Bloomington, IN: Indiana University Press, 1984), p. 17.
3. See analysis of John Mill in *On Liberty.*

Bibliography

Books

Abbas, Ferhat. *L'autopsie d'une guerre*. Paris: Garnier Frères, 1980.

———. *La Nuit Coloniale*. Paris: Julliard, 1962.

———. *Le Jeune Algérien*. Paris: Garnier Frères, 1981.

Abun-Nasir, Jamil. *A History of the Maghrib in the Islamic Period*. Cambridge: Cambridge University Press.

Abun-Nasir, Jamil. *The Tijaniyya*. London: Oxford University Press, 1965.

Aflaq, Michel. *Fi sabil al-baath*. Baghdad: Dar al-hurriyah, 1986.

Ageron, Charles-Robert. *Histoire de l'Algérie contemporaine*. Tome II. Paris: Presses Universitaires de France, 1968.

———. *Les algériens musulmans et la France, 1871–1919*. Paris: Presses Universitaires de France, 1968.

Aït Ahmed. *La guerre et l'après-guerre*. Paris: Minuit, 1964.

Al-Ahnaf, Mustapha, Bernard Botiveau, and Franck Frégosi. *L'Algérie par ses Islamistes.*Paris: Karthala, 1992.

Al-Banna, Hassan. *Al salam fi al-islam*. Cairo: Dar al-fikr al-islami, 1957.

Al-Farabi, Abu Nasir. *Ara ahl al-madina al-fadila. Al-Farabi on the Perfect State*. Translated by Richard Walzer. Oxford: Oxford University Press, 1985.

Al-Ghazali, Abu Hamid. *Ihya ulum al-din.N.p., N.d.*

Al-Jazairi, Muhammad ibn Abdel Qadir. *Tuhfat al zair fi tarikh al jazair wa'l amir Abd al-Qadir.* Beirut: Dar al yaqadha al arabiyya, 1964.

Al-Mawardi, Ali ibn Muhammad. *Al-ahkam al-sultaniyya.N.p., N.d.*

Al-Mawdudi, Abu al-ala. *Islam: Its Meaning and its Message.* Translated by Khurshid Ahmad. London: Islamic Council of Europe, 1976.

Al-Wahhab, Muhammad bin Abd. *Al-rasa'il.* Part V. Riyadh: University of al-Imam Muhammad bin Saud al-Islamiyya, 1978.

Al-Wahrani, Muslim Ibn Abdul-Qadir. *Anis al-gharib wa'l musafir.* Alger: Rabah Bunar, 1974.

Alleg, Henri. *Guerre d'Algérie.* 3 Volumes. Paris: Temps Actuels, 1981.

Almond, Gabriel and G. Bingham Powell. *Comparative Politics: System, Process and Policy.* Boston, MA: Little, Brown & Co., 1978.

Anderson, Benedict. *Imagined Communities.* London: Verso, 1989.

Annuaire de l'Afrique du Nord, 1962. Paris: CNRA, 1972.

Apter, David. *Politics of Modernization.* Chicago, IL: University of Chicago Press, 1965.

Azan, Paul. *L'émir Abd El Kader, 1808–1883.* Paris: Hachette, 1925.

Baldick, Julian. *Mystical Islam.* London: I. B. Tauris, 1989.

Balta, Pierre and Claudine Rulleau. *L'Algérie des Algériens: vingt ans après.* Paris: Ouvrières, 1981.

Benachenhou, Abdellatif. *Formation du sous-développement de Algérie.* Alger: OPU, 1976.

Benachenhou, Abdellatif. *L'expérience algérienne de planification et de développement.* Alger: OPU, 1983.

Benhouria, Tahar. *L'économie d'Algérie.* Paris: Maspero, 1980.

Bennabi, Malek. *Vocation d'Islam.* Paris: Seuil, 1984.

Bennoune, Mahfoud. *The Making of Contemporary Algeria.* Cambridge: Cambridge University Press, 1988.

Berque, Augustin. *Écrits sur l'Algérie.* Aix-en-Provence: Edisud, 1986.

Berryman, Phillip. *Liberation Theology.* New York, NY: Pantheon, 1987.

Bill, James A. and Robert Springborg. *Politics in the Middle East.* 3rd. ed. San Francisco, CA: HarperCollins, 1990.

Botiveau, Bernard. *Loi islamique et droit dans les sociétés arabes.* Paris: Karthala, 1993.

Boudiaf, Mohamed. *Où va l'Algérie.* Paris: Librairie d'Étoile, 1964.

Boularès, Habib. *Islam: The Fear and the Hope.* Translated by Lewis Ware. London: Zed Books, 1990.

Boumédiène, Houari. *Discours du Président Boumédiène, 19 juin 1965–19 juin 1970.* Vols. I-II. Constantine: Ministère de l'information et de la culture, 1970.

———. *Discours du Président Boumédiène, 2 juillet 1973–3 décembre 1974.* Vol V. Constantine: Ministère de l'information et de la culture, 1975.

Bourges, Hervé. *L'Algérie à l'épreuve du pouvoir.* Paris: Bernard Grasset, 1967.

Boyer, Pierre. *L'évolution de l'Algérie médiane.* Paris: Adrien Maissonneuve, 1960.

Brubaker, Rogers. *Citizenship in France and Germany.* Cambridge, MA: Harvard University Press, 1992.

Bulliet, Richard. *The Patricians of Nishapur.* Cambridge, MA: Harvard University Press, 1972.

Carter, Gwendolyn M. *African One-Party States.* Ithaca, NY: Cornell University Press, 1962.

Chaliand, Gérard. *L'Algérie: est-elle socialiste?* Paris: Maspero, 1964.

Charif, Abed. *Octobre.* Alger: Laphomic, 1990.

Chikh, Slimane. *L'Algérie en armes.* Alger: OPU, 1981.

Churchill, Charles Henry. *La vie d'Abd el Kader.* Translated by Michel Habart. Alger: Entreprise nationale du livre, 1991. (Originally published in English in 1867.)

Coulon, Christian. *Le Marabout et le Prince.* Paris: Pédone, 1981.

Coulson, N. J. *A History of Islamic Law.* Edinburgh: Edinburgh University Press, 1978.

Cour, Auguste. *L'établissement des dynasties des Chérifs au Maroc et leur rivalités avec les turcs de la Régence d'Alger.* Paris: Leroux, 1904.

Courrière, Yves. *La guerre d'Algérie.* 4 Volumes. Paris: Fayard, 1968–1971.

Cruise O'Brien, D. B. *The Mourides of Senegal.* Oxford: Oxford University Press, 1971.

Dadsi, Driss and Lazhari Doukali. *Algérie: les années de tous les dangers.* Paris: Présence Africaine, 1994.

Dahmani, Mohamed. *L'Algérie: légitimité historique et continuité politique.* Paris: Le Sycomore, 1979.

Danziger, Raphael. *Abd al-Qadir and the Algerians.* New York: NY: Holmes & Meier, 1977.

Delzell, Charles F. *Mussolini's Enemies.* Princeton, NJ: Princeton University Press, 1961.

Depont, Octave and Xavier Coppolani. *Les confréries religieuses.* Alger: Adolphe Jourdan, 1897.

Dersa. *L'Algérie en débat.* Paris: Maspero, 1981.

Destanne de Bernis, Gérard. *L'Afrique de l'indépendance politique à l'indépendance économique.* Paris: Maspero, 1975.

Di Palma, Guiseppe. *To Craft Democracies: An Essay on Democratic Transitions.* Berkeley, CA: University of California Press, 1990.

Droz, Bernard and Evelyne Lever. *Histoire de la guerre d'Algérie, 1954–1962.* Paris: Seuil,1982.

Duchemin, Jacques C. *Histoire du FLN.* Paris: La Table Ronde, 1962.

Easton, David. *A Systems Analysis for Political Life.* New York, NY: John Wiley & Sons, 1965.

Emerit, Marcel. *L'Algérie à l'époque d'Abd el-Kader.* Paris: Larose, 1951.

Esposito, John L. *Islam and Politics.* 3rd ed. Syracuse, NY: Syracuse University Press, 1991.

————. *The Islamic Threat: Myth or Reality?* New York, NY: Oxford University Press, 1993.

Esterhazy, Walsin. *De la domination turque dans la régence d'Alger.* Paris: Gosselin, 1840.

Étienne, Bruno. *Algérie, cultures et révolution.* Paris: Seuil, 1977.

Eveno, Patrick. *L'Algérie*. Paris: Le Monde, 1994.

Fanon, Frantz. *A Dying Colonialism*. New York, NY: Grove Press, 1967.

——. *Les damnés de la terre*. Paris: Maspero, 1982.

——. *Sociologie d'une révolution*. Paris: Maspero, 1982.

——. *The Wretched of the Earth*. New York, NY: Grove Press, 1968.

Formestraux, E. *L'instruction publique en Algérie (1830–1880)*. Alger: 1880.

Francos, Ania and J. P. Séréni. *Un Algérien nommé Boumediène*. Paris: Stock, 1976.

Friedheim, Daniel V. *The Collapse of East Germany*. Forthcoming.

Geertz, Clifford. *Islam Observed*. New Haven, CT: Yale University Press, 1965.

Goldschmidt, Jr., Arthur. *A Concise History of the Middle East*. Boulder, CO: Westview Press, 1991.

Gordon, David C. *The Passing of French Algeria*. London: Oxford University Press, 1966.

Goumeziane, Smaïl. *Le mal algérien*. Paris: Fayard, 1994.

Gurr, Ted. *Why Men Rebel*. Princeton, NJ: Princeton University Press, 1970.

Harbi, Mohammed. *Le FLN: mirage et réalité*. Paris: Jeune Afrique, 1985.

Harbi, Mohammed. *Les archives de la révolution algérienne*. Paris: Jeune Afrique, 1981.

Hirschman, Albert O. *Exit, Voice, and Loyalty*. Cambridge, MA; Harvard University Press, 1970.

Hourani, Albert. *Arabic Thought in the Liberal Age, 1798–1939*. Cambridge: Cambridge University Press, 1983.

Horne, Alistair. *A Savage War of Peace*. London: Penguin, 1985.

Hudson, Michael. *Arab Politics: The Search for Legitimacy*. New Haven, CT; Yale University Press, 1977.

Humbaraci, Arslan. *Algeria: A Revolution that Failed*. New York, NY: Praeger, 1964.

Huntington, Samuel. *Political Order in Changing Societies.* New Haven, CT: Yale University Press, 1968.

Human Rights Watch. *World Report 1992.* Human Rights Watch.

Iqbal, Muhammad. *The Reconstruction of Religious Thought in Islam.* London: Oxford University Press, 1934.

Jackson, Henry F. *The FLN in Algeria.* Westport, CT: Greenwood Press, 1977.

Julien, Charles-André. *Histoire de l'Algérie Contemporaine.* Tome I. Paris: Presses Universtaires de France, 1979.

————. *L'Afrique du nord en marche.* 3rd edition. Paris: René Julliard, 1972.

Kaddache, Mahfoud. *Histoire du nationalisme algérien.* Tome I. Alger: S.N.E.D., 1980.

Khaled, Emir. *La situation des musulmans d'Algérie.* Originally published 1924. Alger: OPU, 1987.

Khaldoun, Ibn. *The Muqaddimah.* 3 Vols. 2d. Ed. Translated by Franz Rosenthal. Princeton, NJ: Princeton University Press, 1967.

Khomeini, Ayatollah Ruhollah. *Islam and Revolution.* Translated by Hamid Algar. Berkeley, CA: Mizan Press, 1981.

————. *Islamic Government.* Translated by Joint Publications Research Service. New York, NY: Manor Books, 1979.

Knauss, Peter R. *The Persistence of Patriarchy.* New York, NY: Praeger, 1984.

Lacoste, Yves, André Nouschi, and André Prenant. *L'Algérie: passé et présent.* Paris: Sociales, 1960.

Lacouture, Jean. *Charles de Gaulle.* Volume I. Paris: Seuil, 1984.

————. *Charles de Gaulle: The Leader, 1945–1970.* New York, NY: Norton, 1992

Lambton, Ann K. *State and Government in Medieval Islam.* Oxford: Oxford University Press, 1981.

Lamchichi, Abderrahim. *L'Algérie en crise.* Paris: L'Harmattan, 1992.

Lapidus, Ira M. *Muslim Cities in the Latter Middle Ages.* Cambridge, MA: Harvard University Press, 1972.

Laroui, Abdallah. *La crise des intellectuels arabes.* Paris: Prospero, 1974.

Lazreg, Marnia. *The Emergence of Classes in Algeria.* Boulder, CO: Westview Press, 1976.

Lebjaoui, Mohamed. *Vérités sur la révolution algérienne.* Paris: Gallimard, 1970.

Ledwidge, Bernard. *De Gaulle.* London: Weidenfeld and Nicholson, 1982.

Le Tourneau, Roger. *Évolution politique de l'Afrique du nord musulmane, 1920–1961.* Paris: Armand Colin, 1962.

————. *Fez in the Age of the Marinides.* Norman, OK: University of Oklahoma Press, 1961.

Levitzon, Nehemia. *Ancient Ghana and Mali.* London: Methuen, 1973.

L'exode de Tlemcen en 1911. Alger: 1914.

Liebman, Charles and Eliezer Don-Yehiya. *Religion and Politics in Israel.* Bloomington, IN: Indiana University Press, 1984.

Linz, Juan and Alfred Stepan. *Problems of Democratic Transition and Consolidation: Theoretical Perspectives.* Baltimore, MD: Johns Hopkins University Press, forthcoming.

Linz, Juan and Alfred Stepan, eds. *The Breakdown of Democratic Regimes.* Baltimore, MD: Johns Hopkins University Press, 1978.

Luxembourg, Rosa. *Accumulation of Capital.* Ann Arbor, MI : Books on Demand.

Madani, Abbasi. *azmat al-fikr al-hadith wa mubarrirat al-hall al-islami.* Alger: Ameziane, 1989.

Mandouze, André. *La révolution algérienne par les textes.* Paris: Maspéro, 1961.

Maschino, Tariq and Fadéla M'Rabet. *L'Algérie des illusions.* Paris: Robert Laffont, 1972.

McGovern, Arthur F. *Liberation Theology and its Critics: Towards an Assessment.* Maryknoll, NY: Orbis, 1989.

Merad, Ali. *Le réformisme musulman en Algérie de 1925 à 1940.* Paris: Mouton, 1967.

Minces, Juliette. *L'Algérie de Boumedienne*. Paris: Presses de la Cité, 1968.

Nouschi, André. *La naissance du nationalisme algérien*. Paris: Minuit, 1962.

O'Ballance, Edgar. *The Algerian Insurrection*. London: Archor Books, 1967.

O'Donnell, Guillermo. *Modernization and Bureaucratic-Authoritarianism*. Berkeley, CA: University of California Press, 1973.

———— and Phillipe C. Schmitter. *Transitions from Authoritarian Rule: Tentative Conclusions about Uncertain Democracies*. (Baltimore, MD; Johns Hopkins University Press, 1986.

Ottaway, David and Marina Ottaway. *Algeria: The Politics of a Socialist Revolution*. Berkeley, CA: University of California Press, 1970.

Prezeworski, Adam. *Democracy and the Market: Political and Economic Reforms in Eastern Europe and Latin America*. New York, NY: Cambridge University Press, 1991.

Quandt, William B. *Revolution and Political Leadership: Algeria, 1954–1968*. Cambridge, MA: M.I.T. Press, 1969.

Qutb, Sayyid. *Al Islam wa mushkilat al-hadarah*. 6th ed. Cairo: Dar al-shuruq, 1980.

————. *Fi zilzal al-Qur'an*. Rev. ed. 6 Vols. Cairo: Dar al-shuruq, 1981.

————. *Maalim fil tariq*. Cairo: Dar al-shuruq, 1989.

————. *Milestones*. Lahore: Kazi Publications.

Raptis, Michel. *Socialism, Democracy, and Self-Management*. Translated by Marie-Jo Serrié and Richard Sessions. London: Allison & Busby, 1980.

Revere, Robert B. "Consensus in Algeria, 1962–1965." Ph.D. Diss., New York University, 1970.

Richard, Charles. *Étude sur l'insurrection du Dahra*. Alger: A. Becansez, 1846.

Rinn, Louis. *Marabouts et Khaouan*. Alger: Adolphe Jourdan, 1884.

————. *Note sur l'instruction politique musulmane*. Alger: 1882.

Rosenthal, E. I. J. *Political Thought in Medieval Islam.* Cambridge: Cambridge University Press, 1958.

Rouadjia, Ahmed. *Grandeur et décadence de l'état algérien.* Paris: Karthala, 1994.

Rouadjia, Ahmed. *Les frères et les mosquées.* Paris: L'Harmattan, 1990.

Ruedy, John. *Modern Algeria.* Bloomington, IN: Indiana University Press, 1992.

Ruthven, Malise. *Islam in the World.* New York, NY: Oxford University Press, 1984.

Saad, Elias. *The Social History of Timbuktu: The Role of Muslim Scholars and Notables, 1400–1900.* Cambridge: Cambridge University Press, 1983.

Sahli, Mohammed Cherif. *Abdelkader, chevalier de la foi.* Alger: E.N.E.P., 1984.

Sassoon, Donald. *The Strategy of the Italian Communist Party.* New York, NY: St. Martin's Press, 1981.

Schimmel, Annemarie. *Mystical Dimensions of Islam.* Chapel Hill, NC: University of North Carolina Press, 1975.

Schnetzler, Jacques. *Le développement algérien.* Paris: Masson, 1991.

Schurmann, Franz. *Ideology and Organization in Communist China.* Berkeley, CA: University of California, 1973.

Seznec, Jean-François. "The Politics of the Financial Markets in Saudi Arabia, Kuwait and Bahrain." Ph.D. diss., Yale University, 1994.

Shain, Yossi. *Political Exiles in the Age of the Nation-State.* Middletown,CT; Wesleyan University Press, 1989.

Sigmund, Paul E. *Liberation Theology at the Crossroads: Democracy or Revolution?* New York, NY: Oxford University Press, 1990.

The Holy Qur'an. Translated by Abdullah Yusuf Ali. Brentwood, MD: Amana Corporation, 1989.

Taimiyya, Ahmad ibn. *Al-siyasa al-shariyya.* 2d ed. Edited by A. S. Nashshar and A. Z. Atiyya. Cairo: 1951.

Taimiyya, Ahamd ibn. *Le traité de droit d'Ibn Taimiyya.* Translated by H. Laoust. Beirut: 1948.

Tibi, Bassam. *Arab Nationalism.* 3rd ed. London: MacMillan Press, 1990.

Tibi, Bassam. *Islam and the Cultural Accommodation of Social Change.* Boulder, CO: Westview Press, 1991.

Trebous, Madeleine. *Migration et développement: le cas de l'Algérie* Paris: Centre de développement de l'O.C.D.E., 1970.

Trimingham, J. S. *The Sufi Orders in Islam.* London: Clarendon Press, 1971.

Trotsky, Leon. *History of the Russian Revolution.* New York, NY: Anchor Found, 1980.

Vatikiotis, P. J. *Islam and the State.* London: Croom Helm, 1987.

Voll, John. *Islam: Continuity and Change in the Modern World.* Boulder, CO: Westview Press, 1982.

Von Clausewitz, Carl. *On War.* London: Penguin, 1982.

Weber, Max. *Economy and Society.* Vol. 1. Berkeley, CA: University of California Press, 1978.

Zakaria, Rafiq. *The Struggle Within Islam.* New York, NY: Penguin Books, 1988.

Articles

Al-Banna, Hassan. "New Renaissance: The Viewpoint of the Muslim Brotherhood." *Political and Social Thought in the Contemporary Middle East.* Edited by Kemal H. Karpat. New York, NY: Praeger, 1968.

Amnesty International. "Algeria: Deteriorating Human Rights under the State of Emergency." London: Amnesty International, March 1993.

Anderson, Lisa and Eric Goldstein. "Human Rights Abuses in Algeria." New York, NY: Middle East Watch, January 1994.

Arnaud, L. "Histoire de l'Ouali Sidi-Ahmad et-Tidjani." *Revue Africaine* 5 (1861): pp. 473–474.

Bennoune, Mahfoud. "The Industrialization of Algeria: An Overview." In *Contemporary North Africa.* Edited by Halim Barakat. Washington, DC: Center for Contemporary Arab Studies, 1985.

Berque, Augustin. "Essai d'une bibliographie critique des confréries algériennes." *Bulletin de la société de géographie et d'archéologie d'Oran* 39 (septembre-décembre 1919): pp. 193–233.

Bodin, Marcel. "La brève chronique du Bey Hasan: extraite et traduite de Talat-os-Sas-is-Sooud de Mazari." *Bulletin de la société de géographie et d'archéologie d'Oran* 44 (1924): pp. 23–61.

Boudiaf, Mohamed. "La préparation de 1er novembre." In *Les cahiers d'El Jarida,* Organe du Parti de la Révolution Socialiste.

Boyer, Pierre. "Contribution à l'étude de la politique religieuse des Turcs dans la régence d'Alger (16–19 siècles)." *Revue de l'occident musulman et de la méditerranée* 1 (1966): pp. 11–49.

Chatelet, F. "Nationalisme et conscience de classe." In *Consciences Algériennes* (décembre 1950): pp. 110–121.

Chergui, Karim. "La révolte des jeunes à Constantine." *Hérodote* 45 (avril-juin 1987): pp. 61–70.

Chesneaux, Jean. "Les fondements historiques du communisme vietnamien." *L'Homme et la société,* no. 14 (octobre-décembre 1969): pp. 83–98.

Clancy-Smith, Julia Ann. "Saints, Mahdis, and Arms: Religion and Resistance in Nineteenth Century Northern Africa." In *Islam, Politics, and Social Movements,* ed. Edmund Burke, III, and Ira M. Lapidus, pp. 60–80. London: I. B. Tauris, 1988.

Colonna, Fanny. "Saints furieux et studieux." *Annales* 35, no. 3–4 (mai-août 1986): pp. 642–662.

Delpech, Adrien. "Résumé historique sur le soulèvement des Derkaoua dans la province d'Oran." *Revue Africaine* 18 (1874): pp. 38–58.

Destanne de Bernis, Gérard. "Deux stratégies pour l'industrialisation du Tiers Monde. Les industries industrialisantes et les options algériennes." *Revue Tiers Monde* XII, no. 47 (juillet-septembre 1989): pp. 545–563.

Demaeght, L. "Notice sur la mort de Sidi Mohammed al-Kabir et-Tidjani." *Bulletin de la société de géographie et d'archéologie de la province d'Oran* 13 (1893): pp. 150–152.

Djeghloul, Abelkader. "Le défi de la crise." In *Le Monde Diplomatique,* novembre 1986.

Encyclopedia of Islam, 1913–1934 ed. S.v. "Kadariya."

———— 1913–1934 ed. S.v. "Rahmaniyya."

Esposito, John L. "Islam and Muslim Politics." In *Voices of Resurgent of Islam.* Edited by John L. Esposito. New York, NY: Oxford University Press, 1983.

Farsoun, Karen. "State Capitalism in Algeria." *MERIP Report,* no. 35 (February 1976).

Gallisot, René. "Abd el-Kader et la nationalité algérienne." *Revue Historique* 233 (avril-juin 1965): pp. 339–368.

————. "La guerre d'Abd El Kader." *Hésperis-Tamuda* (1964): pp. 119–141.

Goodhart, Arthur L. "Case Law in England and America." *Cornell Law Quarterly* 15, no. 2 (February 1930): pp. 173–193.

Hourani, Albert. "Conclusion." *Islam in the Political Process.* Edited by James P. Piscatori. Cambridge: Cambridge University Press, 1983.

Lacheraf, Mostefa. "L'avenir de la culture algérienne." *Les Temps Modernes,* no. 209 (Octobre 1963): pp. 720–745.

Lawless, Richard. "Algeria: The Contradictions of Rapid Industrialization." In *North Africa.* Edited by Richard Lawless and Allan Findlay. London: Croom Helm, 1984.

Linz, Juan. "The Religious Use of Politics and/or the Political Use of Religion." [photocopy].

Mus, Paul. "Insertion du communisme dans le mouvement nationale vietnamien." *Les Temps Modernes,* no. 78 (avril 1952): pp. 1796–1809.

Nadir, Ahmed. "Les ordres religieux et la conquête française." *Revue algérienne des sciences juridiques, économiques et politiques* 9 (décembre 1972): pp. 819–872.

Nellis, John R. "Social Management in Algeria." *Journal of Modern African Studies* 15 (December 1977): pp. 529–554.

Nghe, Nguyen. "Frantz Fanon et les problèmes de l'indépendance." *Le Pensée,* no. 107 (février 1963): pp. 23–36.

Pervillé, Guy. "Le panafricanisme du FLN algérien." In *L'Afrique noire française*. Edited by Charles-Robert Ageron and Marc Michel. Paris: CNRS, 1992.

Ragau, Christiane. "Ho Chi Minh et l'internationale communiste." *Partisans,* no. 48 (juin-août 1969): pp. 44–55.

Rahman, Fazlur. "The Implementation of the Islamic Concept of the State in the Pakistani Milieu." *Islamic Studies* (Karachi).

Rouzeik, Fawzi. "Algérie, 1990–1993: la démocratie confisquée." *L'Algérie incertaine*. Edited by Pierre Robert Baduel. Aix-en-Provence and Paris: CNRS/IREMAM, 1994.

Shoshan, Boaz. "The Politics of Notables in Islam." *African and Asian Studies* 20 (July 1986): pp. 179–215.

Sprecher, Robert A. "The Development of Stare Decisis." *American Bar Association Journal* 31 (October 1945): pp. 501–509.

Stora, Benjamin. "La guerre FLN/MNA." In *Le drame algérien*. Edited by Reporters sans frontières. Paris: La Découverte, 1994.

Vatikiotis, P. J. "Tradition and Political Leadership: The Case of Algeria." In *Man, State, and Society in the Contemporary Maghreb*. Edited by I. William Zartman. New York, NY: Praeger, 1973.

Vallin, Raymond. "Muslim Socialism in Algeria." In *Man, State, and Society in the Contemporary Maghrib*. Edited by I. William Zartman. New York, NY: Praeger, 1973.

Vandevelde, Hélène. "Le code algérien de la famille." *Maghreb-Machrek* 107 (janvier-mars 1985): pp. 52–64.

———. "Où en est le problème du code de la famille en Algérie." *Maghreb-Machrek,* no. 97 (juillet-septembre 1982): pp. 39–54.

von Moschziker, Robert. "Stare Decisis in Courts of Last Resort." *Harvard Law Review* 37, no. 4 (February 1924): pp. 409–430.

Von Sivers, Peter. "The Realm of Justice: Apocalyptic Revolts in Algeria (1849–1879)." *Humanoria Islamica* 1 (1973).

Wallerstein, Immanuel. "The Decline of the Party in Single Party African States." In *Political Parties and Political Development*. Edited by Joseph LaPalombara and Malcolm Weiner. Princeton, NJ: Princeton University Press, 1963.

Zartman, I. William. "The Algerian Army in Politics." *Man, State, and Society in the Contemporary Maghrib*. Edited by I. William Zartman. New York, NY: Praeger, 1973.

Newspapers and Magazines

Al Ahram

Al Asala

Al Jarida

Al Ma'rifa

Al Sha'b

Al Shihab

Alger Républicain

Algérie-Actualité

Combat

Demain

Dépêche Algérienne

El Mounquid

El Moudjahid

El Ouma

El Watan

Islah

L'Afrique Française

L'Écho d'Alger

L'Entente

L'Humanité

La Défense

La Lutte Sociale

La République Algérienne

Le Monde Diplomatique

Le Parlement Algérien

Libération

Liberté

Moniteur Algérien
Parcours Maghrébins
Petit Parisien
Révolution Africaine
The New York Times
Tribune d'Octobre

Constitutions, Statutes and Legal Documents

Code de la famille 1984. Alger: OPU, 1985.

La Charte d'Alger 1964, Front de Libération Nationale.

La Charte Nationale 1976, République Algérienne Démocratique et Populaire.

La Constitution 1976, République Algérienne Démocratique et Populaire.

La Constitution 1989, République Algérienne Démocratique et Populaire.

Loi du 18 juillet 1873

Loi du 23 décembre 1875

Loi du 22 avril 1887

Plate-forme de Soummam, 1956.

Statuts du parti du FLN. Alger: Ben Boulaïd, 1980.

Statistical Studies

Annuaire statistique de l'Algérie, 1939–1947.

Annual Statistical Bulletin, 1980. Organization of Petroleum Exporting Countries, Vienna, 1981.

Collections statistiques no. 36: situation d'emploi 1990. Alger: ONS, 1992.

Démographie algérienne 1989. Alger: ONS, 1989.

United Nations Demographic Yearbooks, 1970, 1974, 1983, 1985, 1991, 1993

Index